The Step Back

SUNY SERIES IN
CONTEMPORARY CONTINENTAL PHILOSOPHY

Dennis J. Schmidt, editor

THE STEP BACK

Ethics and Politics after Deconstruction

DAVID WOOD

STATE UNIVERSITY OF NEW YORK PRESS

Published by
STATE UNIVERSITY OF NEW YORK PRESS
ALBANY

© 2005 State University of New York

For information, address
State University of New York Press
194 Washington Avenue, Suite 305, Albany, NY 12210-2365

Production, Laurie Searl
Marketing, Anne M. Valentine

Library of Congress Cataloging-in-Publication Data

Wood, David (David C.)
  The step back : ethics and politics after deconstruction / David C.
Wood.
      p. cm. — (SUNY series in contemporary continental philosophy)
  Includes bibliographical references and index.
  ISBN 0-7914-6463-6 (alk. paper) — ISBN 0-7914-6464-4 (pbk. : alk. paper)
  1. Violence—Moral and ethical aspects. I. Title. II. Series.
  BJ1459.5.W66 2005
  179.7—dc22

                                                                    2004014216

                10   9   8   7   6   5   4   3   2   1

This book is dedicated to my father

Derek Rawlins Wood (1921–1997)

who knew how to step back.

Contents

ACKNOWLEDGMENTS   ix

INTRODUCTION
    Toward a Negative Capability   1

PART I
Philosophy and Violence

ONE   Identity and Violence   11

TWO   The Philosophy of Violence ::
        The Violence of Philosophy   27

THREE Where Levinas Went Wrong:
        Some Questions for My Levinasian Friends   53

ADDENDUM
    Twenty Theses on Violence   69

PART II
Singular Encounters

FOUR   The First Kiss: Tales of Innocence and Experience   73

FIVE   Thinking God in the Wake of Kierkegaard   85

SIX   Dionysus in America   109

Part III
Ethics and Politics after Deconstruction

Seven Notes toward a Deconstructive Phenomenology 131

Eight Responsibility Reinscribed (and How) 139

Nine What Is Ecophenomenology? 149

Ten Globalization and Freedom 169

Postscript
Philosophy: The Antioxidant of Higher Education 189

Notes 195

Index 229

Acknowledgments

Chapter 3, revised version of "Some Questions for My Levinasian Friends," in *Addressing Levinas*, ed. E. Nelson et al. (Evanston: Northwestern University Press, 2005).

Chapter 4, revised version of "Tales of Innocence and Experience: Kierkegaard's Spiritual Accountancy," in *The New Kierkegaard*, ed. Elsebet Jegstrup (Bloomington: Indiana University Press, 2004).

Chapter 5, revised version of "Thinking God in the Wake of Kierkegaard," in *Kierkegaard: A Critical Reader*, ed. Jonathan Rée and Jane Chamberlain (Oxford: Blackwell, 1998), 53–74.

Chapter 7, "Notes towards a Deconstructive Phenomenology," in *JBSP* (Journal of the British Society for Phenomenology), 1998

Chapter 9, revised version of "What is Eco-Phenomenology?" in *Eco-Phenomenology: Back to the Earth Itself*, ed. Ted Toadvine and Charles Brown (Albany: State University of New York Press, 2003).

I am grateful to all copyright holders for permissions granted.

And I want to thank my graduate student Aaron Simmons for his exemplary work in preparing the index.

Toward a Negative Capability

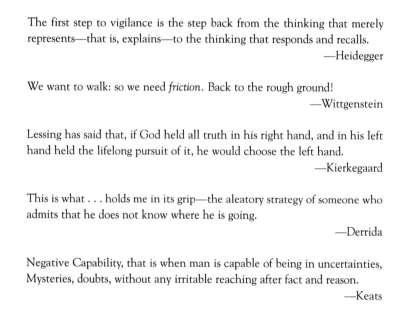

The first step to vigilance is the step back from the thinking that merely represents—that is, explains—to the thinking that responds and recalls.
—Heidegger

We want to walk: so we need *friction*. Back to the rough ground!
—Wittgenstein

Lessing has said that, if God held all truth in his right hand, and in his left hand held the lifelong pursuit of it, he would choose the left hand.
—Kierkegaard

This is what . . . holds me in its grip—the aleatory strategy of someone who admits that he does not know where he is going.
—Derrida

Negative Capability, that is when man is capable of being in uncertainties, Mysteries, doubts, without any irritable reaching after fact and reason.
—Keats

Whether we try to speak about Ethics or take up a specific ethical topic such as justice or responsibility, it is not hard to conclude that we have arrived on the scene too late, that our access to what is fundamental to these issues is fading. While we can still speak about these things, even in interesting ways, it can seem that something vitally important has been lost—as if all one knew about plants came from frequenting a shop selling cut flowers.

The sense of having arrived too late is close to what contemporary thought calls the "always already"—that the origin is structurally recessive, that it cannot be represented within the conceptual level at which its absence is nonetheless being felt.

The implications of this sentiment for ethics are profound. It does *not* proscribe thematic or conceptual reflection. And yet it suspects that such reflection may itself both rest on and occlude its own conditions of possibility. Our continuing debt to the unthematized and the impossibility of finally discharging that debt is one of the central motifs of phenomenology. But the interminable need to "step back" is not the Sisyphean "bad infinity" but rather the ongoing persistence of life, and our contemplation of it. It is no more a sign of failure that this movement must be repeatedly undertaken than that we cannot eat the breakfast to end all breakfasts, or say "I love you" in a way that would never need repeating.

The illusion of a certain mastery at the conceptual level, a relation to language in which the author would be in control, was thematized by deconstruction. Before Derrida had marked this limit, Heidegger wrote about the need to listen to the speaking of language. This was not to recommend passivity, but rather to remind us of how agency is grounded in receptivity, and how easy it is for us to forget this.

꧁ꕥ꧂

A professional philosophy publication recently included the following ad from a Texas company called Cycorp seeking new recruits for an ongoing project:

> Our "Ontological Engineers" rapidly apply metaphysical distinctions to describe common, practical concepts, then represent those descriptions as predicate calculus sentences. An efficient inference engine (theorem prover) helps them perform/check their work. Our goal: the world's first generally intelligent artifact.[1]

Such a vision needs a more considered response than open-mouthed incredulity. Those who insist that the world as it stands won't play ball may be missing the point. There must once have been similar objections to the rectilinear grids of highway engineers. The issue is not whether these mappings fit the land, but whether the habits through which humans engage the real can be reconfigured in such a way as to allow these new grids to reflect them accurately. Grids are not descriptive, they are prescriptive. And they do not prescribe this (new) pattern rather than that (old) pattern. They prescribe what will often be a legally enforced *conformity* to such a pattern. Driving cars demands precise rules of the sort that walking or horse riding never did. While the parallel between conceptual schemes and road grids is illuminating, the stakes are dramatically raised when it comes to thinking. For we are not especially well prepared to protect the ways we think from colonization by such operationalized concepts.

Yet it is particularly important that we do so. Operational thinking is far from being just a lower grade of thinking that we can just brush aside when it fails to deliver. It has the distinct virtue of facilitating constructive complexity in a certain kind of human engagement with the world. Once we are assured of the viability of its key concepts in a particular region, it offers a powerful tool for constructing and managing possible future scenarios,[2] just as the ability to price commodities allows all sorts of virtual transactions to take place. The issue is not simply one of the accuracy and adequacy of such technical concepts; it is rather one of the promise and possibilities offered by the form of life that it opens up. The classic example is perhaps the imposition of distinct property lines on lands inhabited by nomadic tribes, or by hunters. The resulting disputes reflect deep rifts in habits of land use and social organization between indigenous people, on the one hand, and new settlers on the other. Instead of resigning ourselves to an empty relativism, we would do well to focus on the distinct and often compelling virtues of each mode of inhabiting the world. The constructive/conceptual/operational mode can generate extraordinary interlocking complexity of human/machine/program interaction (think of airline traffic). Conceptually fixing each "layer" allows another layer to be built on top of the assured stability of the previous layer. Such layered complexity gives rise to combustion processes—engines—planes—airlines—flight schedules—holiday villa construction—vacation patterns, etc. etc.

The other mode of engagement could be called, in a naive way, deconstructive, in the sense that instead of constructing layers of controlled conceptual operations one on top of the other, it moves in the other direction, maintaining links, input, feedback, from levels of engagement presupposed by conceptuality, but not wholly captured in concepts—such as history, embodiment, nature, perception, social relations, and the texture and weight of language itself. It is in this direction that we find the privilege that Hegel gives to the slave (over the master) in his engagement with nature, that Nietzsche gives to sensation (over "language"), that Kierkegaard gives to faith (over Christendom's outward conformity) and subjective knowledge (over the objective variety), that Husserl gives to intentional consciousness (over the natural attitude), that Merleau-Ponty gives to perception (over science)—his name for this movement was *hyper-reflection*—that Wittgenstein gives to the "rough ground" of actual language use (over our conceptual schemes), that Heidegger gives to "the thinking that responds and recalls" (over representation),[3] that Kristeva gives to the semiotic (over the semantic), and that Derrida gives to disseminating textuality or *différance* (over logocentric schematization). In each case we may say that the movement in question is one in which the recessive dimension interrupts the pretension to independence, autonomy, or closure of the dimension that has captured the space of representation. This is the movement I call the *step back*.[4] It claims not that the truth has been left behind, and that we must return to it; rather, that something like *phronesis* lies in maintaining a circulation, or at least a possibility of further nourishment, perhaps a challenge, from the recessive dimension. The step back is in this sense a movement away from the rush of dialectical enthusiasm for moving forward and overcoming. The step back does not argue for a new foundationalism in which the dependence (say) of culture on nature, or language on sensation is grounded in some formal way. Rather, it insists on the danger of closing off such a connection, or attempting to subject it to a law or a rule. The step back marks a certain shape of philosophical practice, one that does not just resign itself to, but affirms the necessity of, ambiguity, incompleteness, repetition, negotiation, and contingency. I have revived Keats's expression *negative capability* to capture this array of concepts.[5]

This is not the time to offer a fullblown account of the value of the negative. Despite the lonely protest of a Bergson, most European philosophers after Hegel have embraced the significance of negativity in one way or another, though they have often felt the need to explain themselves to a skeptical public. The fundamental idea is that the various negative sounding conditions or operations we listed above (ambiguity, incompleteness, contingency . . .) shed light on social and intellectual formations that would otherwise just appear in their "positivity." That is, they would otherwise just seem to exist naturally. This positivity gets disturbed when it is pointed out that things need not be the way they are, which makes visible the possibilities of transformation, whether through art or revolution. Such an imaginative illumination relies on our "negating"—setting aside, imagining otherwise—the ways things actually are. Time itself seems to embody a kind of ongoing negativity, casting aside each passing moment in favor of the next. It is not unreasonable so to suppose that everyday life, as well as reflection on it, is subject to pressures to define, to name, to label, to pin down, and to clarify the way things are. If so, one of the dimensions of the real that will be excluded by such pressures is *the very existence of such pressures*, as well as the way they operate to simplify, even distort the real. What we have called the step back calls into play a negative capability when it resists these pressures to prematurely resolve complex questions, when it refuses to pretend that boundaries that have been constructed are just *there*, when it refuses to agree that the way things are is the way they must be, and when it consequently affirms the responsibilities of critical reflection and patience that flow from these refusals.[6] By negative capability I do not mean what Hegel would call the work of the negative, which would take shape as dialectical progression. Negative capability, rather, liberates philosophy from the naivete of those established discourses and practices it finds itself faced with, and it protects philosophy from its own tendency to a new kind of positivity—that of conceptual construction. In such liberation and protection negative capability can be seen to have a fundamentally ethical dimension, not in the sense of prescribing or proscribing first order rules or virtues. But rather in focusing our attentions on the space of possibility within which our practical engagement in the world takes place. To be clear, the sense of "possibility" here is not just that of the empirical options (typically consumer choices) we are offered, but rather has to do with the further possibilities both of constructing meaning, and of acknowledging the incompleteness of the narratives with which we provide ourselves.

This book is a response to many different ways in which contemporary philosophers have marked the ethical and (often) marked a distance from bestowing upon it any positivity. Maintaining this position is not always comfortable. Every time *the ethical* is "marked," the cry goes up, "But where is your ethics?" For Kierkegaard, the ethical is doubly inscribed—both as opposed to the aesthetic, and as superceded by the religious. In a broader sense, what Kierkegaard means by the religious is a sense of the ethical that cannot be circumscribed by rules, or by any closed economy, and the willingness, as Nietzsche would say, to affirm, not merely to accept this. Wittgenstein, in his turn, offers us important ways of translating between the religious and the existential, marking the ethical, again, as a space of contextualized practices not fully able to be articulated. For Heidegger, the challenge of the ethical is to think it in a broader sense than that traditionally offered by humanism, a way that eludes representation, a way closer to the Greek sense of *ethos*, or way of dwelling. When Levinas tells us that ethics is "first philosophy," it soon becomes clear that he is not speaking of ethics, but of the space within which the ethical at first arises, a space that in our view is colored with ontological choices and constraints. We could say that for Levinas, the ethical is the space of infinite responsibility for the other man. And the word *responsibility* captures the centrality of the ethical in Husserl's vision of phenomenology as alone adequately honoring (or responding to) the contours of our experience. For Derrida, this responsibility takes on a more general openness to the sites at which otherness—and not just the other man—is occluded in our thinking and writing.[7] And we have plotted this exemplary accentuation and suspension of the ethical in the work of that Nietzsche in America, Charles Scott, whose concern with both response and recall nonetheless closely captures Heidegger's sense of the step back.

Scott attempts to extend our response-ability beyond the human to our relation to the stars, to the most inhuman, the mineral. We argue that the avoidance of the first order morality of guilt—central to his concerns here—does not require this move, that our responsibility to the living of all sorts can be thought of without guilt.

Stars aside, there is no doubt that "nature" in its many levels does constitute a dimension of essentially incomplete conceptualization, one on which we continuously depend, and which solicits in so many ways our response and acknowledgment. Something like an eco-phenomenology, which lays bare some of the natural forces constituting the boundaries of the real, both in space and time, also makes a contribution to a negative capability. Nature becomes visible both as constructed, and as participating in its own construction, and as such solicits a different kind of response.

With the theme of globalization, we return to the concrete ethical and political questions with which we began. The central issue we confront is that of freedom. Globalization is the site for the most powerful ideological contestation over the question of freedom. For some it is precisely what brings freedom to countless people drawn by its opportunities into the circle of trade and development. For others, globalization heralds a new era of economic oppression and servitude. Does it help to be told that the very idea of freedom is tied to the eminently deconstructable subject? And is this "subject" a creature of metaphysics or of the West? Does globalization teach us the vanity of the hope that the third world might provide sufficient force to resist the march of the one-dimensional man of commodity capitalism? We argue that globalization forces a return to thinking through the material conditions of freedom, while exposing the folly of supposing that some particular oppressed group will spearhead the revolution.

Finally, a word about violence, which is a constant concern of the book. If we identify philosophy with "reason" then continuing public violence can appear both as a challenge to reason and an indictment of its impotence. And yet we might think that it is precisely the fact of violence, quite as much as wonder and astonishment, that has led men and women to philosophize, to try to construct models of state and community in which cooperation would replace conflict. Continuing violence raises the question as to whether philosophy has failed to implement its vision of reason, or whether that vision was flawed in its very conception. Some (such as Lyotard) have argued that modern violence is precisely the consequence of attempts at implementing Enlightenment ideals, perhaps even the consequence of the very belief in the implementability of these ideals. The suggestion is that when such ideals move to being implemented they are turned into utopian blueprints by which the real is violently coerced. And those who resist, or who do not fit, become the victims of violence.

Negative capability here takes the form of recognizing the complex mediations between the ideal and the real, the aporetic space of progress, bearing in mind that very often the game may not be worth the candle. Where violence erupts from the clash of national or ethnic identities, it may not help that philosophers have up their sleeves less rigid ways of understanding identity. But the processes by which peace is negotiated, (or conflict prevented), typically involve a dismantling of the hysterical affirmation-at-any-price of tribal identities, and a search for alternative guarantees of peace and security.

The suggestion here is not just that philosophy has a role in thinking through the constructions of identity and difference that can foment violence, but that the way we understand and practice philosophy has a direct bearing on its power and promise for peace. I argue that the step back, the promulgation of negative capability, is the key to philosophy serving the ends of peace, rather than promoting the unthinking identifications whose defense leads to violence.

There is perhaps one aspect of negative capability that deserves special attention, an attention already evident in the quotations that head this introduction, and that is the relation between negative capability and time.[8] We misunderstand the philosophical enterprise if we identify it with some sort of goal-oriented activity that could be achieved once and for all, like climbing Everest. Instead, we are directed to an ongoing process or practice, the character or quality of which is itself the achievement. The achievement, then, is not a *terminus ad quem*, not a point in time, but a different way of relating to time. It suggests that what we most value are dispositions of engagement, ways of carrying on, which can of course be acquired, and in that sense accomplished, but whose value and significance come from being repeatedly deployed. And in stepping back from the fantasy of a "final solution," or an irreversible achievement attained at some point in time, we find a luminous example of the affirmative aspect of negative capability. Negative capability here means letting go of the seemingly attractive idea of reaching an end, never having to struggle again. Negative capability is both a conceptual and an existential achievement—the recognition of ongoing contingent engaged temporality as the plane on which we all must make our fragile sense.

It is not uncommon to hear that a concern with the *way* one philosophizes suffers from vagueness, that it appeals to lazy minds and muddy thinkers. (Concerns about "method" might seem sterile but at least they demonstrate a commitment to rigor.) The usual response is to remind one's critic of Aristotle's remarks about the importance of matching one's demands for precision to the subject matter. But that might seem merely to justify rather than contest the charge of vagueness. The more radical response would contest the very terms of the indictment. The difficulty that some people have with mathematics or logic shows or at least suggests, that the question of precision must be raised at two different levels. Logic is all too precise in its own terms. What some people just *don't get* is not just how to think that way, but why one would want to do so. While mathematical or logical operations can be explained precisely, the same cannot be said for the disciplines of mathematics and logic themselves. Those who are logophobic may have failed to connect with the *very idea* of precise, calculable representation. Consider the terms in which we might critically compare the respective values of a strictly mathematical approach to gardening, with a more intuitive approach that sticks a finger in the air or tastes the earth for sweetness? One could not introduce "precision" as the decisive value without begging the question. It is true that quantification might maximize yields. It might enhance "crop management efficiency." But it is still an issue as to which way of gardening is "better," because the *practice* of gardening does not itself have a technical definition, any more than fishing. People happily "fish" all day without catching anything. Would their fishing be "better" if large trout were attached to their hooks by unseen underwater assistants? The appropriateness of this analogy to philosophy depends not just on how we define philosophy, but whether we think of it as appropriately "definable" at all. It is not for nothing that Nietzsche wrote: "Only that which has no history can be defined." Philosophy would be nothing if it were not intrinsically, and at many levels, historical. If it resists definition, it is not because it is "vague," but "precisely" because, as a historically invested and situated practice, it is not primarily an object of taxonomic scrutiny. It is historical even in its essential capacity to reflect on or step back from its own time, in a certain fashion, the better to contribute to it. This way of thinking and talking about philosophy is precisely what cannot be avoided. And it has nothing to do with vagueness.

I have not tried to position the "methodological orientation" represented by this book on the contemporary map. While I deal with many of the usual suspects, the reader will find few of the usual signposts, those that would mark our distance from postmodernism, or deconstruction. At times it may seem that lines of philosophical correctness have been crossed with a promiscuous disregard for boundaries. I have argued for a deconstructive phenomenology, where many would hear a *contradictio in adjecto,* I have upheld the language of critique and its importance, even though I have not endorsed its traditional philosophical underpinnings. The subtitle of this introduction comes from an English romantic poet. I have reworked many of the ethical motifs of contemporary deconstruction, while taking Levinas and Derrida to task for their residual humanism. It matters to me how we read others and I have tried to read the various philosophers dealt with here in a constructive way. The philosophers who have most influenced me in this respect are Ricoeur (for his ecumenical generosity), Heidegger (for his sense that to read another is ideally to recover the scene of *their* encounter . . .), and Derrida (for his sense of our incomplete mastery of the language we write in). As I suggest in the *Postscript,* I understand the achievement of philosophy to lie in reintroducing difficulty quite as much as solving problems. It requires a double vision, with one eye on the glistening texture of the real, and the other turned to the margins, the background, the conditions of possibility, and the possibilities of transformation. In a different key: There are many who can pick out a tune on the piano with one hand, but playing the piano, like thinking, requires the coordination of the right hand with the left.

If to some the resulting performance sounds like heresy, so be it.

PART I

Philosophy and Violence

ONE

Identity and Violence

Many a man has cherished for years as his hobby some vague shadow of an idea, too meaningless to be positively false; he has, nevertheless passionately loved it, has made it his companion by day and by night, and has given to it his strength and his life . . . until it has become as it were flesh of his flesh and bone of his bone; and then he has waked up some bright morning to find it gone, clean vanished away.

—Peirce

MY CANDIDATE FOR SUCH a cherished idea is the connection between identity and violence, and the hope that understanding such connections might, albeit indirectly, enable philosophy to make a contribution to peace. Rather than waking up one morning to find it vanished, I wrote this chapter to try to rescue at least one clear idea from the rank growth that had sprung up around it. I hope to show that understanding identities as constructions makes it possible to find ways of transforming the brittle, over-rigid identity formations that breed violence. Recent history is generous with examples. Not long ago war raged in what was Yugoslavia, while in Ireland bombs exploded regularly, killing and maiming. In Rwanda in 1994 the world stood by while some half-million Tutsis were slaughtered by Hutus. Only yesterday it seems, Israeli tanks fired shells into market squares in Hebron, while Palestinian teenagers blew themselves up in crowded Jerusalem restaurants. And cars packed with explosives plough into new police recruits in the streets of Baghdad, where Sunni/ Shia rivalries threaten civil war. In Yugoslavia, it was hard to believe that such violence could follow so closely on the heels of the collapse of a relatively liberal, well-educated society. The link between violence and identity is writ large in what is called "ethnic cleansing," in which forced eviction, terror, and genocide are employed to bring about regional racial purity. And the tragic Israeli-Palestinian situation in which identity has become a daily matter of life and death makes this connection even sharper. Ethnic difference is understood in terms of the alien, the other, and the deployment of such a category is then used to legitimate extreme brutality. It is as if an entire economy of mutual recognition and accommodation collapses into a tribal, and strictly speaking, primitive economy of rigid identification. The rigidity with which community identity is understood and the resulting fanaticism of identification (allegiance to the group), forces the most disturbing reflections. I put to one side here the possibility that such forms of ethnic fanaticism might simply be ancient myths exploited by evil politicians, though this must play a part. The question I wanted to answer was this: If the quest for identity, its maintenance and enhancement was, and still is, an independent causal factor in bringing about such horrors, what does this tell us about the relationship between personal and group identity, or about the scope of such relationship? More ambitiously, can philosophers say anything distinctive about the conditions under which less rigid identity constructs flourish? It remains my abiding conviction that it is one of philosophy's particular strengths to be able to think productively the ways in which identity is not threatened by difference but bound up with it, woven by it, and so on.[1] My ambition here is modest: to begin to conceptualize certain of the looser shapes in which personal identity is increasingly to be found, and some of the consequences that flow from the range of external conditions on which identity depends.

On reflection, everyone agrees: Identity is not one thing. When philosophers come to consider the question of identity they enter a scene already populated by forensic scientists, genetic engineers, social psychologists, regional politicians, advertising agencies, and customs officials.

We are accustomed to supposing that these senses of identity can all be gathered together under the umbrella of the empirical—but this unreflective homogeneity may well be an illusion. Within philosophy, of course, matters are no easier. Identity figures in different ways in logic, metaphysics, and philosophy of mind. And it is commonly thought indispensable to begin by distinguishing, for instance, numerical and qualitative identity, not to mention personal, social, political identity, etc.

A philosopher will then wonder whether underlying all these senses there might not be one basic conception. Perhaps, "Everything is what it is, and not another thing."[2] But even in such an innocent formulation, a distinction is already being made. Identity is being defined in opposition to difference. Numerical identity is being identified by *distinguishing* it from qualitative identity, suggesting that there is an intimate connection between identity and difference. Perhaps the bare fact of such intimacy undermines from the outset any simple sense of identity. And the particular way in which some contemporary philosophers have come to understand difference—as (to speak somewhat unguardedly) a productive principle, generating chains of connections—would bring identity and difference closer together, even as they are "opposed to one another."

Few philosophers today would insist on the status of identity as a logical or metaphysical primitive; they are much more likely to understand it in terms of a symbolic function. Identity has acquired a life beyond its significance for logic, but it always operates at the symbolic level, where it functions as a site of repetition, overlapping, transformation, condensation, etc. And as such, identity has become complex, internally differentiated, suspended in matrices, constituted, derivative, even dispersed, distributed. Identity has become spiral, even fractal.

Is this so new? Did not even Plato have a tripartite account of the soul? Perhaps we are still trying to shake off that sense of the simple self-transparency of the self-as-subject to which Descartes introduced us. At any rate, it has become clear that no account of identity and selfhood will do that fails to acknowledge: that we try to make sense of our lives, that the ways in which we do this are subject to interrogation and doubt both from ourselves and others, that we are mortal and know it, and that we want our lives to be publicly as well as privately intelligible. But more significantly, that the means available for us to make such sense are becoming increasingly ragged, unreliable, fragmentary, and local.

The idea of a soul, an immaterial substance, the essence of me, which never changed, would certainly guarantee identity through time. But even if such a notion were intelligible, it would prove too much, and reveal too little.[3] It would prove too much in that it would make the deepest anxieties about personal identity unthinkable. And it would precisely not tell us how our fragile and contingent selfhood is constructed. Essentialism drives out both doubt and complexity.

What then is required is an account of personal identity that offers not just metaphysical security, but real ability to articulate the fabric of our lives. Difference functions as a sign for what we could call a problematizing account of the constitution of identity. The key dimension of problematization is precisely over whether identity is being compromised (at the extreme, destroyed), or whether it is being thought through more carefully, more critically. I lean toward the second view: the issue at stake is not whether something exists or not, in any straightforwardly decidable way. The issue about identity is whether the forms of intelligible coherence that we can still sustain, will do the work we want of them. "Is agency still thinkable for a deconstructed self?" is not a factual question (like "Can a three-legged dog still run?"), it is about what impact certain reflections on the constitution of the self have on the ways we think about agency.[4]

For the sake of argument, I will take for granted that the self must, in one way or another, be thought of as complex, as constituted. I will leave this sufficiently open even to include the idea that such constitution might take the form of an endless deferral of finality. When Kierkegaard reflected on the question of selfhood, he concluded (in *The Sickness unto Death*) that the question was not whether the self was constituted or not. It was clear to him that it was. The question was whether this process of constitution involved the self alone, or whether it had to pass through a relation to another being. He argued that unless we accept that the self is constituted by another, we cannot account for the existence of that form of despair in which we do not just give up our lives, but carry on, albeit anxiously.

We could not understand how doubt and interrogation about its nature could be part of the weave of our lives. Only an original entanglement with something outside of ourselves would transcend the despair of immediacy; moreover, such constitution would make us no longer transparent to ourselves.

Our age is characterized by the most profound mistrust of the transcendental, of there being deep conditions of possibility for anything. This mistrust is only partly alleviated by the gradual separation of the transcendental and transcendence, to the point at which we realize that conditions of possibility may be met by empirical phenomena, without sacrificing their status.[5]

A HERMENEUTIC INTERLUDE

Are there any "transcendental requirements for identity"? And if so, how can they be met? I would claim that "lived-identity-through-time" has to negotiate some sort of relation to the conditions of continuity. The connection between personal identity and "horizons of continuity" may be obvious, but it is worth filling it out just a little. For each of us to be ourselves, we need to be able to project possibilities, to recall the past and to be able to continue to act and make sense of our relation to the world. When any one of these dimensions is weakened, so too is our capacity for selfhood.[6] And each of these dimensions is essentially horizonal. To project possibilities is already to take for granted the continuation of technical means, personal connections, one's own physical and intellectual capacities, desires, etc.—all within the framework of our assumed mortality, for which we have both all the evidence we could want, and none at all. Our capacity and the shape of our capacity to recall the past will depend both on how (adequately?) we originally experienced it, but also, crucially, on the continuity (and sometimes on the discontinuity) of our powers of seeing and understanding.[7] And these powers are not immune from the loss or transformation of public meaning. Some of these considerations are captured in the claim that if you can remember the '60s, you weren't there: Dramatic changes in conceptual or social space can block or transform our capacity to remember, and, just as interestingly, our capacity to draw on the past as a resource for self-interpretation and motivation.[8] Our capacity to continue to act in particular ways is clearly bound up both with our sense of self and with conditions that exceed each of us. We desire not just self-images but the capacity to earn a living, and the whole pattern of our productive engagement with the world derives from our being able to continue to act in certain ways. This is why unemployment is so devastating, striking at the heart of our being-in-the-world, effecting a discontinuity over which we often have no control. And it is not surprising that with loss of productive engagement with the world comes loss of self-worth. I would also mention here those possibilities of action and interaction bound up with friendships and loved ones, the loss of which can force a renegotiation of one's self-understanding, and *in extremis* our willingness to carry on.

Moreover, there is the horizon sustained by our capacity to make sense of our relation to the world. We rely on our grasp both of what, in broad terms, is happening out there, and on what it might mean, in being able to define the intelligibility of our behavior. In an extreme form, experiences of religious conversion, for example, can transform the self because they transform the ultimate horizons of significance. And these can of course be positive and revelatory as well as deeply unhinging.[9]

Finally I would add to this brief sketch of the essential horizonality of our being, the importance of place.[10] A place is a site of both public and private memory. To dwell in a place is to engage in a continuing exchange of meaning through which one's identity becomes, at least in part, a kind of symbiotic relationship with where one dwells. This is true not just of those places of whom people speak fondly, but of bleak, inhospitable places too. Place here is another way of talking about past and future, about opportunities for action and interaction. The more we accept the importance of place (and correlatively "home," and even the sacred) for the construction of identity, the more we will grasp the full significance of "homelessness," "loss of nationality," and the worldwide problem of refugees. Clearly, there are powerful nomadic possibilities of identity construction. While some are simply tied to place in an extended sense, for others, traveling, wandering, "going places" clearly serves as a rich narrative resource in itself.[11]

To sum up here: Self-identity is constituted rather than given and our capacity to construct it depends on all sorts of openness to and being sustained by "horizons of continuity"—in which material conditions and existential and hermeneutic functions coincide.

If such horizons of continuity do provide the conditions for projection, sustaining meaning, self-worth, self-understanding, and self-location in ways I have suggested, it is equally clear that it is impossible to separate the question of continuity from questions about the predictability and guarantees of such continuity. For the greater the dependence of selfhood on these horizons of continuity and intelligibility, the more one has to lose if they are disrupted, and the more one will invest in mechanisms by which such horizons can be guaranteed. Complex social life rests on a mix of legitimate expectations and guarantees of constancy—which generate a kind of "second nature." Common language, patterns of civility, a common range of values, laws, a stable currency—these are all interconnected. Some are maintained by habit, some by informal personal interaction, some by market mechanisms, some by strong state management.

If "lived-identity" is dependent on this whole range of legitimate expectations and guarantees of constancy—horizons of predictability—then the disturbance of these conditions, these horizons, can be expected to precipitate an identity crisis.[12]

I have implicated a range of institutions from the state downward in the maintenance of horizons of permanence that make lived-identity possible. This relationship is often indirect and partial. Our capacity to enter into exchange relationships with others depends on a common currency, and on some control over inflation. But how far this is, can be, or should continue to be a state function is a matter of considerable debate, for example in Europe, where questions of national identity are now loudly debated. Equally, those institutions of state and civil society (army, local government, the press, schools, universities) that one might have hoped would buffer state crisis or disintegration can be so heavily dependent on the state that they fail too. The return to ethnic or religious loyalties is a return to identity-bestowing affiliations that have one vital ingredient—they are reliable, and promise an end to what turned out to be a fragile dispersal of identity functions. Linking faith and power, such identity providers guarantee or claim both horizons of ultimate significance and the stable material conditions by which identity is sustained.

But one might ask: Is not the risk of death a serious objection to the claimed reliability of such affiliations—to those young men who join factional armies? The answer, of course, is absolutely not. If anything, the risk of death, as Hegel knew, is precisely what such identification deals with best. At this level, the risk of physical death is wholly secondary to the risk of loss of self. As Nietzsche put it, man would rather will nothing, than not will. And it is no accident that both religious belief and the military ethos give death the highest significance (death with honor, self-sacrifice), by which not merely through identity, but as a hero or martyr, one obtains a permanent place in the hall of fame. Only in such a disturbing light can we make sense of suicide bombers. The promises of heavenly bliss and expected payments to one's family may lubricate the wheels. But it is surely no secret that under conditions of extreme material deprivation a challenge to one's sense of identity can trump even one's fear of death, and is not to be suppressed by tanks and humiliation.

There is no doubting a kind of "logic" connecting death, identity, and sacrifice.[13] One version is played out in Lévi-Strauss's account of cannibalism as a symbolic relationship, one in which a young man can acquire a name (and hence an identity) only by killing and ingesting an existing name-bearer. Hostile reviews of books in journals might suggest that such a way of making a name for oneself lives on in a symbolically transformed way.

There have certainly been societies or circumstances in which such patterns of behavior have made a positive contribution. The transformation of death into sacrifice really does make something out of nothing.[14] But if we can acknowledge that with all its grotesqueness such economies are still human, we can still ask: To what problems do they constitute a solution, and what alternative solutions are there? And if we think of them as "logics," "economies," or even "forms of life," we must not forget how the bright young faces of the Bosnian, or Serbian, or IRA soldier, or member of the Al-Aqsa martyr's brigade triangulate death, identity, and sacrifice in a space they help to replenish with pain, suffering, starvation, violation, etc.

Questions of identity are powerfully implicated in the recent politics of Eastern Europe and the Middle East. If anything like the analysis I have given is correct, we would be led to accept that the role of the other in the constitution of identity is far from being a matter of transcendental social psychology, but is of the deepest political importance. On our account, the story of the conditions on which we develop a distinct and individuated self is one in which the shape of our bonds to the community and to the state is of crucial significance. It would not be too perverse to treat Kafka's novels as explorations of an identity to which the state's contribution has become an overwhelming problem. But what for Joseph K. is a nightmare and the peoples of Eastern Europe an unthinkable horror does not allow us to describe our contemporary position as bearers of a distributed identity in the classical language of alienation. If I am right, the fact that our developing identities are made possible by their dependence on external guarantees is a description of the human condition. The fact that in Western countries it is often an array of state and other apparatuses that sustain this order rather than a local community bound together by a common faith,[15] creates both deep potential instabilities but also new possibilities of identity and selfhood.

The real justification of Western democracy as a political system is that it promotes and guarantees freedom to its citizens. But there is an obvious gap between formal, legal freedom and what Isaiah Berlin long ago called positive liberty. The communitarian approach both to identity and to social values—the tradition from Aristotle through Burke, Hegel, Marx, Taylor, MacIntyre, Sandel, and Walzer—makes this point even more clearly. The "unencumbered self" is a fiction blind to its own social constitution. Treating social relations as instrumental is an epistemological error, as well as moral myopia, even in those societies that seem to encourage it. Many if not all the goods we seek are essentially relational goods. It may be important to recognize, if only to understand the attractions of the liberal alternatives, that the *illusion* of individual autonomy—not unlike what Nietzsche called "active forgetting"—may well at times be productive for a community. To be able to choose is not just a formal condition, but one deeply dependent on other (e.g., material) conditions. If our own society is not to become riddled with pockets of violence, it has to provide above all opportunities for selfhood—that is, for recognition,[16] individuation, and development.[17]

NARRATIVE AND THE CONSTITUTION OF IDENTITY

I want now to return to the question of the constitution of identity. Suppose we agree that identity, or selfhood, is not given, not simple, but constituted, complex, dependent, etc.—without necessarily at this stage agreeing on a particular analysis of this. Suppose we add that identity is a distinct, often overriding human concern[18] and that whether and how such concerns are met can be of enormous political significance.[19]

Given these premises, what can we learn from contemporary philosophical discussions of identity—particularly those that would deny it, or deconstruct it? My view is that deconstruction quite as much contributes to the highly traditional philosophical task of interrogating the nature of the self as to any denial of selfhood. And one suspects that some of those most hostile are not philosophers at all, but the very same kind of people who found Socrates' questioning tiresome.

To ask whether constructed (or de-constructed) selves are adequate substitutes for the genuine variety is of course deeply question begging. I propose to assume, heuristically, that selfhood is best thought of as constructed, and in some important sense incomplete and relational. We can then return to our question as to what if anything contemporary accounts of the self teach us.

First, however, I would like to bring narrative on stage. In recent years there has been a strong sense that narrative could supply for the identity of persons and states what a metaphysical self could no longer underpin. And moreover, that it would do so in a way that was flexible, open to development, and knitted together the personal and the social, experience and language. Surely, in principle at least, narrative would provide a softening of the outline of a viable identity, one that would reduce those grounds, at least, for violence. Matters are not, of course, that simple. One of the most interesting aspects of Edward Said's *Culture and Imperialism* for example is that narrative is presented not so much as a way out of the violence of essentialist identity, but rather as the plane on which struggles take place. He writes:

> [S]tories are at the heart of what explorers and novelists say about strange
> regions of the world . . . they also became the method colonized people use
> to assert their own identity, and the existence of their own history . . . as one
> critic has suggested, nations are themselves narratives.

If the main battle in imperialism was over land,

> these issues were reflected, contested, and even for a time decided in narra-
> tive . . . [and] the power to narrate, or to block other narrations from form-
> ing and emerging is very important to culture and imperialism and consti-
> tutes one of the main connections between them.

I shall return to Said shortly. But first I discuss the distinctly different
approaches of both Ricoeur and Derrida to the status of narrative, looking in
particular at those readings Derrida gives of Nietzsche and Blanchot that
probe the silent identity framing, and hence exclusion, that makes narrative
construction possible.

Identity is a product not an origin. And it is important epistemologically
as well as politically to grasp the constructedness of narrative; it matters that
the construction of narrative intelligibility is a selective process, and leaves
things out. Exclusion from representation, marginalization, and indeed elimination in the name of a narrative—collectivization, racial purification, liberation, Westernization, perhaps even enlightenment itself—are central concerns on every agenda. But there is another side to this: Narrative is not just
a vehicle for generating silence and forgetting but often an indispensable aid
in the service of memory and commemoration—helping others who were not
there understand what happened.[20]

There are two straightforward arguments for continuing to take narrative
seriously, and for treating the deconstruction of narrative as what, after
Wittgenstein, we might call a reminder.

First, there is a strong sense in which what is forgotten or left out by one
narrative calls not for skepticism about narrative but another narrative, for it
to be adequately represented. Much political activity in both Argentina and
the former Yugoslavia has centered on recording the stories of those whose
sons and daughters, husbands and wives have disappeared. To fit the Holocaust into the story of Germany may be to compromise its singularity. But we
must not forget that it is often precisely because dead men (and women)
don't talk, tell no tales, that they are killed in the first place.

Second, it is arguable that even being forgotten or left out is itself a status we can only understand and then try to correct, because it too has a com-
prehensible narrative form. What then would be the force of the reminder
that the deconstruction of narrative constitutes for us? It could transform our
reading, listening, understanding. We would begin to see the framing as well
as the frame, just as we have to learn to read advertising, and see how we are
being manipulated. We might simply bear in mind that there are "always
many sides to the story," that a plurality of stories can be told of the same
event (think of the film *Rashomon*, or *Groundhog Day*, or of Kierkegaard's
retellings of the Abraham story in *Fear and Trembling*). We might keep our
eyes peeled for squashed marginalia, the failures of history, the things that did

not happen, but could have, the awkward facts that remain unaccounted for, the events that cannot be made part of history without having their singularity threatened.

But these suggestions are all compatible with the thesis that narrative in some broad sense is the inescapable space within which even its own failures are represented. Moreover, it would follow that narrative is never itself the problem. The problem is its mode of presentation—how we understand its scope, etc.

Ricoeur's position here is interesting. He understands man as a self-interpreting being. Through narrative we configure and, when we apply this to life, refigure this process of self-interpretation. Ricoeur could be said to be offering a solution to the following question: If to be a self is to somehow synthesize, bring together, the private and the public dimensions of the self, then in the absence of the package deal provided by religious community, how is it that through language, myth, fiction—a whole range of public forms of intelligibility—we weave selves?

What is extraordinary about Ricoeur's work—and this appears near the end of both *Time and Narrative* and *Oneself as Another*—is his recognition that the various dialectical processes that he sets in train—between the reflexivity of the self, the opposition between selfhood and sameness, and filling the self/other relation—are never resolved. Aporia, and indeed tragedy, remains, and he leaves us with a vision of peace marked by the possibility of ineliminable conflict. We will return to these issues in the next chapter.

For Kierkegaard, Hegel, and others, selfhood requires a constitutive relation to an other, a Power. And we can translate Kierkegaard's remarks about despair into Ricoeur's terms: Selfhood deprived of the symbolic resources to weave a narrative of self-interpretation will know only desperation. A selfhood for whom such resources are available may still feel despair but that despair will be mediated by a symbolic engagement with the social. Kierkegaard's despair at willing to be oneself—what I have called desperation—is one in which the horizon of the future has withered away, as the tracks of symbolically mediated self-interpretation have been torn up. Despairingly willing to be oneself—carrying on, albeit in despair—is continuing this process of self-interpretation even when the story seems bleak, or the story line implausible.

What our translation of this problematic into Ricoeur's language opens up is the whole area of what we might call anxiety about the self, and its relation to the forms of temporalizing engagement available. For if narrative self-interpretation offers an interweaving of the private and the public, one that fuses both symbolic and temporal horizons, this articulation of what narrative provides also allows us to thematize how it is that less complex or completely satisfying forms arise, and may indeed have become the norm.

I am taking it as axiomatic that selfhood requires some sort of identity through time. It is a well-worn position that bodily continuity is not sufficient. Nor is the continuity of memory. One common objection to memory playing this role is that it is question-begging. "Whose memory?" we might ask. But it is not clear whether that should count as an objection or rather a spur to recognize the necessity of some sort of fundamental hermeneutical circularity. And the kind of questions we have run into would have to be drawn into those broader considerations. Memory is not simply a private phenomenon. Its public dimension is to be found not just in the importance of its being corroborated by others, it is a memory woven with public symbols—places, names, times, conversations—which locate it in various series and matrices of meaning. I do not have to sustain the clock, the calendar, the map of the earth, the lexicon of names. I freely draw upon these in my weaving. I have suggested, too, that if we take into account the role of economic and institutional factors, there are further orders playing a normative role—such as exchange rates, national boundaries, shared and contested histories, different levels of industrialization, and access to communication networks. I mention these kinds of "material" factors again simply to keep them on the agenda, for the capacity of such "systems" to supplement the traditional resources for identity construction and maintenance presents philosophical thinking with both a challenge and an opportunity.

If we understand nihilism as the disintegration of all absolute values, and of any transcendental grounds for identity formations, and if we accept that what Nietzsche called nihilism captures if not the state of things today, at least a pervasive concern, or tendency, then our contemporary challenge is that of coping with the *contingency* of identity, as Rorty would put it. Identity will have to be woven from whatever material is available rather than from a kit in which everything is provided. This is not simply a problem for philosophy, it is increasingly a problem for humanity. Certainly within cultural studies, and queer studies, new concepts of multiple and decentered subject formations, dispersed identities, are being forged to cope with this phenomena conceptually. The question I would like to pose, finally, is what limits there are, if any, to our ability to imagine substitute identities, bricolage identities rather than those logically engineered, to rework a Lévi-Straussian distinction.

RENEGOTIATING IDENTITY

Identity is so often treated corrosively, skeptically, not because the young bloods of philosophy have got hold of powerful weapons they don't really know how to handle, but because the shapes that identity takes today reflect a massive and general externalization, decentering, dehiscence, and articulation of all constituted beings. If there is any longer any sense in talking about the meaning of history, its latest phase is surely a ruthless penetration, or at least threatening, of all established boundaries, and their dynamic reconstitution in accordance with diverse economies.[21] I have great sympathy with

Gilles Deleuze when he talks of philosophy as having the task of inventing new concepts, and hence of tracking, as far as this makes sense, the contours of contemporary experience. The truth is no longer the whole, as Hegel would say, or rather the whole has to be understood as diverse, and plural, with many centers of order and significance. When Kristeva suggests in "Women's Time"[22] that we need to think of time as cyclical and monumental, as opposed to the standard linear time—of progressive and ends-oriented time—she is in effect talking about alternative local ways in which identity trails are set up. There need be no grand synthesis of how all these fit together.

The thought that we can entirely eliminate what we might call transcendental questions is misplaced. For there is an inevitable tension between new formations of identity—to which we have to respond—and our continuing sense of the transcendental as the background against which such formations take place. And this issue is bound up with questions we cannot relinquish—of the intelligibility of a human life. We cannot let go of these questions, because—and here Kierkegaard and Heidegger were right—anxiety accompanies us at every stage of our lives and of our endeavor to make sense in the absence of a priori guarantees. At the very least, we owe ourselves a discourse, a language, perhaps even a conceptual scheme in which to think the very fragmentation we have adumbrated.

To return, then, to violence. While there will always be violence only accidentally connected to identity, my hypothesis is that there is much that is deeply internally connected to it. The violence referred to in Derrida's discussion of Levinas in "Violence and Metaphysics" is the violation of the other, the violence toward the face of the other, brought about by a metaphysical or ontological neutralization of all being, which would eliminate the essential asymmetry of human relating. But we need not swallow this formulation whole to see that if identity is concerned with the boundaries and sequencings of the self, threats, or perceived threats, to those dimensions will be threats to our very being. And these will be understood as threats of violence, and will provoke violence in their turn.

It has been recently suggested to me[23] that identity today is just a negotiable commodity, to be bought and sold, that identities are just various forms of investment. When I hear this, I am challenged, because I have already talked about subjects, selves, being located within various economies. It is easy to respond to such a model by asking "for whom" is identity a negotiable commodity, as Ricoeur asks of Parfit "for whom" is identity no longer the issue.[24]

But if I am honest there is something chillingly premonitory about this suggestion. Are we, as Julia Kristeva suggests the first civilization to witness the widespread breakdown of the family, and hence the breakdown of those Oedipal forms of strong identity cathexes that went with it? Or are we witnessing the (re-)emergence of a diversity of forms of family life that deserves support and encouragement? Is there perhaps a positive rather than a merely nihilistic sense in which we can think the negotiability of identity?

Amartya Sen, for example (see his *Reason before Identity*, Oxford University Press, 1999), reaffirms the Rawlsian position that a universal sense of justice trumps a slavish respect for local moralities. And as a corollary, that cultural and political identities are not just bestowed upon us, but can in part at least, be chosen or, as we have put it, "negotiated." It is tempting to think we need to choose between a liberal and a communitarian position here, or else to attempt some general synthesis of the two. It may be more productive, however, to recognize that one of the common (but not unprecedented or universal) consequences of globalization (see chapter 10) is the dislocation of populations, as well as destabilizing cultural invasions of populations more geographically static. And while there are obvious opportunities for new historical processes—such as cultural hybridization—for individuals caught up in these changes, identity must often present itself as a choice, as a matter for negotiation. But this is not a choice of a wholly autonomous independent unencumbered being. It is rather the choice of a multiply encumbered being thrust into conditions in which one's social constitution is no longer just a matter of a single tradition. Sen's own position as an Indian academic, Master of Trinity College, Cambridge, would seem exemplary. But we do not surely have to understand choice here in terms of the agency of some abstractly rational being. The agent here is multiply embedded. And the grounds for identity choice may be, but need not be some universal principle of reason. It may well be true that, if you are in the business of weighing and adjudicating the competing claims of local moralities, at *some* level universal principles are unavoidable. But this is a logical not an ethical truth.

One's first reaction to a boundary threat, a continuity threat, can be expected to be a violently defensive one in which it is the rigid form of one's identity, so to speak (the paranoid self), that is responding. It is, precisely, a reactive response. But if boundaries and horizons are constituted, then, at least in principle, they can be transformed. The subject of such a reaction may not be the self in its dynamic aspect, but rather a boundary guard. Negotiable identity does not mean that every boundary has its price. But it does mean that a more mobile capacity for identity formation and transformation can plausibly be regarded as a better "defense" than the unconditional maintenance of rigidities. If we apply the principle proposed earlier—that we must will the conditions of what we value—then we must ask under what conditions such negotiable identity could best flourish. It may be said that our contemporary rich diversity of stories, languages, cultural symbols, etc. is no substitute for tradition, that one cannot just buy and sell roots, tribal bonds, etc. But one serious response here would be that a culture of dynamic identity modification is a culture, a tradition itself.

I claim, then, that identity is a construction, that narrative supplies the most powerful forms of such constructedness, that narrative does not eliminate but elaborates and restages the possibilities of violence and confrontation, and that a certain "deconstruction" of narrative serves to moderate its capacity to be harnessed for violent ends.

If I understand Derrida's readings of Nietzsche and of Blanchot correctly, he is arguing, as did Nietzsche himself, for the fictionality of the identities constructed through (say) autobiographical writing, and the fragility of the narrative unity wrought by a text. And this fictionality operates through the proper name, through the idealizing functions of names themselves.[25] What this suggests is something of a double strategy: the affirmation of the move away from essentialism toward narrative, but at the same time, the maintenance of a certain interrogative space within which narratives operate. This would argue for the necessity of Narrative, but also for the pitfalls and dangers of taking any one narrative too seriously.

Edward Said emphasizes the heterogeneity in every culture. Once spoken, it is obvious, but its enabling power rests on the fact that the construction of identity involves positioning oneself within countervailing identities. And at this point the elision of differences within the other culture is almost automatic. A *critical political culture* (and it is this above all that is needed) would have to think *against the grain*, it would deconstruct these illusory unities, and keep open the dynamic possibilities of narrativizing. Such a political culture would not just preserve a multiplicity of narratives and encourage differential articulations within perceived unities, it would also have to recognize and promote what we could call the critical space of narrative, which is not "just another narrative." If it is a narrative, it is a narrative about the limits and scope and significance of narrative. And if the Enlightenment escapes the charge of being just another grand narrative, it is because it can be understood as a principle regulating, moderating, even deconstructing the pretensions of individual narratives. If Said is right about the intrinsic heterogeneity of every culture, we might perhaps take that a stage farther and argue that versions of this recognition of a critical space of narrative, as I have called it, can be found everywhere. It would not, then, be a matter of imposing some Western concept of enlightenment, but of seeking out and encouraging local forms of such a space wherever it appears. This would not be just another grand narrative, because the plurality of narrative calls for interpretation for its possibility even to be intelligible. If the intrinsic heterogeneity of any culture will sustain a plurality of narratives, this is not so much another "grand" narrative as an account of how this intrinsic plurality of narratives is to be understood.

This is no more another grand narrative than was Lyotard's original thesis about the end of grand narrative.[26] The explanation we give is in terms of the non-natural constructedness of identity, which opens up the plurality of grounds.

By the critical space of narrative I do not just mean the space of scholarship, but that dimension of any culture that acknowledges and affirms the constructedness of its artifacts, and does so without falling into an ironic consciousness.[27] For it is this fate that haunts every attempt to acknowledge plurality. Once we hold our deepest beliefs in the same spirit as we wear brand-name T-shirts, once our deepest beliefs become mere matters of taste, something essential has been lost.

I am now in a position to complete the quotation from Peirce with which I began, for its true scope has become apparent. Recall his description of the man who has for years cherished some vague shadow of an idea; he continues:

> [A]nd then he has waked up some bright morning to find it gone, clean vanished away like the beautiful Melusina of the fable, and the essence of his life gone with it.

The question we face, putting Peirce into bed with Nietzsche, is whether the essence of a life is reconstructable now that the chimeric Melusina, the beautiful fable of a strong and coherent self-identity, has vanished.

TWO

The Philosophy of Violence ::
The Violence of Philosophy

<hr>

INTRODUCTION: AMBIVIOLENCE, SOME REMINDERS

AT FIRST SIGHT, violence makes a mockery of everything philosophy stands for, scorning both the reasonable and the rational. Might it not even have been the fear of violence that spawned a philosophy cast as an antidote, or countervailing force? One source of caution, then, would lie in the sense of a profound genealogical intimacy between philosophy and violence, an intimacy that a naive enthusiasm for the connection might miss. On this reading, philosophy's encounter with violence would have always already occurred, a lost origin. But there is a more worrying possibility, one more or less common to the thinking of Derrida, Adorno, and Lyotard—that philosophy, or a certain mode of philosophizing, might be more intimately entangled with violence than it would like to admit. How, in the first place, do we come to speak of "violence" as one thing? Is not the unity wrought by conceptualization itself a violence?

The philosophy of violence must never forget the violence of philosophy. When we say "the philosophy of violence," we begin to imagine that "we," we philosophers, are on the side of the angels. With this reversal, a reversal that appears at least to upset the direction of Hegel's speculative proposition, we begin to see that being an angel requires a new labor of the negative, and old virtues, such as patience and humility. I will argue that a philosophical reflection on violence cannot escape reflection on the temptations to a certain violence of philosophy itself. And I believe that this hyper-reflection takes us a step forward in understanding the shape and significance of nonviolence. Nonviolence, I will argue, is a disposition that is recursively and reflectively attuned to the multiple displacements that violence undergoes, to the forms and conditions of its continual resurgence, and to the ineliminable ambivalence that surrounds the issue of violence—what I have called ambiviolence.

This nonviolence is another name for the responsibility of philosophy, the practice of philosophical memory. This memory is that capacity to "keep in mind," to "recall, in the sense of bringing to bear on one's actions." Philosophy understood in this way is a complex "how," a meta-modality of practice. What I hope to do here is, as Wittgenstein put it, to assemble some "reminders." If I am successful, it will become clear that the question of violence is central to our very understanding of philosophical practice. But also that only when philosophy understands this can it positively contribute to an understanding of violence.

The injunction—"Never again!"—has now acquired a familiar association with the Holocaust. And yet, that very familiarity brings with it the danger that we might remember the slogan but forget what it enjoins. Ever since Plato made anamnesis central to philosophical knowledge, the problem of memory has been central to philosophy, even though its theme has had to be recalled repeatedly under different names—repetition, "assembling reminders," reactivation, *destruktion*, deconstruction, and so on. We need new names, in part to counter precisely the dangers of familiarization. In these repeated renewals of philosophy, of philosophical method, of philosophy always in conflict with mere method, and in the issues raised by this need for a perennial resurgence of the *physis* of philosophy, it is hard to know whether we are dealing with ethics or ontology, or whether the event of philosophy was not always prior to that distinction. If "Never again!" is the measure of our contemporary responsibility, it is also a call for the renewal of philosophy as memory, as a practice of recalling, reminding ourselves, of commemoration.

This chapter pursues three different threads: First, what I call the ineluctability of violence—the ways violence is connected to the fragility of peace, and the pathologies of time, and recognition. Second, some of the moral ambivalences of war, genocide, and revolution. And third, the idea that violence is endemic to philosophy itself (especially its humanistic expression), though it can be diminished.[1]

THE INELUCTABILITY OF VIOLENCE

Violence in its ordinary sense typically reflects a conflict of interest, one which is pressing, and one for which there is no obvious peaceful solution.

It might be thought obvious that the goal of those who seek peace would be the cessation of violence by agreement, by reconciliation. It is, however, all too easy to relapse into a "pre-critical" and naive sense of the nature of such agreement. Even if there can be "agreement" of a kind in some cases, nothing guarantees it in all cases, not least because interests may be irreconcilably "in conflict." It is not that agreement is never possible, but that it cannot be guaranteed. And there are many ways for an apparent consensus to break down. This does not mean that there never is any consensus, but rather that all consensus is conditional and hence fragile.[2]

That there are no guarantees of consensus or of its permanence can be made apparent when we understand how it is that interests can be "irreconcilable." There are clear cases of reconcilable conflicts (two nations may both want a piece of land—one for water, the other for security; two people may want one lemon—one for the juice, another for the zest). But cases of irreconcilability can arise for both practical and principled reasons.

Practically, the situation may be one in which it is only "accidental" that the two parties cannot both be satisfied. Two friends find a $100 bill, each with their heart set on buying some object that, as it happens, costs $53 and $57 respectively. Had their desires cost $53 and $47, everything would be fine, but. . . . And if the two friends fall in love with the same woman, or two tribes believe that the same city (and its sacred sites) is the capital of their respective state, then we have a case of principled irreconcilability.[3]

Principled irreconcilability arises through nonnegotiable interests. Let us call these nonnegotiable interests *absolute* interests. Why are absolute interests nonnegotiable? First, there are some goods, in some contexts, that are, or seem to be, irreplaceable. For the army general, a soldier may be replaceable. For the soldier's daughter, he is not. For the insurance company, the fatal auto accident is a cost; for the family of the victim, the check may be welcome, but "is no substitute."[4]

And sometimes the condition for the negotiation of loss is the recognition of its nonnegotiability.[5] The question of interest (in conflict resolution) is complicated because there are secondary interests as well—the mediators, and other third parties, who have an interest in the resolution of the conflict—and those (e.g., arms dealers, terrorist gangs) who have an interest in the perpetuation or renewal of conflict. As we saw in the last chapter, these latter typically serve to fan the flames of regressive identity formations.[6] Obviously, the implication of all this is that violent conflict is most likely where the interests at stake are least negotiable. So what makes interests nonnegotiable?

It is easy to identify negotiability with calculation, and in the world of insurance companies and legal compensation, with money. In this Benthamite world, in principle, everything can be measured.[7] The attempts to translate quality into quantity (estimating the cash value of a slur on someone's reputation) are often ludicrous. And yet, of course, the very idea of money presupposes the general if not universal possibility of such translations—$ for land, $ for food, $ for human organs, $ for sexual services, $ for medical care. . . . Even barter presupposes a making equivalent of things that are in some sense "incommensurable." We might speculate that the ubiquity of money-based exchange relations has bankrupted the defensive posture of philosophical essentialism, which attempts to find some sort of hard currency within language, or even outside it. The abandonment of that project opens up to philosophy a different goal—learning how to deal, negotiate, even draw lines, in a world where everything is fungible and nothing bolted down.

It is tempting to say that there is much more to negotiating than the direct or indirect exchange of goods, than buying, selling, or bartering. But of course there is already much more to buying and selling itself than meets the eye: the value of the currency—how "negotiable" it is!—for example, the presence and power of a central bank, and the political (and military) power to maintain the stability of the global market. All this is the background—more or less visible—against which commercial and financial transactions everywhere take place. It is a commonplace that political uncertainty produces a loss of value in a currency. These remarks can now be conceptually generalized.

The general significance of background conditions on other forms of negotiation suggests an important principle—that any force capable of representing or projecting itself and that has the capacity to alter significantly the background conditions of a negotiation, is potentially a party to those negotiations. We might want some sort of legitimacy constraint to be added here, but history teaches us, if I dare put it like this, that this is precisely the point at which legitimacy is not so much required as created. Consider the inclusion of Sinn Fein in negotiations over the future of Ireland, over the objections of those who would not "negotiate with terrorists,"[8] or Israel's refusal to negotiate with Hezbullah. It is not simply that "might is right," but that the sustained capacity to deploy force toward an end that has a political character (i.e., would establish new forms of legitimation) typically does affect the background conditions of any negotiations that would *exclude* them by preventing those negotiations from succeeding.

The role of background conditions in deciding whether negotiation can succeed is very complex. Some of these conditions are "natural"—the absence or presence of rivers, mountains, seas that give some rationale to national boundaries (e.g., making them defensible or intelligible), and the regularity of nature—we assume that oil fields will continue to produce oil and not turn into milk. But these physical conditions are not, in principle, capable of being made party to an agreement. Whereas those that involve human beliefs and practices can be.

There are many ways in which agreements that resolve (or prevent) conflict can fail. They may be based on assumptions that seemed reasonable at the time but which turn out to be false, or on background conditions that were not even considered but turn out to be decisive. War between nations over water rights may be averted by agreements that fail to anticipate substantial reductions in total water flow. Human relationships founded on unconditional love may falter after incapacitating illness or accident.[9] And it is a mistake to suppose that one could anticipate all such contingencies. Even if one could, it is not possible to predict one's affective response to them.

Here, then, we see that hidden background conditions provide opportunities for consensual breakdown. Put more strongly, events can lead even the parties concerned to question not merely whether they still like the agreement, but what the agreement really means.

This is obviously a field day for lawyers, but lawyers are not to blame for the phenomena they deal with. Semantic incompleteness is not the result of carelessness, it is the consequence of various features of language: First, the meaning of words is inseparable from the complex and changing network of human practices. Words are human institutions, tied up with the practices in which they operate. And second, however else we think about words, there is always a moment of application (recognizing this as an instance of x) for which there will be no rules. It may be said that there will always be clear cases, unambiguous cases. But one does not know the meaning of a word if one can only use it in unambiguous situations and has no idea how to deal with marginal cases. Meaning is inseparable from extension. It might be thought that what is missing from this account is what Kant and, later, Gadamer appeal to as "good will"—the willingness or desire or motivation to resolve such difficulties as do arise.[10] But, curiously, this supplemental thought falls to the same objection. We can all bring to mind cases in which renegotiations maintain agreements through a certain give-and-take that we attribute to good will. But nothing guarantees how far good will can take us. There is nothing so *apparently* pure as a good will!

GOOD WILL

There is clearly work for "good will" to do. One of the key principles of negotiation theory is to focus not on positions but on interests.[11] The implication is that positions are particular ways of realizing underlying interests, and clashes of positions may mask the possibility of harmonizing of interests. We know, for example, that there are situations in which a conflict of interests can be resolved—by introducing new considerations (such as long-term interests), or new ingredients (a third party could change the terms of the dispute by a generous offer), or new information (you want the land, I want the house). But it would be blind faith to believe that all conflicts of claimed interest are reconcilable. It might be proposed then, that some test could be devised to determine whether any particular claimed interest was legitimate, allowing some higher authority to decide the matter.

If we could devise a test for legitimate interests, nothing guarantees that this would prevent conflict, or violence. Nothing, that is, guarantees that all conflicts of claimed legitimate interest can be arbitrated, whether to the satisfaction of impartial arbitrators, or to the satisfaction of the parties concerned. It is an unwarranted assumption to suppose that legitimate claims are all, as Leibniz would say, compossible.

It is quite proper, and a vital ingredient of a true pacifism, to believe that it is always possible to resolve disputes without violence. But "always possible" does not imply "possible always."

TARGETING THE BACKGROUND

The significance of background conditions for understanding the fragility of agreement and the possibilities of consensual breakdown and violence can be made apparent by considering the pathologies opened up by the very structure of action. The exercise of the will in action always involves the attempt to change some aspect of a situation against the background of certain assumptions about what will stay the same. These background conditions may be relatively recessive or inoperative, or they may include the very material being acted on. A supple negotiation of this relation to the background we call *phronesis*; blindness to it is folly.

What is distinctive about war, revolution, and genocide is the way in which, increasingly, background conditions both account for the outcome of wars and are the targets of violence and hostility. The concept of total war rests precisely on the idea that the civilian population can be targeted, not because it is part of the army but because it supplies the army, and because army morale is undermined by civilian losses. Genocide targets the very population from which future resistance might flow and attempts to eliminate even the memory of atrocity. The frightening fact is that while the logic of war as conquest of people would set limits on the destruction of populations, war over other resources (territory, water, oil) knows no such limits. As horrific as death camps, rape camps, nuclear war are, it should not escape notice that war is increasingly tied to capital flows, and specific human lives do not figure significantly in these equations.

VIOLENCE AND TIME: THE ETERNAL RETURN OF RESSENTIMENT

The ineluctability of violence has many sources, but none so potent as the shape of our inhabiting of time. For the tradition that includes Heraclitus, Nietzsche, and Heidegger it is clear that violence needs to be understood not merely empirically but ontologically. The structure of Nietzsche's account of ressentiment is quite exemplary in this respect. The closer we can link violence to ressentiment and trauma, the more violence becomes visible as a disease of time, as a chronopathology.

Nietzsche's account of ressentiment operates on our most basic existential/ ontological condition—the passage of time. While there will be other stories to be told, what ressentiment does is to provide us with a ground logic for violence. We philosophers have a tendency to think of violence as a form of intentionality, even when it incorporates efficiently inhuman means in which no "recognition" takes place: nerve gas, machine guns, rail transportation. Arguments that link enlightenment to totalitarianism and genocide (e.g., from Adorno and Lyotard) correctly link enlightenment to the project of willing the destructive transformation of any and all regressive background conditions without considering the price to be paid for the substitute mechanisms required to sustain the new background conditions (e.g., a totalitarian state).[12] But this sounds like a discovery, a meta-truth about enlightenment that ought to be able to be fed back into enlightenment to create an enlightened enlightenment. If this did not happen, I suggest (contra Lyotard, for example), it is because enlightenment took a hysterical form, characterized by ressentiment, one that did not allow the past to be affirmed for fear that its traumas would (merely) be repeated, which is why the theme of repetition becomes central for both Nietzsche and Heidegger. Nietzsche discusses ressentiment in terms of our taking "revenge" against time and its "it was."[13] What is interesting here is that it sounds, at least, as if Nietzsche is talking about a pathological response to a central dimension of the human condition—that time passes, and that the past and the passage to the past, are both irrevocable. What would it mean to take revenge against this fact? And what could determine this or a different shape of response?

First, note that if ressentiment is understood as revenge against time and its "it was" it cannot in principle be successful. For any particular act of ressentiment will itself be engulfed by the very time it rails against. The frustration of ressentiment is essential because its impotent rage can only produce imaginary and temporary reversals to what it opposes.

But while it is vital to understand ressentiment at this ontological level, it is hard to resist asking whether the very level at which this phenomenon operates is not symptomatic of the problem. Suppose, for example, that ressentiment was a response that, as Freud describes melancholia, does not actually engage the traumatic event, but rather rehearses the aporetic structure it generates. If this were so, the ontological dimension of ressentiment would be deeply significant, but significant as a *symptom* of a certain opacity about the specificity of the trauma.

Nietzsche's "solution"—affirmation of all that ever has been, and its eternal recurrence—itself needs interpreting. We might think that it is defective for precisely this same reason—that it fails to engage the specificity of the past. But interestingly, it might be thought to be precisely the right response, indeed the only response, for a condition in which the specificity of the trauma is genuinely unavailable, like a broad-spectrum antibiotic used for an infection that has only roughly been identified. It might be that trauma can only be targeted in certain ways if it is *not* identified.

This connection between ressentiment, trauma, and its necessary failure provides at least the skeleton, or a possible logic, of the frustration expressed in much violence. We often lament the lack of recognition, lack of respect for the person involved in violence. But do we ever pause to reflect that this lack of respect, etc. may be essential. When violence is a displacement of frustration, the frustration of being locked in traumatic repetition, then the actual object of the violence[14] is precisely not respected, not just because the act is one of violence but because the real object lies elsewhere. If so, then violence in general, or at least this kind of violence, calls for a kind of psychoanalytical phenomenology to analyze the displaced intentionalities at play.[15] But is also suggests that the release from violence may be a never-ending task.

VIOLENCE AND RECOGNITION

In Kant, Hegel, and Sartre we can find extraordinarily suggestive accounts of what we might call the social contradiction, one from which violence all too freely flows.[16] Here is the contradiction: For our purely selfish purposes we nonetheless need the help of others. Sometimes this assistance, or provision, could equally well be provided by an apple tree, a spring, or a shady place. In these cases it is not necessary that the Other be human. But there is a whole class of cases in which what is at stake is recognition. And this cannot straightforwardly be given by nature.[17] Recognition is something we need from others, but this very need creates its own ambivalence. I may need your recognition, says a son to a father, but I resent needing it, I resent the structure in me that needs it. Why? Because this very achievement of a certain independence is seen to be dependent on the Other, and hence outside my direct will. When all goes well, this dependence may be unproblematic. But when difficulties arise, we find ourselves primed for violence.

For Sartre, this predicament leads to a dialectical sequence of clear but unstable positions (sadism, masochism, . . .) .[18] If we ask ourselves what drives this sequence, the answer surely is a demand for resolution, which generates a series of unstable positions, "resolutions" that each prove to be chimerical. The instability of this demand for recognition is reflected not just in a neat quasi-logical series of stepping stones, but in the potential for displacements of various sorts, displacements that have the character of disguising their own fragility. Or at least of facilitating our failure to look farther, to anticipate the breakdown. Here, we can see how the violence that mutates along this chain of transformations is the result of a certain deep structure of demand for resolution. This demand is nothing but a disease of time, a demand for the end to a contradiction that in itself is irresolvable.

Sartre puts the basic structure very well when he talks of love's need for free recognition on the part of the other. To the extent that it is free, I cannot control it. To venture down the path of nonetheless trying to control it is fatal. Here, a nondialectical solution is called for. One of the most suggestive sources here is to be found in Keats's idea of "negative capability."[19] Another would be Heidegger's *Gelassenheit*.[20]

But these "solutions" raise a serious question: Can they genuinely function as solutions for the psychic structures in question, or do they require a change in psychic structure in order for them to become solutions? Suppose, for example, that rape and racist attacks are both symptoms of a pathological recognition deficiency, that the perpetrators of these crimes feel that the world (parents, economy, history, . . .) does not value them sufficiently, does not acknowledge them, recognize them. The violence of these acts is complex. For the recognition may come from below, from the fear, the terror, the suffering perpetrated on the other, or it may come laterally—from the solidarity of the group (e.g., the gang). But either way, this recognition is unstable, permeable, etc. A forced recognition is all too close to a refusal of recognition. And the solidarity of other group members is all too vulnerable to a wider public refusal of social recognition to that group. The frustration inherent in these "difficulties" of recognition can be expected to result in greater violence. This condition of recognition deficiency is complex, because all young adults, by definition, have to deal with this, however successful their upbringing. Economic, intrapsychic, and personal independence is a considerable achievement for anyone. For those with "deprived backgrounds" there is a double burden. Not only may there be little personal foundation for achieving recognition, there may be few available steps toward recognition that would even hint at its possibility. And a generally recognition-deficient culture not only breeds crime, it also breeds a psychic structure ripe for cooption into hierarchical institutional structures that exert control by managing recognition.[21]

The violence of hierarchical institutions may be invisible, and sometimes harmless. But its exemplary form is to be found in military and other totalitarian structures, such as what are called "intelligence" agencies. And in the military, of course, we find classic instances of directed violence, where the need for recognition is harnessed to lethal ends. Unfortunately, the military imperative—the apparent need for modern industrial states to sustain armies, or defense agreements with states that sustain armies—suggests that there are institutionally countervailing forces to those that would strive for a broader culture of recognition. For healthy cultures would not provide the recognition-deficient fodder of anomic young men for incorporation into institutional structures of violence. Here, we see another way in which states have an interest in the perpetuation of evil.[22]

The tantalizing prospect held out by Kant's concept of "unsocial sociability," and by the accounts of the dialectics of recognition in Hegel and Sartre, is that we might find therein certain rational seeds of violence. The watershed reflected in Hegel's account of the life-and-death struggle lies in the fact that it presents to us the connection between violence and the need for recognition. The eagle that catches, kills, and eats a lamb does not seek from the lamb recognition of its strength, its magnificent wingspan, etc. We believe, at least, that the eagle is hungry, or that its little eaglets are hungry. Fighting stags seem to be concerned with something else—we may call it territory, mating rights, and it is hard to avoid here the language of recognition, even rights. Victory is followed by the flight or subservience or acquiescence of the loser, who will not, for a while, challenge the victor. And among humans, it seems that "recognition" is the name not for a specific social act, but for an entire dimension of relationality, to which a whole class of violence is attached. Terror, sadistic torture, rape, football violence, humiliation, are all crimes of recognition, in which at least part of the point of the action is to force the recognition on the part of the victim of, minimally, one's strength and "superiority." "Conventional" war is perhaps characterized by the possibility of victory or defeat, that is, by recognition. It may be that the horror of genocide is tied to the fact that no recognition is required on the part of the victim. At "best," the elimination of the Other is part of a process of (pathological) self-recognition.[23] Genocide is war without recognition, and without remainder.

VIOLENCE, WAR, AND GENOCIDE

FROM HEIDEGGER TO DERRIDA:
THE INDETERMINACY OF INAUGURAL VIOLENCE

So far I have been trying to demonstrate the deep ineluctability of violence, along various dimensions, from the fragility of peace to the pathologies of lived time, to the instabilities created by "unsocial sociability" and the struggle for recognition in recognition-deficient cultures.

With our discussion of time and its pathology, we touched on a dimension of violence that is deeply disturbing, that gives us pause when we assume that all violence is to be understood negatively. The experience of a hurricane, a volcano, an earthquake, a tidal wave is in each case the experience of a frightening disturbance of an order. And yet we know, and we would not wish it otherwise, that the shape of this earth, the Rhine and the Mississippi, the Rockies and the Alps, the bedrock on which we build our cities, are the products of mighty forces that did not politely seek permission for their violence. It is as if there is a metaphysical slope, with our sense of the timeless and the unchanging at the top, our sense of cycles of change and process halfway down, and our grasp that both nature and human affairs are shaped by violence at the bottom. We typically try to climb up the slope, away from the recognition of the inaugural power of the event.

It is perhaps helpful to distinguish empirical history from inaugural history. Empirical history is an affair of causality, whether it be slow developments, chance accretions, dramatic configurations, or unavoidable consequences. Inaugural history, on the other hand, would concern itself with the significance of what emerges, with the field (if any) that it commands, with the possibilities that it opens up (and closes down), and so on.

This distinction will, I believe, help us to understand inauguration, and hence inaugural violence, better. Violence, understood as a dimension of the empirical, seems (obviously) opposed to slow development. Violence is typically abrupt, allowing no opportunity for a mediating response. In this sense violence is only one of the shapes in which many orders of things come into being. Villages and towns, like stalactites, and English case law, characteristically grow by accretion. The empirical forms of inaugural violence—forced resettlements, a military coup, political assassination—are cases of violence as empirical event. And empirically, the new can arise by process as well as by event. Here, violence is one option among many. But in terms of inaugural history, we might think it was not. Whatever the shape of empirical time, the institution of the new is something that opens up a future, a realm, a world of possibilities. What is true, in principle, of the maturation of every human individual, takes on a wider significance when we are dealing with social institutions, traditions, nations, works of art, treatises, etc. Here, violence is not an option, for what we mean by violence is precisely the eruption of an identity where before there was none, or the displacement of what once was there.

As Heidegger has shown in "The Origin of the Work of Art,"[24] such events cannot just be characterized empirically, both because they open up possibilities of empirical identification (they open new worlds) and because their success in doing this, and hence their very status as inaugural events (poetry he describes as projective saying), rests on their reception and preservation.

When I speak of the "significance of what emerges" I am referring to this power to bestow a kind of significance, or this distinctive responsiveness to a level of significance. It is with such phrases that I attempt to capture what Heidegger is getting at when, on a number of occasions, he talks about violence. I suggested in the previous chapter, "Identity and Violence," that in the war between rigid and dynamic identity, the "blame" for the conflict lies with those who promote rigid identity. In this light, Heidegger's use of the language of violence is revealing.

Heidegger talks of violence (Gewalt-tatigkeit) in many places. In Being and Time,[25] for example, it is associated with an interpretation that tears away the veil of man's everydayness. Sometimes he uses the word in scare-quotes, sometimes without. "The Anaximander Fragment"[26] marks this same association. Violence is used to describe both what is required of interpretation and what has already been suffered by the object of interpretation. The truth of man's being has been violently suppressed and must be violently recovered. This double inscription of violence is at the core of the most extraordinary discussion of originary violence to be found in Heidegger's An Introduction to Metaphysics.[27] As it would be hard to find a better example of what could be meant by instituting violence, I will present a short account of what he says here. Heidegger has challenged the traditional view (to which Nietzsche succumbed) that would oppose Parmenides and Heraclitus, and insists that we need to break open the lost significance of Parmenides' claim that thinking and being are one. To do this, he suggests we explore "the poetic project of being-human among the Greeks"—to wit, Sophocles' Antigone, beginning with the lines: "There is much that is strange [Deinon], but nothing / that surpasses man in strangeness," which, he comments, "shatters at the outset all everyday standards of questioning and definition."[28] What Heidegger tries to show in his commentary is that Sophocles is giving voice to an original Greek sense of man's relation to the cosmos, as having to respond to the challenge of what threatens to overpower him. Violence is original and ontological, and is not to be thought simply in commonsense (and negative) terms as a "disturbance of the peace." Rather,

> Man is the violent one, not aside from and along with other attributes but solely in the sense that in his fundamental violence he uses power [Gewalt] against the overpowering. He is . . . violent in the midst of the overpowering.[29]

This relationship cannot be reduced to a simple opposition. Commenting on a later passage Heidegger writes:

> What is now named—language, understanding, sentiment, passion, building—are no less a part of the overpowering power than sea, earth, and animal. The difference is only that the latter, the power that is man's environment, sustains, drives, inflames him, while the former reigns within him as the power which he . . . must take upon himself.[30]

Heidegger identifies the violent with the creative, and insists that the possibility of disaster is a permanent possibility at every stage of "the conflict between violence and the overpowering."

Heidegger is offering us a strong account of instituting violence. On his account it is only through such violence—which he identifies with the Greek experience of being—that man was invented. Given the subsequently overpowering burden of tradition, violence needs to be repeated in the form of interpretation to recover even the sense of our having an origin.

It is worth adding here that Heidegger also strongly distinguishes his (and philosophy's) interpretive activity here from that of historiography. What he calls primordial history seeks to uncover violently inaugural beginnings.

> The beginning is the strangest and the mightiest. What comes afterward is not development but the flattening that results from mere spreading out . . .[31]

> That strangest of all beings is what he is because he harbors such a beginning in which everything all at once burst from superabundance into the overpowering and strove to master it.[32]

In brief, Heidegger is offering us an account in which institutive violence is not only distinguished from mere destruction, but strongly opposed to it as a creative force. This violence is moreover constitutive of what it is to be human, the most fundamental identity. And it requires an approach distinct from history to recover its significance. Philosophy itself, then, is implicated in an economy of violence to the extent that it understands its vocation in terms of a response to the kinds of questions Heidegger is asking.

There is something importantly right about what Heidegger is saying here, and something importantly wrong, or at least limited and misleading. There is a difference in type, as I have suggested, between a historical account and one that concerns itself with the possibilities opened up by inaugural acts. Heidegger is raising the stakes in saying that this difference is radically determinative for our understanding of the human project, for understanding what kinds of beings we are who might ever engage in historical understanding.

What is less satisfying is the role attributed to the Greek experience, ambiguous at times it is true, in Heidegger's writings. Philosophy as we know it, we might say, just *is* Greek in inspiration. But insofar as Heidegger does talk of founding mythology, it suggests that philosophy may have or might have taken different forms. More important than this is the fact that Heidegger privileges a past origin. For the logic of his position does not preclude (indeed, it may require) that origination be a recurrent phenomena, distributed perhaps (potentially or actually) over every moment. This would be tantamount to generalizing what he has to say about the origin of the work of art to institutive acts in general, and at different levels. It would offer us a very different model of philosophizing from that proffered in An Introduction to Metaphysics.

We would be confronted by a world not just of dead tradition in need of resuscitation, but of inaugural power itself on the wane, and perhaps in need of rethinking. It may be that the *es gibt* and *ereignis* are attempts at thinking just this. In particular, we would find ourselves surrounded by inaugural temptations, possible beginnings that have yet to prove themselves. Heidegger is not good at working in such uncertain conditions. (He did not say: Hitler just might be an inaugural moment.) We need here to develop (as Derrida has suggested) new concepts—of risk and strategy. The story of Greece is a story of a completed inauguration that has proved itself (though some, like Levinas, might judge its contribution differently). Heidegger thereby avoids all the problems of how we decide which horses to back, how to confront the renewal of renewal, the possibility of a radical displacement of tradition. Even when he deals with works of art, Heidegger seems to be dealing with an existing canon, the worth of which is established but needs interpreting.

A generalization of Heidegger's concern with inaugural violence, without necessarily being opposed to Heidegger's intentions, would find violence (or at least the question of violence) arising at every instant, both in the sense that the very passage of time is a continual rupturing of complacency, but also in the sense that every instant opens up the possibility that truth will break out. And the most powerful insight here would be that violence in this generalized inaugural sense is not something to be abolished or contained. Pure nonviolence could, perhaps, only be obtained by . . . violence.

Much has been said by others about Derrida's extraordinary essay on Levinas, "Violence and Metaphysics,"[33] but one thing Derrida does seem to be insisting on is that the peace that Levinas proposes for an eschatology is not possible within history, that we live in an economy of war, and not just in some fallen dimension of "totality." Derrida also seems to be casting doubt on Heidegger's attempt to read Anaximander as an account of the concealing and revealing of truth, rather than as an account of the creation and destruction of natural (and other) beings.

With the recognition that the ontic and the ontological are tangled together comes the recognition that inaugural violence may not be limited to the days of Sophoclean Greece, may not always be heroic or great, and may not be completed and served up for judgment. If we find ourselves being defined and redefined by our participation in an economy of violence, then the issue will always be what kind of violence. The repudiation of violence in favor of what Heidegger certainly thought of as a vapid commitment to peace, is a refusal to face the reality of struggles not only for truth and enlightenment, but also for survival, for health, and for justice. Violence cannot be contained to one side of an opposition, or to one level (e.g., ontological/empirical). To adapt what Derrida says elsewhere, we have to go through the undecidable when thinking violence practically and philosophically.

Inauguration and violence are intimately bound together in Heidegger's thinking of *destruktion*—one of the central antecedents to deconstruction. *Destruktion* seizes and breaks open positive possibilities from within passively received tradition, challenging the power of what has merely been handed down. And it does so in favor of those who can make traditions sing, who can help to reestablish a tradition of inauguration. The task for the philosopher here is immense, because what deconstruction brings in its wake, or perhaps pushes in front of it, are transformations in those temporal horizonalities that have traditionally constituted states, persons, identities of all sorts.

Heidegger's destruction of dead tradition, however, works almost entirely through the idea of resuscitation of an original destiny and direction for man. "The beginning is the strangest and the mightiest." But might not this very model of return and renewal, of remembering what we have forgotten, be itself part of what needs moving aside? The paradox that then faces us is this: Such a prospect—the loss of the prospect of the recovery of meaning—threatens to overwhelm us. It is hard not to respond to a future that takes the form of absolute danger[34] as reproducing the very condition of violent response to overwhelming power that Heidegger had found in Sophocles. So the loss of the model of return and renewal of origin would return us to the original condition of cosmic challenge.

It is to a strangely parallel position, I believe, that Derrida takes us in his essay—"Force of Law: 'The Mystical Foundation of Authority'"[35]— largely a discussion of Walter Benjamin's 1921 essay "Critique of Violence" (Zur Kritik der Gewalt). This is far too rich a paper to summarize here. Derrida finds Benjamin resuscitating, as an alternative to the Greek problematic of violence and the law that it founds, a divine violence that calls for a justice beyond all established law. In ways demonstrating certain convergences with his treatment of Levinas in "Violence and Metaphysics," Derrida takes the opportunity to develop and explicate here the complex logic of deconstruction—a critical sensitivity to necessary forms of contamination between textually constitutive oppositions. What I would highlight for my purposes here is Derrida's insistence on the undecidability of a revolutionary violence that seeks to constitute a new order. Revolutionary violence rests on a promise, and the logic of the promise entails that one does not know whether the promise will actually be fulfilled. Inauguration, in other words, may have its origin in an act, but no act has its meaning in itself. That significance will always need confirmation. Needless to say, it would seem obvious that there are forms of revolutionary violence— attempts to establish a tyranny, for example—that would be less likely to trigger a detour through undecidability!

Violence, then, however immediate, points beyond its own instantaneity. Founding events are never complete. But the broader implication—in which Derrida, I think, would concur—is that the structure of such originating violence is the structure of events as such. Weaning ourselves off the Greeks, we may perhaps rediscover the opportunities, responsibilities, and uncertainties of inauguration itself. For good or ill, philosophy does not solve the world's problems. But a recognition of the uncertainties and responsibilities of inauguration would surely temper the prospects of fanaticism.

I draw five conclusions from this discussion of violence and inauguration:

1. In its inaugural form (at least), violence is creative, identity-forming.
2. While inauguration may be the beginning, it is only the beginning. It requires preservation, continuation, repetition.
3. Inauguration need not be limited to major past Greek events—it is, one might say, the ethical dimension of all events—their inaugural power.
4. Inauguration, as Derrida says in Force of Law (and this is a consequence of its dependence on preservation), is a future perfect event, and as such, undecidable.
5. This has unsettling consequences for the judgment of violence too, where an inaugural role would redeem it.

We can effectively pursue further a number of these questions through the kinds of connection that other thinkers have established between identity and "narrative." If I am right, it allows us in particular to develop productively the consequences of thinking violence in connection with nonessentialist, and in that sense, nonrigid senses of identity. One of the recurrent themes of this chapter is that of the challenges violence sets us. We deny it, mislocate it, fail to deal with it. These misprisions continue even when we talk about genocide.

GENOCIDE AND THE END OF RECOGNITION

When we speak of genocide, we speak of something that "they" engage in, something from which "we" would dissociate ourselves at all cost. We would like the problem to be one from which we can dissociate ourselves, one of which we can wash our hands. And if we must pay for the sins of our fathers, let us pay, and make a fresh start.

What should give us pause here is the way in which the drive to extinguish the memory of genocide repeats some of the central psychic mechanisms of genocide itself—exclusion, projection, separation, a refusal and inability to engage. Strangely, however, the acknowledgment of guilt can perform precisely the same function, becoming a routinizing mechanism for relieving us of the need for ongoing reflection and vigilance.

I say these things as a philosopher born into a once great imperial state, who now lives in the most powerful country the world has ever known, a nation constitutionally committed to freedom and tolerance, and yet founded, historically, on the repression and extermination of its native population, on the forcible transportation and enslavement of African people, and on their continuing oppression through geographical, educational, and institutional segregation. You can buy land in Tennessee from pacifist Mennonite descendants of Anabaptists who fled persecution in sixteenth-century Germany only to profit from the genocidal expropriation of the land of the Cherokee Indians in the New World. Speaking about genocide is not without its dangers.

I want now to say something that is difficult enough to write, and may be even harder for some to read—about Heidegger's silence, and the notorious bad taste of such remarks as he did make on the Holocaust. As we all know, Heidegger (in 1949, quoted in his *Der Spiegel* interview) compared the concentration camps to "mechanized agriculture," suggesting that what was really in evidence was the rule of planetary technology, the mechanization of death rather than the killing "as such." It is easy to conclude that for Heidegger the Holocaust was nothing more than an illustration of a particular destining of Being. Understood in this way, the remark can seem obscene, a kind of high-minded numbing detachment from human horror. But reading

Kant again, in particular his "Idea for a Universal History for a Cosmopolitan Purpose," has led me to formulate a not implausible defense of Heidegger's remarks, which I shall follow with some even more outrageous reflections on Kant's essay.

It is too simplistic to demand that philosophy entirely disentangle itself from theology, not least because the very existence of theology may be a function of the culpable self-impoverishment of philosophy. But it is hard, at least, not to be chastened by Nietzsche's nose for the more offensive intrusions of theology into philosophy. And surely rational theodicy is one of these intrusions.

There is a long history of apologetics in which theologians try to reconcile the evil of the world with the existence of a beneficent God. The Holocaust has even been claimed to be God's way of bringing about the state of Israel, surely the height of obscenity! If justifying the ways of God has any plausibility it comes from the important truth that actions can have unintended consequences, that bad actions can have good consequences, and that good can flow from evil. The fallacy is to suppose that, because some narrative can be constructed that highlights these good consequences, what was not intended by the agents themselves should be thought as intended by some higher being, as if there operated some principle of the conservation of meaning. Kant warns us, in terms that themselves are symptomatic of the immaturity of mankind, that the only alternative is meaninglessness and chance.

Kant's argument here deserves long and careful dissection and exposition. If I may, I will extract just one of the strands—the claim that human conflict unintentionally serves the cause of human progress. Kant's caution about examples in his first *Critique* might have served him well here too. For his account of human conflict seems to waver between (1) what we could call recognitional conflict (which Hegel develops in his account of the life-and-death struggle in the *Phenomenology of Spirit*), (2) "natural" conflict, and (3) recognitional conflict as having natural consequences. Kant gives the example of trees in the forest which, he says, grow tall to deprive each other of light, etc. This is a strange analogy, because it seems as untrue of trees as it is an implausible account of human rivalry. Trees may grow tall and straight to get light, but depriving other trees of light is surely a consequence, not a purpose. And even if there are some forms of human achievement with a zero-sum form, it is not an essential purpose in winning to deprive the other of victory. There is surely here a confusion of purpose with necessary consequence or corollary. When Hegel talks of struggle, when Nietzsche talks of the value of enemies, when Heidegger speaks of battle,[36] they are each, I believe, taking up the sense of recognitional opposition as, in one way or another, healthy, productive, and intensifying, whether for the parties involved or for successive generations. This is not, in fact, a general justification of war, or struggle, or conflict. The triumph of evil may not be enlightening, barbarians sometimes win, and so on.

For all the horror of modern war, in which, increasingly, soldiers die without even seeing the enemy, we still cling to the idea that conflict can be ennobling. Sport allows us to dramatize conflict in a way in which principles of deep human significance are still at stake (the boxer v. the fighter; flair v. organization; speed v. style; risk v. patience; etc.). Sometimes "recognition" is crucial to the contest (e.g., when the wrestler submits, or the team "knows it's beaten, and hangs its head," sometimes it is central for the audience). But what is characteristic of twentieth-century war and conflict is the growing irrelevance of recognition or the face-to-face situation. Bombing from the air, gas warfare, torpedoing shipping, land mines, artillery shells—none of these involve recognition, tests of resolve, bravery, etc. This conflict is not for the most part ennobling. It is anonymous, face-less, etc.: "What passing bells for these who die as cattle" (Wilfred Owen). War has always been traumatic, but the apparent senselessness and inhumanity of modern war produces a trauma of a different order. And with this facelessness, war moves away from being large scale human conflict to being mass killing, such as genocide, where it is not so much human values or ideals that are at stake, more a high-tech process of eliminating competition for scarce resources. Heidegger's remarks about the death camps should, I believe, be understood in this sense—they symbolize the splitting apart of war and struggle. It is not just that the Jews did not here struggle. Nor did their guards or captors. For all the idealization involved in stories of the heroism, bravery, courage of war, there is still some possibility at least of redemption here. The Holocaust is different not because of the numbers killed, but because it extinguishes the only redemptive hope that conflict keeps alive, by eliminating conflict from killing, transforming death into a technological process. Is this not what Heidegger was saying?

VIOLENCE AND PHILOSOPHY

The inner connection between violence and philosophy can be thematized at many levels. To the extent that philosophy can be identified with a discourse of mastery,[37] with a representational view of language, with the symbolic (rather than the semiotic), to use Kristeva's distinction, then the violence of exclusion is constitutive of philosophy itself.[38] I will take up just three of the many strands that present themselves here: the violence of concepts, the violence of philosophical discussion, and the silent violence of humanism.

THE VIOLENCE OF CONCEPTS

Concepts serve to constitute fields of discourse. It might be thought that this would preclude the attribution of violence to concepts—if violence presupposes the law, then the constitution of a conceptual space—which brings the law to phenomena—could never be violence. So how can the suggestion that concepts are themselves instances of violence be sustained? We might look to Nietzsche for a clue here. The basic argument of his "Truth and Falsity in their Ultramoral Sense" (1872)[39] seems to be this:

1. Sensation has an unsynthesizable multiplicity.
2. Language (concepts) involves a violent destruction of that multiplicity in the name of a certain control over phenomena.[40]

The usual objection is to ask what access Nietzsche has, or could have, to this sensuous multiplicity. How can he compare language to the world that it is said to distort? He might reply that the fact that we use the same word *leaf* for so many different individual leaves is proof enough. We can see the differences, even use color and shape language to point out these differences. But where is the violence? In the case of *leaf*, we may indeed wonder. Leaves do not suffer from loss of individuality, misrecognition, etc. But it may well be the very fact that conceptualization at this level is a "victimless crime" that lures us in to allowing that people can innocently enough be grouped together as blacks, gays, Arabs, etc. And as such can subsequently be targeted for violence. How is this possible? Here we discover an extraordinary phenomenon—that what must here be thought of as a double violence (e.g., a racial attack) often bears a genuine relation to people's self-understanding. The leaf does not say to itself: "I am a leaf, and proud of it," but anyone watching the Olympics will be able to attest to the connection between identity, and identification, and (at least in this case) national pride. Should anyone (should "we") be surprised to find that this kind of identity typically comes through identification, which seems like a voluntary abdication of one's singularity? We seem to find the same phenomenon in both man and leaf—that conceptualization and both identification and self-identification each involve what we could call constitutive or institutive violence, a violence that produces something from the sacrifice of singularity. But what is the loss, and where is the violence?

Perhaps true loss does not lie in the movements of conceptualization /identification, but in the forgetting of that movement, the inability to engage in what Merleau-Ponty called hyperreflection,[41] a return, not to some primeval presence, but precisely to a preconceptual sensuous multiplicity, one in which various possibilities of conceptuality still simmer. Blockage of that movement, the refusal to acknowledge that reflective truth has an origin, a ground—is violence. And one of the reasons this matters is that whatever difficulties we may have in thinking this through, there is no denying that there can be competing conceptualizations. The argument against this possibility would deny any possible independent point of comparison, and hence any direct opportunity for conflict. But there are many layers of conceptualization. American Indians and European settlers may have had incommensurable ways of understanding "property rights," incompatible *Weltanschauungen*, but that did not stop them from fighting over land—there was still something they were fighting over, even if it was the right to think of and use the land as they saw fit.

What I am claiming is that the "violence of conceptualization" is a complex phenomenon, that it cannot be dismissed by a priori arguments, that it is compatible with conceptualization having an instituting role, and that the greater violence may lie not in the concept as such, but in a certain genealogical aversion, a blindness to the fact that concepts have histories, take sides, need replenishing, etc. Here, as elsewhere, dogmatism is violence. That suggests that at a certain point what we call the violence of the concept may recede into a quasi-transcendental status, allowing us to focus on the comparative care and attentiveness that distinguish some cutting and shaping of the world, from the absence of it elsewhere. If violence is necessary, callousness, gratuitousness, and cruelty are not.

Violence in Philosophical Discussion

I once replied to a conference paper by a well-known American phenomenologist. He had focused on the peculiar spatiality of place, and I tried to open up the constitutive significance of time and history. Afterward, a notoriously pugnacious analytic philosopher asked me why, having injured my protagonist, I did not go in for the kill. (Actually, his formulation was much more vulgar.)

In informal discussion prior to a conference in Germany at which I once presented a version of this chapter, I was told that if I said this or that, I might be "attacked," indeed that my philosophical style might be alien to other participants in the conference. I do not wish simply to note the irony of being advised that my cultural, national, linguistic, philosophical background might single me out for attack at an international conference on violence. Rather, I want to draw attention to what I would call the fractal nature of violence— that it seems to reappear at every level, and (most embarrassingly, I would say) even in discussions, or as the very shape of discussions, on violence.[42]

Let me put this in the form of a question: What if our discussions about violence were to reproduce the very structure(s) of violence? This is not necessarily a contradiction. We can talk about language in language. And can we not ask questions about questions? Or talk peacefully about peace? Why should it be an issue that we might engage (perhaps routinely, silently) in violent confrontation discussing violence? Should we be concerned?

We might say that philosophical discussion has the same justification as football (and diplomacy), that it is the continuation of war by other means. And as these other means are less deadly, they are to be preferred. But this position is deeply implausible. When Heidegger says it is impossible to "think" in the French language, it is hard to see this as a symbolic substitute for war—that if philosophers stopped trying to refute each other, international conflict would break out. Or even personal conflict. It is just as likely that certain kinds of (e.g., dogmatic) philosophical formulations (and religious doctrines) have often served to license conflict, so that instead of being substitutes, they fan the flames of violence. Instead, I suggest that every activity has its own possibilities of violence, and, correspondingly, its own ways of overcoming or limiting violence.

THE SILENT VIOLENCE OF HUMANISM

Many of the most prominent postwar European philosophers (Heidegger, Levinas, Foucault, Derrida) have attempted to set aside, move beyond, redefine, or critique what has traditionally been called "humanism."[43] One might have thought that suspension of the metaphysical privilege of "man" would involve some sort of renegotiation of the way in which the distinction between man and animal has operated, particularly in legitimating the practice of certain kinds of systematic violence by humans on animals. The record, however, is disappointing, although Derrida begins to make some of the right moves.

In his discussion with Jean-Luc Nancy, "'Eating Well,' or the Calculation of the Subject,"[44] Derrida extends the sense of philosophy as a discourse of mastery to the broader verdict that Western philosophy shares with the culture in which it is embedded a pervasive carnophallogocentrism, an ugly word for a not too pretty thing. Part of the argument is that our culture is not carnivorous by accident, but rather that the eating of meat belongs to the same symbolic register as the privilege of reason, the phallus, presence, etc. If we accept that meat eating is itself, or is connected to, a kind of violence, the connection between carnivorousness and a certain shape of the symbolic might take us a step farther in understanding Heidegger's apparent lack of sensitivity and proportion in comparing the death camps to factory farming, and what some have more broadly described as the "animal holocaust." For, again, it is what we might call the symbolic dimension[45] of factory farming that is at stake. We have referred already to the essay ("Idea for a Universal History . . .") in which Kant develops the idea of man's unsocial sociability as the mechanism that allows man's distinctness from the animal to emerge. I proceed by launching another raid on Kant's essay, to try to effect a disturbing reversal of his argument.

Kant's essay, which centers on the unexpected benefits that flow from man's "unsocial sociability," is structured around the idea that man is distinct from the animal in that man can only fulfill his natural capacities in society. And such a society must allow "continual antagonism" among its members, within the rule of law. Kant goes on to argue that the follies of international conflict will require that states will renounce war within a greater international order. This cosmopolitan order will then allow the development of our original human capacities. This whole sketch of a "universal history" rests on the fundamental idea that man is distinct from the animal by virtue of having capacities that require social life for their development. What is curious about this argument is that this development takes place essentially through conflict, which is ultimately regulated only by the establishment of an international order.

But if the shape of this international order will itself be determined by the support given to it by powerful states (it is not administered by Martians), it is hard to see how such an international order could ever, in principle, be able to extricate itself from the power relations of those states it seeks to regulate. And that suggests that what counts as successful regulation may well end up being defined by these same powerful states, or the interests for which those states may be proxies.[46]

The skeptical conclusion would be this—that if Kant is right that distinctive human capacities can *only* be developed in an international order of the sort he describes, if he is right that this is the only way of redeeming the conflictual process from the law of the jungle, then reasons to doubt the possibility of such an order would be reasons to *doubt the productive development of distinctive human capacities*. If we add to the equation the global dissemination of nuclear technology, and the technologies of nerve gas and biological warfare, not to mention the dissolution of the state as the unique representative of power, we have a recipe for disaster. The disaster here is not just physical. It is the permanent deferment of the ideal of a world order that would allow us to be distinctively human. If that is so, then unless we were to recalibrate the distinctive human capacities that Kant talks about to *include* the development of weapons of mass destruction, etc., we might have to conclude that the conditions that would allow man to distinguish himself from animals by the development of his distinctive talents do not exist. Or if they do, that so many of those talents are so toxic we would wish they did not.

It is worth adding here that the idea that the distinct virtues of other animals are not developed in social life has simply been disproved in case after case. Animals have many "instincts" that make possible further social development. And, according to Vicki Hearne,[47] humans can further socialize animals to develop capacities they would not otherwise have.

Maintaining a blanket distinction between humans and animals is fraught with danger. Heidegger's comparison of death camps to factory farms has been thought obscene in part because it seems to repeat the same assimilation of man to animals that might be thought to have legitimated genocide in the first place. Jews, communists, and gypsies were, in fact, not only described as animals, but as vermin, as bacilli, as viruses, as the "animals of the animals," so to speak, just in case the first-order animal label would not sufficiently legitimate mass murder. But while the apparent comparison of the treatment of Jews with the fate of animals in Heidegger's account may be obscene, so too is the implication that these sort of practices would call for a quite different judgment if we were "just" talking about nonhuman animals. It has been argued that the architecture and logistical organization of the death camps was not, in fact, invented specially by the Nazis. It was stolen, or borrowed from the successful designs of the Chicago stockyards, also fed directly by the railway system. If the industrialization of killing was first perfected on cattle, and then applied to humans, we have not an obscene analogy, but an obscene piece of history. Should we not also be horrified when sentient beings of other species are treated in this way, species that themselves altogether lack the capacity for evil, and are in that sense truly innocent? If there is a worry that the distinctiveness of the human gets lost in such a comparison, there is an equal worry than the refusal of such analogies perpetuates our all-too-human blindness to the systematic violence we habitually inflict on other creatures.

The expression "animal holocaust" is taboo in many circles. Even those without religion will defend at any cost the scraps of the sacred to be wrested from recent history. And that includes the singularity of the Holocaust. This is puzzling. While the word *Shoah* does seem appropriately limited to the Jewish holocaust, the word *holocaust,* which means sacrifice/destruction through burning, dates back at least to the fifteenth century. It may at times be counterproductive to speak of the animal holocaust—we do not always see more surely what is thrust in our face—but is it inaccurate, or ill-chosen? The expression may well provoke the very resistance it seeks to overcome, but the expression is not used unthinkingly, or irresponsibly.

It could be argued on principle that the Holocaust is a singular event, such that the word could and should never be used generically. But what does insisting on its singularity signify here? Is there a concern that it might become just another event in history, that we forget its uniquely horrific nature, or that we just forget it altogether? All of these things would be unforgivable. But if we say, as so many have said, "Never again," it would be crazy to respond that we need not worry, that as a singularity it could not happen again. In one sense every historical event is a singularity. And it may be that the extermination of Jews (and, in smaller numbers, gypsies, communists, and homosexuals) in Nazi death camps, is more than that—a particularly unique event, one that particularly demands to be burned into our memory, rather than being classified under some general category. Into *our* memory, note. We are proud inheritors of the Western tradition (now a little chastened), a tradition wedded to a sense of its own progressive values. But is it obviously wrong for a Cambodian to speak of the genocidal terror of the Khmer Rouge as a holocaust? It would be plain wrong to refuse to allow the survivor of such terror any language at all that could point, however hopelessly, to what for them too must have been unthinkably horrific. I cannot imagine saying: "Use any word you like, but *holocaust* is already taken." Perhaps there is a better word, but we could not in all justice insist on reserving a singular word for the Holocaust, while happily dispensing generic words to other reigns of the unthinkably horrific. The victims of horror have a right to whatever language they can find. And for those of us who are not in this sense victims, I wonder if our gestures of sacred singularity are not as much a testimony to our hopelessly unassuagable guilt, as to any other propriety.

The sober justification for the expression "animal holocaust" would be this.[48] The development of modern industrial methods of breeding, fattening, killing, and consuming animals, coupled as it is with a rapid acceleration in the extinction of species after species of living creatures, species many of which are wiped out before they are even named and classified, is, if anything is, a singular event. Nothing remotely like it has ever happened since the Ice Age, something in which man played no part. It might be thought more appropriate to use a phrase such as "animal slaughter." But this suggestion suffers from precisely the opposite problem. Animal slaughters—even mass slaughters—are a dime a dozen. To use the everyday word *slaughter* for the whole historical epoch of the calculated and unprecedented transformation of animal life into the stuff of an industrial process (and the killing of thousands of millions [sic] of animals for food every year in the United States alone) would be precisely to fall foul of those same demands to grasp singularity that led to the dismay at the apparently generic use of the word *holocaust*. It is not a generic use. It is not trying to say that animals are the same as humans. (Animals are not even the same as each other.) It is, however, a claim that the scale and scope of the undeclared enslavement of and war on other sentient beings, needs to be marked as a singularity, and for the same sort of reasons as the Jewish Holocaust—that it is in a strong sense a unique historical Event, that the pain and suffering of these creatures is genuinely unthinkable in both quantity and quality, as is, many would say, our blindness to and complicity with this Event.[49]

For this is without doubt mass violence, mass killing. It is legal, vehemently opposed by a substantial minority of humans, but tolerated, even endorsed, and profited from by the masses.[50] I will not attempt to argue here against these practices, but if we want an example of silent, invisible violence, one that bubbles and oozes beneath the waiterly calm of our restaurants, and the *gemeinschaftlich* Sunday lunch, we need look no further than here.[51] What would we say in a principled way to an alien from another planet, a planet that had long since realized Kant's ideal of a cosmopolitan society, when he explained ever so reasonably why he and his compatriots, for whom human flesh was a real delicacy, felt that our necessarily underdeveloped state justified them in eating us now, and taking back a few specimens to farm?

CONCLUSION

I began by assembling some reminders to accompany our thinking about violence. I grouped these reminders under three headings. First, the ineluctability of violence—the ways in which violence is connected to the fragile background conditions of peace, the indeterminacy of the terms of our
agreements, the pathologies of time, and the prevalence of recognition-deficient cultures. Second, discussing war, genocide, and revolution, I followed
Heidegger and Derrida in highlighting the difficulty of judging inaugural or
creative violence. I argued that what is distinctive about genocide is the
absence of any question of recognition, the reduction of war to a process (of
extermination). Lastly, I suggested that violence cannot be eliminated from
philosophy itself, though it can be abated.[52] And I pointed to some glaring
holes in the project of undoing the silent (and silencing) violence of a
humanism that continues to be embarrassed by the existence of other animals. Violence is a fractal and recursive phenomena. I have tried to engage
in some boundary disruption, with the express purpose of showing how our
very demarcation of the limits of violence may itself be scrutinized as evidence of a further silent or structural violence. The conclusion I draw is that
true nonviolence is a recursive willingness to expand our sense of the scope
and structure of violence. (This, I take it, is the impetus behind many of the
Eastern religions' commitment to nonviolence, at many different levels.) To
seek peace requires that we recognize and find ways of dealing with the
repeated ambivalence of violence—that violence can be creative as well as
destructive, and that we cannot always know which in advance.

THREE

Where Levinas Went Wrong

Some Questions for My Levinasian Friends

THOSE OF US DISAPPOINTED with Levinas's position on animals might con-clude in a moment of exasperation that it clearly shows that ethics is *not* first philosophy for Levinas. What comes first is a commitment to other humans, especially those in need. And that this discrimination is framed in terms that are philosophically unremarkable—the capacity to speak, for example. We might add that his view of the feminine makes it equally clear that Levinas's ethics disguises a further quite specific ontological commitment, even virility. We might conclude that, for all Levinas's opposition of ethics to "ontology," his ethical opening precisely rests on an ontology. I want to pursue precisely this thought, suggesting

1. that Levinas's ethics rests on an ontology, one that is importantly flawed;
2. that his relation to Heidegger is at least symptomatic of his blindness to his own ontological commitments;
3. that if the climate of Levinas's thought is marked by the asymmetry of the ethical relation, we need to move on;
4. and that we need to open ourselves to an *other* event, one in which the event of otherness explodes in many directions.

Levinas writes that I am infinitely obliged, I more than others, that I am even responsible for the others' responsibility. And that the face of the other is the command "Don't kill me." This seems like a specific formulation of the ethi-cal. And it is surely essential to ask whether there is concealed in these for-mulations a response to the particular circumstances of imprisonment, degra-dation, and genocide.[1]

What if the very formulation of the ethical provided by Levinas, and the implicit proposal that vigilance is the only answer, are as much symptoms of the problem as responses to it? And in particular, what if the hyperbole in Levinas's formulations were a sign of the impotence of the stance rather than of its significance?

Levinas's formulation of ethics as first philosophy seems, in part, to rest on his reading of Heidegger. I would not be the first to wonder whether his readings of Heidegger can be seriously defended. But I would like to ask a more complex question—whether his opposition to Heidegger, and the formulation he gives of his own position, would not profit from a better understanding of what is involved in reading another philosopher, an issue on which Heidegger himself offers valuable guidance. This has consequences on two levels—first supplying a better model of how to read than Levinas perhaps practices, but also opening up, through reflection on that relationship, an ethical dimension that may have escaped Levinas.

In *What is Called Thinking?* Heidegger distinguishes between two ways of reading another thinker: going counter to them (through critique, polemic), and "going to their encounter."[2] What does it mean to go to the other's encounter? I understand this to mean entering, or trying to approach, the space of the other's relation to alterity. Which requires a certain generosity, and not just for the other's sake, but for the sake of the encounter itself, the space into which one has entered. By generosity I mean foregoing the temptation to oppositional thinking, trying to see where the other person may have already addressed the question you are raising, not just to do justice to him, but also to thinking itself, and to the very idea of respect.

Let me just take one example to begin with. Levinas writes: "What seems to have escaped Heidegger—if it is true that in these matters something might have escaped Heidegger—is that prior to being a system of tools, the world is an ensemble of nourishments."[3] Levinas presents this as an objection to Heidegger's totality system (almost as Kierkegaard would have referred to Hegel). There are three responses to be made to this. First, we must ask whether Heidegger had simply failed to grasp that the world was an ensemble of nourishments, or had perhaps recognized the significance of this in a different way. Second, it is important to grasp the status of Heidegger's account of the "world of tools" in *Being and Time* and its place in his subsequent path of thinking. Thirdly, we might want to ask whether understanding the world as an ensemble of nourishments can really be sustained in the way Levinas suggests.

1. In *What is Called Thinking?*, it is precisely through the theme of nourishment that Heidegger attempts to expand and displace Descartes' image of the "tree of knowledge," with a detailed focus on the question of the relation between the roots and the soil. Indeed, one could say that the entire language of the "gift" as Heidegger introduces it is a recognition of being itself as nour-

ishment. Second, while there is no doubt that in *Being and Time*, the world is first described as a referential complex of instrumentalities, Heidegger has a very specific target here—that of displacing the Cartesian sense of the world as a kind of "extended stuff." For that he needs to be able to demonstrate our participation in a space which has a kind of nonconstructed wholeness. For this our instrumentally interconnected world, in which we engage whenever we pick up a pen to write, without explicitly positing that world, works very well. Elsewhere in *Being and Time*, Heidegger speaks of the world of public interpretation, the ways in which historical triumphs of world understanding get threatened and lost, and so on. Here, at least, Levinas seems to be siding with the pragmatist reading of Heidegger, losing sight of the specific strategic significance of those formulations. In subsequent writing, Heidegger will discuss the ways in which art and poetry open worlds, and how technology enframes them. The world could not, in an important sense, be an ensemble of nourishments, because an ensemble is not a world. Thirdly, and lastly, there is something strangely one-sided about the very idea of nourishment. We may imagine everywhere mothers feeding their children, where nourishment is an act of love. But the truth of the matter is otherwise. The world of nourishment, if we want to call it that, is just as much the world of death and violence, the jungle, the Discovery Channel[4] (mostly sharks, lions, and packs of hyenas), and the meat industry, which in the United States alone accounts for hundreds of millions of animals fattened (nourished) for food, then killed and eaten every year. (See longer discussion in our previous chapter.) Here, perhaps, we find a "world of nourishment." If Levinas objects to the idea that Heidegger is talking about nourishment when he speaks of the gift, because it is too ontological, let us talk ontically. Not only do we find that nourishment is not neutral, but it has victims. And for all its own limitations, we should look again at Derrida's interview with Jean-Luc Nancy, "Eating Well," where he introduces the idea of carnophallogocentrism.[5] My nourishment may be the other's death. (As, to be fair, Levinas acknowledges when he speaks of our drinking Ethiopian coffee.) To the extent that nourishment is a system, or a world, and even if we prefer to think of more primitive forms of rural agriculture—(grazing, farming, crops)—we are tied up with the very world of tools (from ploughs to tractors) that Levinas wants to make secondary.

When Levinas says that Heidegger's position is a philosophy of being, and contrasts this with a search for the good beyond being (having praised *Being and Time* for its "intellectual vigor, and . . . steadfastness"), Levinas asks nonetheless, "Can we be assured, however, that there was never any echo of evil in it?" And goes on to speak of the diabolical as "endowed with intelligence." Such a question, I have to say, betrays the logic of the Inquisition and worse. "Can we be assured that . . . never . . . ?" Of course not! The charge works by insinuation. It is not without a certain sense of strong irony too, when we think that this distinction—between mere intelligence and something deeper or more responsible—is one deployed regularly by both Hegel and Heidegger.

Levinas claims Heidegger's is an ontology of Being. But how does this correspond to what Heidegger himself thinks he's doing? In *Being and Time* Heidegger says he is trying to ask the question of the meaning of Being. Why? Because he claims we have lost contact with the question in the very process of trying to come to terms with Being. He describes metaphysics as modeled, unhelpfully and misleadingly, on the particular kind of beings we come across in the world. And Heidegger believes we can come to some understanding of the meaning of Being by opening up the horizon of time. It is by this move, as I see it, that Heidegger claims precisely *not* just to be offering a philosophy of Being in the traditional metaphysical fashion. So, I suggest, the question of whether Heidegger's philosophy of Being is susceptible to Levinas's charge will depend on what Heidegger can eventually do with the horizon of time and temporality.

Perhaps the salient question raised by Heidegger's account of time in *Being and Time* is the significance of being-toward-death. Why is this such a big issue? Because here each man faces his mortal condition and the fragile possibility of realizing himself. What is wrong with genocide? With gas chambers? With war? We are appalled that our fellow human beings can engage in these practices. But what is it that horrifies us? The desensitized camp guards. And the technological rationality with which the rounding up and killing took place. It is not just the outcome, the numbers of dead, the selection of the Jews and other marginal groups. We are horrified at the thought that the perpetrators might not be so different from us, as we too have largely embraced lives of limited ambition within desensitizing techno-instrumental complexes. But we must not lose sight of the fact that these innocent people were degraded, imprisoned, worked to death, tortured, and killed. The many layers of evil here—and the point, I take it, of Heidegger's unhappy comparison with factory farms—come together in the fact that humans are *not* just animals, but are here being treated in the way we do treat animals. Many believe it is also a crime to treat animals in this way.[6] But the particular reason it is evil to treat humans like this has do to with the kinds of lives it is taking away. It is precisely because we are not just biologically alive but place a value on our own lives, and that we typically do value life, liberty, and the pursuit of happiness, that mass killing is so horrific. What was cut short was in each case human hope and fulfillment. (In this sense, being stripped of rights, jobs, property, is a full part of this terrible process.) The Other, whom we fear for, whom we protect, whom we may harm, is always a being capable of pain and suffering, of joy, and of a certain fulfillment. Each time we leave something off this list, we do violence to the other. If, as with Mill, we think of the other simply in terms of the capacity for pleasure and pain, we do violence to them at the very point at which we seem to take account of them. How we understand the other is essential to our capacity to honor, respect, and protect them. When Descartes, after la Mettrie, compares the cry of a cat to the squeak of a carriage wheel, the only reason not to step on its tail would be to protect our ears from sharp sounds. The implication of all this of course is that we cannot separate ontology from ethics. If so, ethics cannot be first philosophy. Or if it were, ontology would have to be equiprimordial.

Suppose someone says to me that each I is infinitely obliged to the other. I reply that I agree, which is why I leave the bats undisturbed in my roof, why we should ban hunting, why I gently remove the daddy longlegs from the bathtub, and why stands of ancient oaks should be preserved.[7] I am then corrected, and I am told that it is only humans that infinitely oblige me. If I then scratch my head, I may be told that of course I can extend this sense of obligation to nonhumans if I wish. But it would be an analogy. This puzzles me, because I thought part of the point of the account of the face-to-face relation was to circumvent the analogical transfer Husserl describes in the Fifth of his *Cartesian Meditations*.[8] How strange that it should turn up again a little farther down the line. Of course, we can give an *account* of why the other is first and foremost human. We may think that is what metaphysical principles are for. We no longer say that man is rational. Somehow that doesn't seem so convincing. Now we say that the human other can speak. Or that the human other is aware of his mortality. Or belongs to a species, many members of which can speak or "die" in the full sense.[9] But it is hard not to conclude that what all this comes down to is "beings like us." That would not make Levinas's position ontological in any explicit sense. But it does suggest that it operates on implicit humanistic premises, premises from which Buddhism's generalized respect for sentience, for example, seems free. And the strangest thing is that the principle of my fundamental exposure to the other is precisely the kind of principle that we need in order to breach the repeated roadblocks in the way of our respecting the various modes of otherness of the other. What does this tell us about the significance of ontology for ethics? I am tempted to say that ontology without ethics is empty, and ethics without ontology is blind. I suspect that it could be shown that ontology is not possible without at least such proto-ethical concepts as openness, relation, and other. But just having an ontology does not alleviate blindness. We need to recognize the ways in which one's ontological commitments and prejudices can both inform the kind of respect and response proper to different kinds of beings, and, where missing, can limit one's capacity for responsiveness.

And what is true of the various species of otherness is quite as much true of oneself. My capacity for response to the other's needs will depend to a considerable extent on the health and expansiveness of my understanding of myself, and what it is to be human. It has been said that Levinas's aversion to psychoanalysis is based on the fear that a divided self would encourage alibis for nonresponsiveness. Perhaps too it might undermine the distinctively ethical character of any self-constitutive opening to the other. Yet again, it might cast a troubling light on the images of height, command, face, and obligation with which my relation to the other is articulated. And finally it might be thought that psychoanalysis is but a moment of self-absorption, deflecting us from our primary obligation to the other. But surely a better response would be this: My obligation to the other is inseparable from my acquiring the insight (and even knowledge) that would enable me to reach out and help the other. Ethical commitment is no substitute for medical training when you're faced with a road accident victim. And it is essential to have grasped some of the complexities (projection, identification, etc.) involved in therapeutic assistance to the other. Now these claims might be thought to be uncontentious. But if they entail that the quality of my response, even my capacity to respond at all to the other, may depend on the way I understand and relate to myself, and on my sense of what it is to be human (or, more complicatedly, what it might be like to imagine being a horse, or a herring, or to recognize important limits to my imagination in these cases), then ontology is central to ethics. When Heidegger distinguishes between that mode of concern that involves "leaping in" and taking over the other's project, and "leaping ahead of" the other, the key to the second response being superior is that it addresses the other in their freedom.[10] And that is an ontological discrimination. A common everyday example of this—one that touches again on the problematic question of nourishment— is the saying that if you give a man a fish you feed him for a day, but if you teach him to fish, he will feed himself forever (Mao Tse-tung). These may seem just like two practical options. But they can be seen to address the other in qualitatively different ways. In the first, the other is a passive victim in immediate need. In the second, the other is acknowledged as a being with powers that can be cultivated and encouraged. If this distinction is indeed ontological, then it might seem from Levinas's examples that he made quite distinctive ontological choices in this area too. And the apparent opposition to ontology would only serve to disguise this.

It may be that I am oversimplifying the purported relation between ethics and ontology. Perhaps Levinas should be read not as claiming that ethics is free from ontology, but that it somehow supersedes it. This would involve reading his account of my solitude, my suffering, my recognition of my mortality as making possible an opening onto the other (or the Other) that would transcend any such ontological determinations. I don't know that he can be read in this way, but it would surely not work. Because the motivation and formulation of this ethical opening rests on the ontological formulations that it then supercedes. If we were to contest those formulations, the sense of and the incentive for such an opening would disappear.

Another approach would be to argue that ontology means something rather special to Levinas—the philosophy of light, or the reducibility of being to knowledge, the triumph of a certain positivity. But on this reading, Heidegger would not be doing ontology, and Levinas would have to formulate his

position differently, and would have to engage in dialogue about the ontological grounds of ethics. I do not see him willing to do this.

Take one or two examples: In the formulations of the '40s, in *Time and
the Other*, and in *Existence and Existents*,[11] Levinas begins with the relation
between a solitary existent and being, he begins with solitude, and witnesses
the dawning of a consciousness that tears itself away from the vigilance of the
il y a. In *Time and the Other*, this will start him on the long march through the
experience of suffering, death, otherness, the other person, eros, and fecundity. But these "primal scene" stories somehow do not have the allure they
once did. It has seemed to many that these stories are little more than retro-
spective reconstructions whose artificiality is testified to by the kind of language used in their formulation, language that knows too much, that has
already been to the end of the trail and come back to guide the way for the
rest of us. The child's experience of solitude, for example, is unthinkable
without it being the experience of the absence of its parents. And I for one
would need convincing that Levinas does not betray more of his hand than
he might have intended when he compares my already being hollowed out by
my obligation to the other, to Descartes' sense of the presence of God in me
in the shape of the idea of perfection. The question opened up by such a
Cartesian filiation can best be phrased along Heideggerian lines: If the Cartesian conception of the subject has indeed inherited the mediaeval conception of substance—namely, something that needs nothing else in order to be
itself—do we not have a most powerful ontological prejudice right at the
heart of Levinas's thought? God would be the wholly independent substance,
and man would be a dependent substance, having no essential relations to
other men, but an essential dependence on God. What Levinas helps us navigate, in effect, is his transposition of this relation to God onto my relation to
the other. If this reading were correct, however, it would not just make the
ethical bound up with ontology. The ethical relation would be an essentially
ontological one, indeed onto-theological, as Heidegger would put it.

Now, there is a certain genius in setting oneself the task of thinking God
in and as the relation to the other. Without some such immanence, theology
becomes a branch of stargazing. But two further questions are raised by Levinas's version of this move. First, the sense that this relation to the other is
essentially a relation to the other human, and second, that it is essentially
characterized by an infinite *obligation*, that I am responsible, more than others, and even for everyone else's responsibility, that the other addresses me
from a height, with "a commandment which comes from one knows not
where," etc.[12] It is hard not to conclude that in both of these dimensions, Levinas leaves his always problematic phenomenology behind, and follows the
lines already laid out by the Judaic or Judaeo-Christian tradition. The task
that he sets himself then would be that of transferring the properties of my
relation to God understood within that tradition back onto my relation to

man. Of course, if we thought, like Feuerbach for example, that God had originally been created in the image of man, then we might expect this humanistic reclamation to proceed smoothly. I am indeed tempted by a quasi-Feuerbachian story here. But the question it (helpfully) raises for us is whether many characteristics of God were not in fact *generated* by his original alienation from the interhuman space, with yet other features then acquired in exile. As I see it, it these kinds of questions are hard to avoid when we struggle to make sense of what Levinas says about my relation to the other. For example, we can see "height" as a marker of a kind of relationship beyond mundane everyday human activity, reflecting both the relative position of the sun and the sky, and also of a parent to a child. But the idea that the other person addresses me from a "height"? Is it not possible that the theological transfer of epithets is taking place too swiftly? And the "commandment that comes from one knows not where"? This is surely a piece of the Old Testament looking for somewhere new to land, once it has heard that "the moral law within" is wearing thin.

I pursued this issue out of a conviction that Levinas's reference to Descartes told us all too much about his ontological commitments. I will shortly spell out what I think are the real dangers of the hidden ontological commitments Levinas does have. But before then, I would like to draw attention to another dimension of his fundamental solipsism. This time, the reference would be back to Hobbes rather than Descartes, although in the place I am referring to (his "Dialogue" with Richard Kearney)[13] Levinas alludes to Spinoza, Pascal, Darwin, and Freud. Levinas writes: "Ethics is, therefore, *against nature* because it forbids the murderousness of my natural will to put my own existence first."[14] This is both astonishing and yet not astonishing. It is astonishing in that it reveals in the starkest terms Levinas's commitment to a particular view of the state of nature, and even a particular way of understanding that view. And here, I suggest, Levinas's relation to social Darwinism is most unfortunate. He treats it as articulating in a developed form the biblical truth of the story of Cain and Abel. He takes it to be the truth, but not the whole truth. And yet it is not astonishing, because it makes so much more sense of his general position. But what if his ethical position was not so much a vital corrective to our natural murderousness, but a supplement to a particular, strongly contested view of human nature with its own history, its own ideological background, etc.? I would refer again to Robert Bernasconi's reference to Marx's comparison of social Darwinism to the structure of bourgeois society in nineteenth-century England.[15] If we reject this account of the state of nature, doesn't the appeal of his ethical philosophy wane too? I cannot here mount a full-scale critique of this account of the state of nature, but I would make four comments here:

1. There are plenty of studies that suggest that even in the animal world, individual survival is not an overriding instinct, from the mother par-

tridge who feigns injury as she leads predators away from her nest, to the porpoises who shield a human swimmer from shark attack.

2. The same is true of human beings. One only has to think of the many examples of heroism and altruism, in which people sacrifice their lives for others and for ideas they care about. Even Nietzsche's account of the will-to-power, which Levinas would not approve of, is a critique of the primacy of the will to exist.

3. Much human violence is not the eruption of some natural condition, but the developed response to particular social conditions, of threat, fear, scarcity, lack of recognition, and so on.

4. Even if we were to accept the idea of a primitive "natural will to put my own existence first," it is an extraordinary thing to call this "murderous." This would make no distinction between defending one's family against Charles Manson and being a serial killer oneself.

Levinas's view of human nature as "naturally murderous" is perhaps understandable, even "natural" given what he went through, what he suffered, what he saw. But the fact that other humans who may seem so normal in other ways can do unbelievably horrific things is not an argument for man's naturally murderous condition. Indeed, the many ways in which what too often happened in the twentieth century went *beyond* murder (extermination, torture, psychological brutality and traumatization, etc.) is strangely further evidence for the thought that we are not dealing with some deep facet of human nature but with social pathology.

What alternative account could be given of the human propensity to violence?

It would be a considerable shift in our thinking if we began from the thought that the capacity for the worst violence, the transformation of multicultural toleration into ethnic cleansing, the willingness when provoked to kill, either in defense or in preemptive defense called aggression, is, at least in many cases, the predictable outcome of people finding themselves in or *believing themselves to be* in a desperate situation. If this is so, it suggests a different line of remedies. Allow me to present an analogy.

In England, most Victorian houses are plagued by the actuality or the reality of dry rot, a particularly vigorous fungus that turns healthy structural timber into dry frangible cubes. It thrives wherever there is wood in a house combined with a source of water, or even dampness. Chemical companies mushroomed in the '70s that would spray, inject, and otherwise poison your house to kill off this fungus. In fact this fungus is always present, its spores are airborne, and it is impossible to eradicate it. One all-too-honest contractor told me that you can, however, completely eradicate the development of dry rot just by preventing any contact of any wood with any source of damp. What if violence were best understood in the same way?

To describe a response to extreme conditions as predictable is not to condone it. But there are and always have been conditions under which most humans do not act or feel in ways that reflect anything we commonly value. Wild animals in traps will chew off their legs to escape. Humans in conditions of extreme hunger turn cannibalistic, even if it is only to eat the dead flesh of their companions. And in conditions of extreme fear, even rational humans are driven by what Freud would call "primary processes." When we fear for our lives, or those of our loved ones, and we believe or imagine that others really are hunting us, poisoning us, or sucking our blood, we may do terrible things. But it is hard to see what we can learn from the things that people will do in those circumstances. It would be crazy to formulate principles such as: Killing your neighbors tonight is justifiable when they are planning to kill you tomorrow. And yet I take it that countless ordinary people have found themselves in just this position. The true criminals are not these unfortunate people, but those who fan such fears, pouring gasoline on the flames, or water into the foundations of Victorian houses.

The implications of these claims are at odds with Levinasian ethics in the following ways:

1. We cannot exercise the vigilance captured by the demand that we *not forget* (the Holocaust) unless we know what it is we are remembering. What if thinking of it in primarily ethical terms were a way of forgetting, that is, *not* understanding what happened? What if our ethical response were a *symptom* of our utter revulsion at these events, rather than any kind of prophylactic? It may well be that the Holocaust just would not have occurred without the concurrence of a range of factors, such as:

   a. unemployment and economic hardship in Germany in the '30s (with its own causes),
   b. the concomitant real economic fear and despair of the German people,
   c. the desire for power on the part of Hitler and his friends,
   d. the actual or perceived bankruptcy of the Weimar Republic,
   e. the historic exclusion and marginalization of the Jews in Europe,
   f. the susceptibility of even educated people to believe simple, scapegoating stories about how this situation can be rectified,
   g. a mechanism (SS, Gestapo) for selecting and mobilizing psychopaths to commit horrific acts in the service of the Reich,
   h. a technological capacity for mass killing (gas chambers, railway system).

2. The articulation of these "factors" is not meant to hide or attenuate in any way the horror of what happened, or the responsibility of those involved. If I am right, however, there are important causal preconditions that had to be in place for it to occur, and my claim is that it is

these that should be the focus of our attention. And here we find a real hard case of "responsibility." For it has not to do with "my" infinite responsibility, and me more than others. It has everything to do with getting away from delusional thinking of every sort. True responsibility here consists in accepting that it precisely is *not* "my" responsibility, but ours. And this is not to spread the risk, as they say, not to avoid a responsibility that is properly mine, but to locate it in the only way that will make a difference.

Many factors need to be worked on: new practices of negotiation (if the Vietnam war was unwinnable and so too, in some ways, Kosovo, Afghanistan, Iraq, what strategies and practices would allow for nonviolent resolutions?); the development of new political institutions (educating politicians); changes in our educational practices (through the development of new financial and even military institutions?). But also developing powerful forms of nonlethal intervention in such conflicts. The bottom line here is that we need a different account of our ethical stance toward others for this to go ahead. That is, we need an account that abandons the purity of asymmetry. Asymmetry is an unstable and transformable structure—and includes torturer/tortured, rapist/victim, as well as the relation of forgiver to the forgiven.

The utter repudiation by Levinas of the whole space of negotiation, by associating it with a certain ideal reciprocity and community, and contrasting this with the ethical relation of asymmetry, might plausibly be thought to reflect the trauma of being subjected absolutely to the power of another. I doubt that anyone who has not experienced this can begin to imagine what it is like. But it is important to ask whether the lesson it teaches us is the right one.

The asymmetry of the face-to-face relation seems blind to contemporary threats to our capacities for self-determination—through cultural imperialism, through the invasive deterritorializing infantilization of an economic system that demands our participation at any cost. The need for some sort of workable identity, the struggle for recognition—these do not dissolve in the experience of the face of the other. The danger of Levinas's position is that the substitution that becomes important is not my willingness to substitute myself for the other, but the substitution of these traumatized relations to the other for ones in which the ethical complexity of the self-other relation is allowed to appear.

Levinas believes morality is founded on ethics as responsiveness to the other. But is not the character of our grasp of that responsiveness itself dependent both on knowledge and on ontological commitments?

Levinas says that it was first Bergson and then Heidegger who showed him that "the phenomenological search for eternal truths and essences originates in time, in our temporal and historical existence." Levinas's innovation is to have claimed that the central meaning of the break in totalizable self-presence implied by time, is to be found in my relation to the other. "The relation to the other is *time*," "Time means that the other is forever beyond me, irreducible to the synchrony of the same."[16] I have a great deal of sympathy with the tradition of temporalization which Levinas is radicalizing. But how does he make the move from the relation to the other being merely an important example of the alterity of time, to it being time itself? We have to look back to what Levinas says about death. Eventually he will want to say, against Heidegger, that what is central is the death of the other, not *my* death. But in *Time and the Other*, the critical role that death plays is as my death, where it announces the end of the subject's mastery. And the end of mastery "indicates that we have assumed existing in such a way that an event has happened to us that we can no longer assume." Death is "the impossibility of having a project."[17]

I would like to scrutinize more carefully here the move that Levinas will now make of identifying the alterity, the otherness announced in death, with the other person. But first, it is important to remind ourselves that Levinas is explicitly reworking Heidegger's account of *being toward death*. His basic line of argument is reminiscent of Sartre's objection to this same analysis: that Heidegger appropriates death, makes death work for him, generating "a supreme lucidity and hence a supreme virility."[18] While Levinas's discussion of death places it at the end of a spectrum of suffering. As I see it, Levinas is offering us, once more, a somewhat one-dimensional view of Heidegger. He operates here (and when he comes to describe femininity) with what seems to be a rigid opposition between virility, mastery, lucidity, power, on the one hand, and femininity, ungraspability, passivity, on the other. But to the extent that being-toward-death produces lucidity in Heidegger, it is the lucidity of one who has recognized his mortality, his limits, and resolves not to lose sight of this. As with Levinas, Heidegger's account is not a phenomenology of the experience of dying, but an account of the impact on my self-understanding of recognizing my mortality. As with Heidegger's account of the experience of *angst*, being-toward-death seems to me to bring him closer to Levinas's position than Levinas is comfortable with. We know that with *Gelassenheit*, with the growing importance of the *es gibt*, and with Heidegger's subsequent account of man's relation to language, Heidegger's position becomes ever more clearly a many-fronted critique of the very mastery that Levinas attributes to him. But the point of these remarks here is not just to rub in the extent to which Levinas makes Heidegger into a straw man, or what Bernasconi has called a surrogate. Rather, I think that in this case it is particularly important for Levinas to accentuate his distance from Heidegger—however much they agree on a critique of the "now"—because of the strikingly different way, and in my view, deeply problematic way, he wishes to develop the significance of my becoming aware of my mortality.

Levinas writes that "the end of mastery indicates that we have assumed existing in such a way that an event can happen to us that we no longer assume."[19] This approach of death indicates that we are in relation with something that is absolutely other . . . something whose very existence is made of alterity,"[20] What does he mean by this other here? Is it another person? Is it my nonexistence? Levinas writes that "the other does not possess existing as the subject possesses it; its hold over my existing is mysterious. It is not unknown but unknowable."[21] At this exact point Levinas makes the following argument. He says that all this shows that "the other is in no way another myself, participating with me in a common existence."[22] This claim, which is completely indeterminate as to whether it refers to a god, a rock, a cloud, nothingness . . . is immediately treated as capturing the distinctive characteristics of the other person (alterity, exteriority).

There are of course a whole cluster of argument fragments in the vicinity working somewhat rhizomally toward the same end. Let me just rehearse one more before explaining my resistance to them.

In Part IV of *Time and the Other*, Levinas begins by reaffirming the Bergsonian sense of time as creative. "Time [he writes] is essentially a new birth"[23] (a phrase which of course anticipates its literal accomplishment in his later account of fecundity in *Totality and Infinity*). However, he claims, "The strangeness of the future of death does not leave the subject any initiative." The problem this poses us is that of vanquishing death in such a way as to "maintain, with the alterity of the event, a relationship that must still be personal."[24] Two pages later, this question will have been answered by my relation to the other person, in his or her alterity. And with the examples of the "widow" and the "orphan," this relation is claimed to be essentially asymmetrical. Obviously, these matters get revisited in later texts. But let us just focus on the argument at hand. His problem is to work out how there can be creative time after an experience of mortality that "leaves the subject with no initiative." The strangeness here lies not in the experience of death, but in Levinas's account of its consequence, an account tied up with his outright rejection of Heidegger's account of being-toward-death as virility. But surely Heidegger shows us a much more nuanced account of just how a "subject" can retain initiative in the face of mortality (just as Kierkegaard does in his account of how love and the eternal are embodied in marriage in *Either/Or*—see chapter 4 below). In other words, while Levinas seems at least here to be offering a solution to a problem, the real problem lies in his formulation of that problem in the first place. It is difficult here to follow how the other comes to be specified in terms of the widow and the orphan. I assume it is because my sense of my own mortality brings to my special attention those living close to the limit. But what this shows, importantly, is just how far my own self-understanding is vital in focusing my obligation to the other. And how difficult it is for Levinas to maintain the claim that "man's ethical relation to the other is ultimately prior to his ontological relation to himself."[25] As I see it, everything points to an unavoidable dialectic between the two.

However, it is by these arguments that the path is established that will allow the face-to-face relation with the other person to *be time*. There is no doubt at all that time is inseparable from my relation to the other, but this is not because time is a unitary phenomenon that can be identified with the other person. But rather because time, even when thought of as event—a position with which I have much sympathy—is a multifaceted phenomenon that cannot be reduced to any one dimension. Let me explain what I mean. For Levinas, the identification of the *event* with the *other* seems to take place—at least on one occasion, through the sense that my own death-induced lack of initiative in the face of alterity is redeemed by this alterity taking a human form. The idea of event is tied up both with the human other and with the idea that it is something that happens to me, rather than something I do. Clearly this sets the stage for hearing the command of the other. But the deep acknowledgment of the limits to my active powers can and does take many other forms, some of which importantly complicate the account Levinas gives of my relation to the other person while some supplement it with strange new dimensions. But all of them are ways of making good on Bergson's sense of time as essentially the birth of the new.

Let me present some suggestions in the form of questions for Levinas, and for us trying to read and interpret him.

1. If I experience the erotic relation in terms of a relation to an absolute, recessive, modest, feminine, what would happen if the oppositional frame within which this account is set up were to fall away? It would be an event, an opening onto a brave new world of eroticism, in which the putting into play of this very polarization brings its own delights. Or would the event perhaps be to recognize that it has always been so?

2. If I find myself in the mountains, climbing rocks almost as old as the earth, walking among specimens of the bristle-cone pine dating from before the rise of the Roman Empire, and at night I gaze into the starry sky at points of light so old they no longer exist, the ungraspable other appears at every step—never human, and yet sometimes speaking a strange language, hard to decipher. This importance of this dimension of our experience is acknowledged (within limits), in chapter 6 below: "Dionysus in America."

3. I am reading a philosophy book. I notice the way in which the thinker proceeds by one sharp opposition after the other—ontology and ethics, morality and ethics. I notice something glinting through the cracks. What is it? Could it be the real? The complexity of the real? I wonder why we have stopped listening to that man who knew a thing or two about thinking, who described his style as a dance, an overleaping mockery of symmetries? Was that thought not also an event? I wonder what happened to that other man who suggested we might not be speaking unless we listened to the speaking of language.

4. I am watching a lizard on a rock in the heat of the day. I can see the pulsing of its heart. I watch a spider for hours, spinning its web, waiting for
   flying food to entangle itself. I watch a snake at the water hole. The pan-
   ther in its cage. The snail eating my tomato plants. First event—I notice
   them in their "world," not just in mine. Second event, I realize, shatter-
   ingly, that while I have some measure of access to what they might be,
   and are up to, in other ways, they are utterly incomparable.

I will not multiply examples indefinitely. The point should be clear.
There is a structure to the event, an unexpected transgression of limits that
opens onto an unknown future, one that exceeds any attempt to shackle it to
the human other. What I am calling for is the event of the event, the explosion of eventuation beyond the boundaries to which Levinas confines it. Of
course this is unsettling. And it does not necessarily help us resolve conflicts.
Indeed, sometimes it makes conflicts visible where none were apparent.

Levinas is right to pursue the question of time in relation to the other,
and to show the intimacy with which this relation is worked through. But I
wonder if it is not what Husserl would call a regional ontology, with the word
"ethical" functioning to mark the intimacy of the relation being explored.
And even in relation to the other, even when one understands that relation
ethically, I claim that we cannot merely eliminate the ontological dimension,
as occasionally Levinas admits. We cannot ignore the fact that the positions
Levinas takes up are grounded on analyses of the human condition that are
both ontological and if not plain disputable, at least of limited validity.

I will just indicate what I mean here. I have tried to give some sort of
explanation of how Levinas comes to treat my relation to the other in terms
of height, transcendence, etc. But his further claim is that ethics so understood, as a infinite obligation to the other, is quite distinct from everyday
morality, and yet supplies the basis for that everyday morality. But surely he
makes the same mistake as Kant in supposing that any trace of self-interest is
proof that what we are dealing with are those social arrangements for mutual
benefit that masquerade under the name of morality, and not ethics. The former are characterized by some sort of symmetrical interaction. The latter by
a fundamental asymmetry. Can this distinction be sustained? It is not hard to
see something of what lies behind this thought. The widow and orphan seem
to lie outside any obvious system of exchange. Our response to them must be
motivated by something other than the thought that they are "part of the
community," part of the extended "same" with which I can identify myself.
The stranger, precisely, comes from outside. But the opposition between
asymmetrical and symmetrical is a dangerous one. If we understand the ethical relation to the other as purely asymmetrical, we are establishing this relation on the same grounds, with a reversed valence, as those that allow the
greatest violence. Asymmetry is just what characterizes the relation between

overwhelming power and victimhood. And what worries me here is that focusing on the relation of asymmetry will distract us from thinking about those *complex forms of mutual dependency and interaction* that would block a simple reversal of the valency of the relation. The idea that the obligation is all mine (and mine more than others) may only be meant to define clearly the nature and purity of obligation. But does this not deprive the other of all capacity for moral agency? Or magnanimity? Or generosity? I am sure Levinas's position can be explained in such a way that it does not do this. But the deeper point is that if "Never again!" means "find constructive ways of making it less likely that genocide and every other form of violence will happen again," then I for one want to spend much more time thinking about those impure forms of human relation that do not absolutize the other's alterity, but bring the other in all kinds of ways into relation with us.

Two brief indicators: The principle of hospitality often found in under-developed countries need not be understood as one of pure generosity, for it to be valued and cultivated. There is no reason to think that it does not have a practical value *as well as* giving expression to a capacity to imagine being in the same situation oneself. And interestingly, when the stranger you have helped wants to help you, one is not suddenly stepping out of the ethical when one accepts his offer. Secondly, the other to whom one has an infinite asymmetrical obligation *must* be thought of in whatever ontological terms are appropriate (bird, fox, plant, man), and *hence in terms of the kinds of further relation that might be possible with that being*, or else it becomes a purely abstract relation. One would have become a guilty monad scurrying out to carry his infinite obligations, then scurrying back. These are meant as examples of how the asymmetrical relation of obligation can be productively conjoined with symmetrical relations (of friendship, cooperation, negotiation, etc.) The ethical cannot and must not be reserved for relations of pure asymmetry. If it is said that the ethical, as Levinas develops it, is not really a relationship at all, but a certain vigilance with respect to any relationship, I would be much happier. This does not, however, fit with much of what he says. And what it demands of us is that we focus on the practical and theoretical tasks of developing those models of interpersonal, social, and political relations that open up ever more complex symmetries, and mixed forms of symmetry and asymmetry. Now that would be an event!

Addendum

TWENTY THESES ON VIOLENCE

1. The philosophy of violence must never forget the violence of philosophy.

2. Philosophy is the only protection against the violence of the concept; it is also the most common victim.

3. Violence is inseparable from the boundaries we insist on maintaining.

4. We should not comfort ourselves by thinking that violence is a failure of recognition. Violence teaches us that recognition is not *one* thing. All violence requires a certain recognition.

5. There is no Other as such, no pure alterity.

6. Otherness is the ground both for infinite peace and absolute violence.

7. The distinction between friend and enemy is already a violence—to our friend, to our enemy and to ourselves.

8. The secrets of violence are locked in the vault called Time.

9. There is no violence without the law.

10. Violence shows us that ethics and ontology are inseparable.

11. Genocidal violence is a war of logics—human destruction and the sedimentation of irrecoverable loss.

12. The boundary between force and violence is always contestable.

13. To try to eliminate force from human affairs would itself be violence.

14. The danger of enlightenment ties not in its ideals of freedom and reason, but in its dream of their unconditioned realization.

15. Every open agreement rests on decisions on which there was no open agreement. In this sense, human affairs are of necessity rationally opaque.

16. Violence is not *just* a failure of imagination, but it involves such a failure, indeed many such failures.

17. Violence breeds violence, but many a peace breeds violence.

18. As certainty is the enemy of truth, so the demand for absolute security is the enemy of peace.

19. "Force is the *ultimate ratio*, and between two groups of men that want to make inconsistent kinds of world I see no remedy except force . . . every society rests on the death of men" (Oliver Wendell Holmes). Does this mark the end of philosophy, or only the end of a certain idealism?

20. Negative capability is the antidote to violence.

PART II

Singular Encounters

FOUR

The First Kiss

Tales of Innocence and Experience

An old proverb fetched from the outward and visible world says: "Only the man that works gets the bread." Strangely enough that proverb does not aptly apply in that world to which it expressly applies. For the outward world is subjected to the law of imperfection. . . . It is different in the world of spirit.

—Kierkegaard, *Fear and Trembling*

When you say the first kiss is the most beautiful, the sweetest, you insult the loved one, for what gives the kiss absolute value here is time and what pertains to that.

—Kierkegaard, *Either/Or*

But healthy love has a quite different worth; it works itself out in time, and is therefore also capable of rejuvenating itself through these outward signs; and—what for me is the main point—it has quite another idea of time and of the meaning of repetition.

—Kierkegaard, *Either/Or*

WHETHER WE DO something for the first time, or repeat what we have done before, the significance of such events, and hence the fate of innocence or experience, is tied up with the ways we inhabit time, and how we count. The philosophical interest in pursuing the "economy" of a thought rests on the supposition that how we count ultimately determines "what counts."

In *Either/Or*, one of his most celebrated books, Kierkegaard seems to pose for us a choice between two ways of life—the aesthetic and the ethical—and makes the question of repetition central to this choice. I argue here that when it comes to choosing between the aesthetic and the ethical, it is not possible to choose between the forms of repetition each enjoins. Rather, what is called for is a grasp of the ineluctable tension between the two. Kierkegaard helps us to see the bare choice as problematic at the very point at which he seems to be recommending the ethical. What is the privilege of the First Kiss?

THE QUESTION OF NUMBER

Throughout Kierkegaard's writings we find him toying with number, typically illuminating unexpected dimensions of a dialectical movement from first to second, in which what is often at stake is the economy of loss amidst progress, the aporias of old and new. And he will pit the whole world of measurement and calculation against that of spirituality, only to reverse the opposition at a critical juncture. In one place,[1] Kierkegaard alludes to magic with the Danish expression *1,2,3 Kokolorum*, an analog of our abracadabra. And I will use this as a point of entry for a brief consideration of the *significance* of number.

Even within mathematics, it is not hard to see that the apparent simplicity of counting 1,2,3, etc. is home to numerous puzzles. For example, there is the question of negative numbers, the question of zero, and the question of the first number.[2] Small numbers—1,2,3, and perhaps a few more—seem to appear even before arithmetic, as fundamental to biology (think of symmetry, cell division), physical sciences (bilateral symmetry), to simple human interactions (conflict, gift, exchange, recognition, intercourse), to systems of justice (law of the talon, restitution), religion (monotheism, the mystery of the Trinity, Manicheanism), cosmology (the war of opposites, struggle of good and evil), and so on.[3] And when we say that two's company and three's a crowd, *c'est mieux avec deux*, or talk of looking after number one—or when, more reflectively, we think of Levinas's insistence on the importance of the third or Peirce's distinction between firstness, secondness, and thirdness—we can see that the significance of small numbers is deeply embedded in our grasp of the primitive structures of human relationality and of relationality in general.

By enumerating these various domains in which the play of unity, duality, and thirdness is so all-pervasive, it is hard not to notice that number seems here to operate prior to its extension into arithmetic, into counting or into abstract seriality, and it is hard not to wonder whether there are not at least some common principles in play, common issues that arise, common solutions, and dilemmas.

Those who have studied the pre-Socratics, pursued the dialectic through Hegel, Kierkegaard, Marx, and Sartre, and even followed its twists and turns in contemporary philosophies of difference (Derrida and Deleuze), may think that these issues have been sufficiently clarified and resolved. And yet the thought that they may have been resolved suggests, not least to Kierkegaard, that it is in the very idea of resolution that the danger lies. So let us rehearse just a little what is at stake.

The binary choice captured by the title *Either/Or* could be said to reflect an opposition between two ways of understanding time and repetition—one we could call external, and the other internal. The external way understands temporal succession in terms of an outer sequentiality, while the internal account not only proposes an inner connectedness, it believes that the external view itself can be taken up as a moment in the development of that internal perspective. And Kierkegaard seems to suggest that it's only on this latter view that various of the normative conditions we imagine to govern the external view are actually realized. Thus, the idea that "those who work get the bread" suggests that there is some sort of natural causality and justice in the ordinary world. In fact, says Kierkegaard, in the real world this principle is often mocked, while in the spiritual world it really is true. "Here an eternal divine order prevails" (FT, 38). For Kierkegaard spiritual work has a direct connection to results, one not mediated by fallible external circumstances subject to a law of indifference. Though it has to be said that the significance of faith does not suggest that if you make the right spiritual moves you will get the right results, for that would reduce spiritual life to a calculable activity, leaving no room for grace. But rather that, as Hegel said, there is no royal road to truth, even if spiritual work is a necessary condition for self-transformation. Whether it is *sufficient* is another story.

THE PHENOMENOLOGY OF THE FIRST KISS

Kierkegaard often ruminates on the significance of the First Kiss. Why is it so difficult to think this through on the ethical plane? The argument rests surely on the phenomenology of the First Kiss, by which I mean not necessarily the very first kiss, or even the first "romantic" kiss. There are kisses one gives and receives as a child from parents and ancient aunts that just don't count. And even romantic kisses can be exploratory, imitative, learning how to do it, what it feels like. By the First Kiss, I mean a kiss that inaugurates a relationship. It is not enough to say that it does so intentionally, for it may precisely be the occasion for the formation of such an intention, and it may happen precisely on the understanding that it not inaugurate a relationship. For the sake of our discussion, I would describe the First Kiss as the experience of the opening of a possibility, as a trembling on the brink of something inchoate but momentous, the experience of the realignment of boundaries. Space and time, self and other, activity and passivity, certainty and uncertainty are all thrown into the air, and caught again, differently. I will not decide here whether one is being kissed or doing the kissing, or whether there is some ideal mutuality. Whatever the general shape, the first kiss solicits the tenderness of a response, a visceral recognition of the desire of the other. But it also asks a mute question, a question every bit as important as "What is the meaning of Being?" And we too (we two) must have become mute, must have run up against the limits of language, at the lips, at the birthplace of words. The kiss draws us deep into the face-to-face, feeding and being nourished by the other's transcendence. "The kiss is the impossible food."[4]

For Kierkegaard's aesthetic seducer, the First Kiss, coupled with the subsequent conquest, presages the end of all interest. A kiss always has a distinct character. "Sometimes," he writes, "it is clicking, sometimes hissing, sometimes smacking, sometimes popping, sometimes rumbling, sometimes resonant, sometimes hollow, sometimes like calico, and so on . . ." (EO, 350). But this sonorous classification pales into insignificance compared to the spiritual and subsequently erotic levels of intensity that Johannes seeks to develop in his Cordelia. The First Kiss, he writes, is indifferent not just to sound, but also "to touch, [and] time in general" (EO, 351).

A little later, Johannes begins to be troubled "that it might occur to her at some moment to consider the future. So far this hasn't happened; I have been too good at drugging her aesthetically. Nothing less erotic is imaginable than this talk of the future, the reason for which is basically that people have nothing with which to fill the present. When I'm there I have no fear of that either, for I can make her forget both time and eternity" (EO, 373).

Finally, we recall how it ends: "Once a girl has given away everything, she is weak, she had lost everything. . . . I will not take leave of her; nothing disgusts me more than a woman's tears and a woman's prayers. . . . If I were a god I would do for her what Neptune did for a nymph: change her into a man . . . now it is over and I want never to see her again" (EO, 376).

Judge William's aim in Part II of *Either/Or* is to show that we do not have to jettison the intensity of the first kiss in marriage. It is not necessary for a woman to "exchange maidenly yearning for marital yawning" (as Johannes Climacus puts it in the *Concluding Scientific Postscript*). On Johannes' aesthetic model, thinking about the future is a distraction from the intensity of the present. And this is easy to understand. It is hard to listen to a fugue while wondering about how to meet the mortgage payments. The aesthetic intensity of the present may be thought to rest precisely on its exclusion of the outside world, of time and space. I am reminded of John Donne's poem, *The Good-Morrow*:

> I wonder by my troth what thou and I
> Did 'til we loved? were we not wean'd til then?
>
> For love all love of other sights controules,
> and makes one little roome an every where[5]

The claim that the First Kiss is indifferent to time, that it is important that she "forget" time, and that thinking of the future ruins everything, etc., may be more complicated than it seems, even before we turn to Judge William's response. Leaving aside the manipulative unpleasantness of "The Seducer's Diary," it is simply not clear that Johannes and Cordelia actually have the kind of encounter that could count as a First Kiss. It is surely not sufficient that Cordelia have no thought of the future. For a true first kiss, even in aesthetic terms, it is surely necessary that Johannes too is "controuled" by love. In fact, he is not really occupying their "little roome." The whole action is contained within a calculative temporal and spatial framework. She may not know this, but he certainly does. Moreover, even if Johannes were fully participating in the First Kiss, which I claim he is not, the idea that we "forget" time in these moments seems too simple. It does not, for example, preclude the possibility that time is operating as one of the grounds of the intensity of the experience.[6] It may well be that time is not being *represented*, or that a certain linear understanding of time is suspended. But that does not mean that time is absent.[7]

Many philosophers, and I am thinking specifically of Heidegger and Irigaray, argue that it is precisely through our reversion to or a transformation into, a more "original" inhabiting of space and time, that new possibilities of thinking and being arise. The experience of the opening of love may not be alone in convincing us of the plausibility of this thought, but it is certainly a powerful source. If love is not the experience of unity, of the dissolution of boundaries (as it is often poetically expressed), it surely involves a dramatic disturbance, or mobilization and interrogation of boundaries—bodily, emotional, and social. It is in this sense that love truly makes us tremble. And this trembling occurs in part because what is at stake is utterly inseparable from time. The feeling of safety, the sense that she is the one you have always been looking for, the sense that whatever this leads to will be good—the tension between the ecstatic exhilaration and the anxiety that this will not last— these are all surely part of the experience of the First Kiss, and of First Intimacy in general. It is not that time is banished. It is, rather, transformed, put into play, renewed. And at the level of fantasy, time operates forcibly whenever we feel or say "forever."

Clearly, any sense we give to the First Kiss is an idealization of some sort. I am proposing that we understand the First Kiss as the event of opening of love, which has a projective and destabilizing dimension, one in which the destabilizing reveals the schematizing parameters of our standardly individuated existence. And it is one that sets in motion powerful desires for connection, and reconnection, desires that themselves almost certainly have archaic origins. As I see it, this account is a corrective of Johannes' sketch of the aesthetic treatment of the First Kiss in two respects: (1) It is no longer wedded to the distortedly one-sided formulation that the manipulative seducer sets up. Once we have genuine mutuality, then a cycle of growing recognition and tenderness is set in motion, which cannot happen in a seduction framed even by altruistic manipulation. (2) Time is not banished at all. Rather, it enters in more profound ways.

THE ETHICAL TRANSFORMATION

The revisionary thesis about first love in Part II of *Either/Or* has many aspects, and it seems important to know if they can be separated. For the sake of speed and clarity I will list some of them:

1. Judge William expresses extreme gratitude that his eventual wife was his first love. This makes first love into only love. But is this necessary? And if he thinks it is, does not that point to a limitation in his whole account of how first love develops?

2. Judge William is clearly seeking to impress on the aesthete that there are dimensions of relationality (in love) that only something like long-term unconditional commitment makes possible. This seems to be a central claim, and an important truth to which a certain kind of aesthete is indeed blind.

3. The aesthete might respond—but there are equally dimensions of hell that only open up under these circumstances. Marriage, he suggests, can be like living in a prison cell. Judge William boldly affirms that these people betray marriage, etc. And he explicitly does not attack divorcees, who at least have courage.

4. We might understand Kierkegaard as arguing for the constitutive role of long-term commitment, or for the constitutive role of an absolute commitment. He is ambivalent precisely because an absolute commitment by one party, even by both parties, does not guarantee constant renewal, which seems at least to be the justification of marriage over a life of mere repetition. In fact, one might argue, it is a condition of the possibility of renewal of the significance of first love (constant rejuvenation) not that one simply occupies the space it opens onto, but that one enacts and reenacts the anxious movement, the trepidation, of opening onto that space, and that one allows the boundaries to be put in play. And *in extremis*, one risks the possibility of the failure of this repetition. The logic here is that of the faith of an Abraham; it is only in being prepared to risk all that one can possibly continue to renew the promise of the First Kiss. Anything less than risking the loss of the whole *guarantees* the loss of the whole. You can only win by being willing to lose everything. And that loss must be not only be possible, it must from time to time happen. (Which is one reason why the Abraham story is problematic, because the story is only allowed to have one outcome, even though Kierkegaard offers various glosses. This leaves open the destructive thought that faith is a sufficient condition for success. But if that were true, and known to be true, it would self-destruct, because it could be relied on, and hence no longer function as faith.)

Let us work this through a little more slowly. The blindness of the aesthete's view of the First Kiss is that it understands thinking about the future only as a distraction from the intensity of the moment, and it fails to recognize that an unconditional commitment to a future life together is necessary for the realization of certain values and virtues. These include loyalty, mutual understanding, honest recognition, a shared context of meaning, everything that is only possible as part of a shared life. The aesthete focuses on the boredom of a life that falls into habit and routine. The champion of the ethical life argues not just that certain values presuppose unconditional commitment, but that we do not need to think of our commemoration of the First Kiss in terms of nostalgia for a lost past. We can find new ways of reopening the space of mutual desire, excitement, and significance. Kierkegaard will call this unconditional commitment the eternal. It is what is missing, he suggests, from the intentional horizon of the contractual five year marriage.

I have already suggested that we need my reworked account of the First Kiss for this story to work, one that would preclude the seducer's kiss, a kiss that is far from excluding time. What is reworked, I claim, is precisely the essential ambiguity and tension about the relationship between present and future, self and other, etc. The aesthetic, in other words, is already more than the aesthetic; it is, rather, constructed by the repression of time and the other. And the same can be said, in its own way, of the ethical. Here, I am on the side of paganism. Certain human virtues are only possible on the basis of unconditional commitment—giving oneself, one's life, to another. Kierkegaard is surely right about this.

The problem is that unconditional commitment is "actually" and essentially conditional, for all promises and conditions are *framed*. This blind spot is usually highlighted in the marriage ceremony in the singular form of death: "Til death do us part." Although this is ambiguous, because one can clearly continue in some sense to love (and even honor and obey) someone who is dead. But there is something strange lurking in this whole structure of double promising. In the typical case of a marriage, whether legally sanctified or not, we find something like a mutual commitment. Each party publicly or privately commits himself to the other, in the context at least of the other's reciprocal commitment. Now, we can imagine a mediating device (such as the institution of marriage) that would contain, guarantee, and distribute all the benefits of such a declaration. And the supposition of such a device may itself make possible consequences that would not flow without such a fiction. If you believe the streets are being policed, you can walk in areas you would otherwise be afraid to walk in. Even if the police are all at home asleep. The belief that one's own commitment or vow is unconditional, and that the other intends his or her's in the same way may make possible all kinds of decisions that facilitate the development of the relationship—such as moving city, changing a job, having children—which would not make sense without those assurances. Death, we say, will part us. But in truth, there are many ways in which relationships "die," and the avoidance of which constitute the tacit conditions of unconditional commitments. The briefest possible way of putting this would be to say that the breakdown of a couple's capacity to reenact the play space opened up by the first kiss would constitute a breach in the conditioned unconditionality of marriage. The basis of this breakdown may be utterly unpredictable and uncontrollable, such that it is not at all possible or meaningful to assign blame. After all, in some sense, this capacity for rejuvenation has to remain a spontaneity, which can of course be cultivated, but cannot be guaranteed.[8] It is perhaps worth alluding here to Kierkegaard's own comments on the whole question of the importance of keeping the habituality of certainty at bay. He first mentions this in the context of explaining the alliance between indirect communication, and uncertainty and becoming, and illustrates this danger by alluding to "the woman who wants to settle herself in legal security as a spouse." If she "lets go of the Idea," she is as unfaithful as if she had found another lover. What this means, however, is that the ethical advance on the aesthetic does not merely continue to feast on the aesthetic in the sense that it repeats and reaffirms the First Kiss, rather than consigning it to the innocence of youth. It also draws on what is arguably the fundamental limitation of the aesthetic—its being embroiled in appearance and illusion. We make unconditional promises we are in no position to make. And yet, in trying to keep them, we make possible things that would not have been possible without them. This, we might say, is a miracle, a paradox. Once we recognize that *it is important not to say this,* for this to remain secret, then we will have unearthed an explanation for the language of eternity, god, etc. It would be the language that concealed the ineliminability of (aesthetic) illusion from the ethical. But in so doing, it would introduce a further illusion.

I am wary of offering these comments as a critique of Kierkegaard. For that to be possible, I would have first to offer a definitive reading of *Either/Or,* resolving the relationship between the aesthetic and ethical perspectives, and then drawing in the question of the religious. Instead, I have treated the two halves as themselves lips that are kissing—whether each other or another I cannot tell (compare here Kierkegaard suggesting that *Either* and *Or* may be treated as an internal debate within one person.). On analogy with my revision of the aesthetic understanding of the First Kiss, I would add that for the kiss to be a real one, there has to be both confidence and uncertainty about the relationship, and neither party can be allowed to be manipulating the response of the other. This is not just to say that the verdict of whether Either or Or wins is to be left open—far from it. I am saying that it is in our repeating *their* First Kiss, that this book continues to be rejuvenated.

5. Kierkegaard is also clear that one of the other key dimensions in which repetition operates in an importantly complex way is that of generational

transmission. First, he says that it is only by having a son that a father can understand his own childhood. Second, he suggests that children inherit and have to work through the sins of their fathers, as the Bible says—to three and four generations. "There's something pleasing about a son's repenting his father's sins . . . it is only in this way that he can choose himself" (EO, 519). Thirdly, he says that the sense in which we come to "know" ourselves is analogous to carnal knowledge—in which one begets oneself, and gives birth to oneself (EO, 549). And again, "the only saving thing, is that always, in relation to his own life, a man is not his uncle but his father" (EO, 556). Here, paternity is being understood, curiously, as a phase in self-discovery and salvation. In this way, having children is drawn into the heart of the sphere of meaning rather than being relegated to a biological or practical matter, such as support in old age. (Compare Nietzsche's "Everything about woman has one solution: it is called pregnancy.")[9] Understanding paternity this way is also strangely limited, suggesting that what is distinctive about the "ethical" perspective is still contained within a temporally extended narcissism. And curiously, at least in the account in *Stages in Life's Way*, Kierkegaard understands the value of marriage for a woman in similar terms. For marriage opens the possibility of motherhood, which transforms a woman from a girl, a "phantom," into the reality of woman. "This is a metamorphosis which has no analogy in the man . . . a woman's development is not complete until she is a mother, only then does she exist . . . in all her beauty."[10] What this suggests, however, is that it is the child who does this for the woman; the man is just a means.

6. Something of what Kierkegaard says about the First Kiss is true of any inaugural event. As we elaborated in chapter 2, "The Philosophy of Violence," such events open up a future, but this will only have happened if that future is welcomed and preserved. This reference to the future makes it clear that while the excitement of the First Kiss may be restricted to the present, its significance lies in the historical possibilities of development that it sets up. A similar event structure can be found in Heidegger's "The Origin of the Work of Art," in which the work of art is said to open and preserve the strife between earth and world.[11] Heidegger too insists on the need for preservers. The parallel deepens remarkably when we notice how Heidegger interprets the shoes as the shoes of a peasant woman, who through her labor is connected to the earth, but who also occupies a world. Where Kierkegaard speaks of the woman supplying finitude to the man's infinity, Heidegger speaks of the peasant woman's shoes as indicating her groundedness in the earth, and animating the relation to world. In each case, it is woman who supplies the grounding corrective. There is perhaps a further parallel to the residual privilege Hegel attributes to the slave whose relation to the earth gives him a kind of intimacy with things that the master lacks.

Kierkegaard's account of generational transference seems wholly patri-lineal. This makes sense if it is only men who, essentially cut off from their natures as they are, suffer the pathologies of the infinite, and need to have that connection restored by their relation to a woman. But we might wonder whether there is not some connection between the role being set aside for women in this model, and the absence of the mother in the generational suc-cession story. The young aesthete who luxuriates in the pleasures of seduction and then moves on to a new conquest could be said to be actually engaged in an internal repetition of an infantile scene, while never allowing the signifi-cance of the event to blossom. But the melancholic recollection that can only seek the repetition of the First Kiss itself needs its narrative filling-out. It is noteworthy that Kierkegaard's most striking accounts of the role of the mother occur in the analogical commentaries he gives to the four variant replays of the Abraham/Isaac story in *Fear and Trembling*. In each case what is at stake is a different strategy of weaning, of facilitating the separation of the child from the mother, different ways of coping with loss: by deception, displacement, shared mourning, and substitution. We might be forgiven for wondering whether the schematic role Kierkegaard offers women in love is not connected to the absence of any account of the relation to the mother, and the absence of any account of the historical relationship of love as a two-way street, as dialogically developing. This is a complex issue. Clearly, the terms in which Kierkegaard understands the relationship between men and women—infinite and finite (women grounding men)—are problematic, even if they are quite capable of supplying the rhythmic background for the narra-tive development of a relationship. The description he gives of the wife whose husband doesn't come down to dinner because he is entranced by an orthographic eccentricity on one of the manuscript pages he is poring over is very amusing. The dot on which all attention is focused turns out to be a par-ticle of snuff that his wife just blows away, bringing him down to earth. But this positioning of woman seems to many readers like a blind spot on Kierkegaard's page that we struggle to blow away without success.[12]

Obviously, we could read *Either/Or* as an extended working through of the distinction he makes in *Repetition* between recollection and repetition. He explicitly ties recollection to Platonism, and to what Freud will call mourning, while "repeating forward" is very close to what Nietzsche will call affirmation. Each could be said to relate to a First Kiss, a founding event. But the former repeatedly, tragically, and impossibly attempts to recapture an imaginary past. While the latter recognizes the distinctive virtues of narrative continuity, of marriage as a kind of co-authorship (with a metaphysical script, e.g., finite and infinite), and the possibility of a continuous reenactment of the founding event—its *preservation* as Heidegger would put it.

I have argued that the phenomenology of firstness would rescue an ade-quate account of the aesthetic from both one-way manipulation and recollective mourning. I have further argued that the religious dimension that brings the framework of eternity and unconditionality into marriage renders the ethical dependent on illusion and aporia. This suggests that the aesthetic and the ethical are interwoven in ways that would make the development from one to the other inherently problematic. And the conditionality of marriage, which Kierkegaard clearly acknowledges, suggests that as well as there being an essential ambiguity between aesthetic and ethical, the truly ethical dimension is one in touch with its own fundamental uncertainty and hesitation.

CONCLUSION

The girl who would be a "phantom" until married, until she became a mother, the scholar who would be studying imaginary punctuation until it is blown away as dust by his wife, all these examples testify to what I would call the economic flow that characterizes Kierkegaard's thought—it is a flow that returns us from appearance to reality, from the secondary to the primary, the derived to the original, from 2 to 1. The aesthete's understanding of the First Kiss is a serial nostalgia—a philandering repetition that gets nowhere, that merely repeats the exhilaration of a timeless moment. The force of Judge William's comment is to release us from servitude to this empty seriality, and open us to the unity of a shared life. The primary effect of marriage on each partner is the fulfillment of each and the elimination of the shadow side, with some acknowledgment of co-authorship of a joint project.

The initial contrast we cited between the real world, in which there is no necessary justice, no balance between effort and rewards, and the spiritual world, where such justice does reign, is precarious. Hard work is neither a sufficient nor a necessary condition for worldly rewards, and yet while it is necessary for spiritual completeness, it is not sufficient either, for there is still grace, good fortune, etc. As for marriage, if the success of that relationship depends on the continuing capacity to recreate, rejuvenate the delights of the First Kiss, then despite the symmetry of the agency of spiritual completion that each can perform for the other, the unity of a shared life will depend precisely on the irreducible duality, twoness, of the relationship. It is not just, as Levinas once said, *mieux avec deux*. It is *impossible sans deux*. Kierkegaard admits the possibility of failure of marriage. He compares favorably the courage of those who divorce to the unfaithfulness of those who linger trapped in their cells. And as much as he seeks for married life the stamp of eternity, and the exorcism of doubt, the logic of both the continuous recreation of the First Kiss and the possibility of faith is that a certain uncertainty must remain, and a certain resistance must continue to the economic reduction of plurality to unity. It is essential to the eventuating excitement of the First Kiss that it cannot ever wholly anticipate what it will open up. *Either/Or* begins with the whimsical thought that it could just as well be understood as a conversation one might have with oneself, which immediately renders the externality of the dialog into something of an artifice. For all these reasons, *Either/Or* does not actually enjoin an absolute choice at all. Not only does it open the way to recognizing the interpenetration of the ethical and the aesthetic. It also problematizes the very terms of the connection between individual and shared fulfillment.

FIVE

Thinking God in the Wake of Kierkegaard

IF EVER WE NEEDED proof of Sartre's genius[1] we could do worse than read his extraordinary essay on Kierkegaard—"The Singular Universal."[2] In this essay, Sartre finds in the character of Kierkegaard's Christian faith the key to his significance even for those committed to the life-long task of "becoming-an-atheist." It would be a commonplace to remark that such a reading revealed "more about Sartre" than about Kierkegaard. But it would also trivialize the stakes of a philosophical engagement.

About thirty years after this profound acknowledgment, Derrida takes up the question of Kierkegaard's God in ways that bear close comparison:

> It is perhaps necessary—if we are to follow the traditional Judeo-Christian-Islamic injunction, but *also at the risk of turning it against that tradition*, to think of God and of the name of God without such idolatrous stereotyping or representation. Then we might say: God is the name of the possibility I have of keeping a secret that is visible from the interior but not from the exterior. Once such a structure of conscience exists . . . once there is secrecy and secret witnessing within me, then what I call God exists.

Derrida develops this thought further:

> God . . . is that structure of invisible interiority that is called, in Kierkegaard's sense, subjectivity. [This gives us] . . . a history of God and of the name of God as the history of secrecy, a history that is at the same time secret and without any secrets. Such a history is also an economy.[3]

Derrida is not merely affirming that the very word/name God is as such problematic, he is demonstrating the logic or economy within which all that we want to say (or not say) about "God" can best be located. He is sharpening the question that Sartre rubs our nose in: Is the specifically religious character of Kierkegaard's *philosophical* reflections not best repeated, revitalized as a recognition of the *passion* of thought? How else could it inspire a militant atheist? I pursue this question—of how to understand references to God—by an indirect route, commenting on the concerns of various thinkers who have found in Kierkegaard a kindred spirit. After some remarks about Wittgenstein, I will return to comment more fully on treatments by Sartre and by Derrida, and then show that this same possibility of an economic reading of Kierkegaard's religious language—a thinking of an excess that explodes all ethical complacency—is anticipated by Kierkegaard himself.

I

The meaning of life . . . we can call God
—Wittgenstein

Some time ago it was fashionable to refer to God-talk. The idea was that the intelligibility of religious (and theological) language might not rest on its having a real world reference, but rather on there being appropriate and shared ways of talking. Perhaps God-talk could best be thought of as a language-game in Wittgenstein's sense, one *bearing witness* to the limits of language from "within." To speak of a language-game is not to abjure all structure to one's discourse. Although there are many kinds of games, they all involve the possibility of distinguishing between acting correctly or appropriately and incorrectly or inappropriately. It is no accident that Wittgenstein wrote sympathetically about Kierkegaard. Having said that he "can readily think what Heidegger means by Being and Dread," and how tempting it is to suppose that one can express our astonishment that anything exists, as had both Heidegger and Leibniz, in the form of a question, he writes, "Everything which we feel like saying [here] can a priori, only be nonsense. Nevertheless, we do run up against the limits of language. This "running-up against" Kierkegaard also recognized and even designated in a quite similar way (as running up against Paradox). This running-up against the limits of language is *Ethics*."[4] Now, we might suppose that we could continue to speak here, because it would be what Ramsey ironically called "important nonsense."[5] But Wittgenstein insists that "it is truly important that one put an end to all the idle talk about Ethics," which suggests that many a philosopher should stop talking. And then he goes on, "Yet the tendency represented by the running-up against *points to something.*" and quotes St. Augustine's advice: "Talk some nonsense, it makes no difference."[6] Where does this leave us?

There is a soft sense of a language-game which marks the local legitimation appropriately bestowed on any linguistic practice tied to some stable social practice, a legitimation that acknowledges that from regular patterns of linguistic behavior norms are born. But Wittgenstein never quite lost the logical or grammatical concerns that were more conspicuous in his early writing, and which surface here in the form of his reference to "the limits of language." If "the limits of my language are the limits of my world,"[7] if "God does not reveal himself in the world" (6.432), then it sounds as if Wittgenstein has a version of Kant's insight—that our impulse to apply reason (language) beyond the bounds of possible experience (the world) is hard to curb and doomed to fail. But Wittgenstein does seem to be willing to make remarks of another grammatical order. Consider some of the following claims:

1. "The meaning [Sinn] of life, i.e., the meaning of the world, we can call God."[8]
2. ". . . we are at any rate in a certain sense dependent, and that on which we depend we can call God. God in this sense would be simply Fate, or, what comes to the same thing, the world independent of our will."[9]
3. "God does not reveal himself in the world."[10]
4. "The feeling of the world as a bounded whole is the mystical."[11]

In the first two cases, it is notable that Wittgenstein does not simply identify or define God by some other form of words. Instead he says, ". . . we can call God," ". . . we are at any rate in a certain sense dependent," "what comes to the same thing," and finally speaks of "the feeling of the world" (my emphasis each time). In each case he signals a decision to accept or acknowledge a certain equivalence, a certain translatability. The final example—"the feeling of . . . as . . ."—is an extraordinary fusion of the cognitive and the affective, in which there is an uncanny echo of Heidegger, for whom it was not through epistemology, not through some constructive act of synthesis, that we could ever get a sense of the world "as a whole," but through mood. Heidegger wrote, "Mood has always already disclosed being-in-the-world as a whole and first makes possible directing oneself towards something," and ". . . the world already disclosed lets inner-worldly things be encountered."[12] Heidegger is articulating as a requirement what Wittgenstein acknowledges phenomenologically—that from our position "within" the world, it takes a rather special shift of perspective to come to grasp the world as such. That shift is brought about by mood (Heidegger) or feeling (Wittgenstein).

While Heidegger does not here speak of God, he and Wittgenstein are clearly on the same wavelength. Why does Wittgenstein move from "the meaning of life" to "the meaning of the world" in the first remark? He is assimilating the question we normally ask to one in which the structure of relation to the world becomes explicit. God appears not in the world, but in or as a way of thinking (or feeling) about the world. We may think of this as a topological remark, or a grammatical one. As a topological remark, we would have to accept that it would be possible to take up some sort of distance from

"the world-as-a-whole," that one could define another sort of space in which
to locate it. As a grammatical remark we would have to allow that the difference between "in" and "about" is such as to allow the appearance of a different order of being.[13] What Wittgenstein (and we) are clearly wrestling with
is the order of grounding here. Might naming (God) or spacing ("aboutness")
or different orders of being simply be ways of folding back into the world (and
into ordinary language) the consequences of moves that would otherwise lead
us to silence? If so, the justification would, perhaps, be that without this folding back, we would not have the means of differentiating different respects or
dimensions "beyond" the world. For that a back projection is necessary. But
equally, we might come to wonder whether there are not different modes of
being within the world in the first place, of which thinking about it would be
but one. Given such reflections, it suggests that the fate of "God" will depend
on the way we construct our topology of the world and what we come to
believe it makes sense to say in or about it. And it is clear that some of what
is in play derives immediately from what are almost logical properties of the
terrain. For example, the world itself is not obviously "in" the world. If we can
only talk about what is in the world, it would seem that the very expression,
"in the world" needed to formulate this claim is both intelligible and unin-
telligible. What this suggests is the more radical thesis that insofar as we can
raise any of these kinds of questions, *we* cannot merely be *in* the world,
whether as facts or as things. It would not then be impossible for the "transcendence" of God to be our way of recognizing the transcendence implicit
in our ability to talk *about* the world. Such a formula would continue a tradition of inscribing "God" in a complex structure of our self-self and self-world
relationality, which would do justice to the important things we know to be
the case—that God is *not* a thing, not "part" of the world—while respecting
Ockham's proscription on multiplying entities unnecessarily.

Before returning to pursue this thought further in Kierkegaard, let us just
mull over Wittgenstein's remark about dependence, another attempt at
thinking God without God, as one might say. First, we note that Wittgenstein again finds a way of understanding God in terms of our relation to the
"world"—as a modulation of our relation of "dependence." This sense of
"dependence" derives from the discovery that the world is not simply a reflection of my will. Things happen that I never willed. My very existence is not,
at least initially, a matter of my will. Somehow, the will provides us with a
route to the unification of the "world" at the very point that its independence
of my will comes into focus. Wittgenstein seems to offer "fate" as an inter-
mediary sense of this unity, from which an identification with God then
arises. Wittgenstein's successive references to our being "in a certain sense"
dependent, to God being "in this sense . . . simply," and "what comes to the
same thing" both record and perhaps mask the process of synthetic unification and substitution by which we can give to the word *God* both a logic and

a kind of phenomenological grounding. Wittgenstein seems to be saying: To the extent that we can conceptualize the world as coherently exceeding my will, we have found a way of understanding how the word God can be intelligibly deployed. This does not, of course, guarantee that all the additional things we might want to say about God would be intelligible or justified. Indeed, the exposure, if that is what it is, of such an origin, might lead one to a theological minimalism. It is interesting to note that the same combination of a phenomenological and what I will call a "structural" sense can be found in Wittgenstein's reference to the experience of "absolute safety," which crystallizes both a separation between myself and the world, and a second order attunement of the two. "Absolute safety" is dependence plus faith (or trust). The word *absolute* alludes both to the scope of the experience (nothing can harm me) and also the power and quality of the experience—that through it we may come to understand how it might make sense to use terms such as "God." The sense of absolute safety is not a proof of God's existence. We might be tempted to say, then, that it rather "opens a world" (to use a Heideggerean expression) in which talking about "God" would make sense. But given that Wittgenstein wants to place God, and the mystical, in the "space" of our discourse "about" "the world," it might be better to say that it opens up "a new way of being *in* the world," that is, one in which "being in" could include rather than on principle exclude "reflecting on," "marveling at," etc. What this suggests is that God-talk is an acknowledgment and witness of the grammatical complexity of being-in-a-world, even if the form of that recognition *may* be systematically misleading.

II

Kierkegaard . . . is my adventure
—Sartre

I want now to work back to see whether these suggestions illuminate not just Sartre's treatment of Kierkegaard, but Derrida's treatment too, and indeed Kierkegaard's treatment of himself. I will try first to show that what I have called Sartre's genius here is to have taken us a number of steps closer to realizing the connection between Kierkegaard's religious discourse and the paradox focused in Sartre's title: "The Singular Universal." I will argue that Christianity supplies Kierkegaard with a way of giving coherence to crucial aspects of our being in the world for which he possessed no more satisfactory form of acknowledgment or unification. It may seem outrageous to broach the matter so directly, but Christ himself supplies Kierkegaard with an important source of distance from what he construed as philosophical detachment (in Hegel, for example). To be a sacrifice is to transform one's individual life into something whose significance transcends that empirical individuality. That is already implicit in Hegel's characterization of the life and death struggle (for recognition). In being willing to risk death, each party demonstrates to the other their status as more than a living being, but as a being *with a relation* to life (and death). It is imperative for Hegel's story that the protagonists do not actually kill each other but rather live to embody a transformed relation to themselves—that they are self-conscious beings. In Christ's case, we may say that this living on is achieved by the public nature of his crucifixion, so that meaning is produced "for us," a "performance" in the technical sense. (Christ died to save our souls.) Death, for a living being, is an absolute. It is not just an event in the world but the limit of the possibility of certain kinds of events (such as *my* experiences). To talk about a limit is to talk about the very sort of thing that constitutes a world. That limits appear *in* the world is how there can be absolutes within the world. To give up one's life for . . . is to take up a relation to "the absolute." To take up a relation to the absolute here, to appropriate one's finitude, is to transform oneself; it is to bring transcendence into being. And so we can see how dialectical thought allows us to develop forms of transcendence within immanence, life folded back upon itself.

Sartre shows exactly how Kierkegaard does this, and the success with which he accounts for Kierkegaard's stance in existential but nonreligious terms forcibly raises the question of whether religious discourse is any more than a way of temporarily coding certain insights that might be better understood in a different way. Wittgenstein says that God does not appear *in* the world. I have responded by suggesting in effect that the very idea of God (here) rests on a narrow sense of what appearing *in* the world might consist in. If we acknowledge ways of being-in-the-world in which the transcendent is folded back into the immanent, the infinite played out in the finite, the absolute found in the contingent, then we may not merely exhaust the impulse for a further religious discourse, but enrich the ways in which we think about *this* world. The general form of Sartre's discovery of the key to Kierkegaard's thought could be put in a number of ways: appropriation, "living as," repetition, bearing witness. Each of these concepts names a way of converting the straw of contingency into absolute gold. The general idea is not difficult. If I "begin" thinking of my existence as contingent (accidental, without ultimate purpose), I may oppose this to the necessity of some postulated absolute being. And yet the discovery of my contingency, and indeed, the contingency of all beings like me, is the discovery of an essential condition, one that *bearing witness to* allows me to rise above. How does this happen? There seem to be four different thoughts interwoven here: First, that being aware of a truth about myself changes the character of that truth. To be beautiful and not to know it is very different from a knowing exhibition of one's beauty. The one can be deeply attractive, the other distasteful. Second, something that is a limitation if one is not aware of it can take on a kind of necessity and distinctiveness, if one is aware of it. It is not difficult to suppose that the fact that humans are not omniscient is some sort of deficiency, until we realize how much of what is good about being human rests on our not knowing everything. If we knew everything life would be totally uninteresting—there would be no surprises, no news, no conversations, no tomorrow in any informational sense. Indeed, it is not impossible that the very idea of omniscience implodes when we think it through. Third, acting on, embodying in one's life, the distinctive and defining nature of one's limitations is a way of transforming *awareness* into a creative and transformative process. Lastly, by publicly demonstrating to others, by bearing witness to such a feature or condition, something new occurs. The acknowledged willingness to sacrifice one's life (or one's son's life) creates a value that had not been there before. Life is no longer just life, but. . . . And here a word such as "spirit" commonly puts in an appearance!

In what sense does something new occur? or a value get *created?* Is this not all a kind of idealism? The fact is that reflection, "repetition" (or appropriation), embodiment, "living as," witnessing are all ways of transforming the economy of significance within which our actions can have meaning when the *considerations brought to bear* on action have to do with our self-understanding, our finitude, mortality, and limits.[14]

Let us now be more specific about Sartre's account of how Kierkegaard effects the moves I have outlined. The first general economy or logic he deploys is that of "Loser Wins." His argument[15] is that Kierkegaard's defeat by history (we can place him within Hegel's system, we can "understand" him to have been psychosexually "troubled," we can teach him in Existentialism classes) is dialectically temporary. For the being that was "defeated" (absorbed, forgotten, objectified, misunderstood, etc.) both anticipated and lived that defeat subjectively, as *despair,* and as such he escapes history.

> [N]o knowledge could express directly, . . . no historical development could salvage it: the failure lived in despair. Those who died of dread, of hunger, of exhaustion, those conquered and executed are wounds of knowledge insofar as they have existed. Subjectivity is *nothing* for objective knowledge since it is non-knowledge, and yet the failure shows that subjectivity exists absolutely. Thus Søren Kierkegaard, conquered by death and taken up again by historical knowledge, triumphs at the very moment he fails, by showing that history cannot take him up again. Dead, he remains the unsurpassable scandal of subjectivity; known to his bones, he escapes history by the very fact that it constitutes his defeat and that he lived the latter by anticipation. In short, he escapes history because he is historical.[16]

Underlying Sartre's argument is the idea that the negative, nonbeing, is not ultimately susceptible to calculation, to identifying history with positivity, with outcomes, with objectification. The negative *can* be merely formal (the antelope *not* on the sofa, the Pope *not* in my seminar) but in the concrete cases that interest us, the negative functions as an economy of resistance that preserves significance against positivity. Sartre contrasts any knowledge we might have *of* Kierkegaard with the singular existence of which we suppose we might have knowledge. If we ask whether Kierkegaard's thinking is not subordinated to the objectification wrought by Christian dogma, Sartre's response is, fundamentally, that there can be no question of proof of the grounds of existential self-determination, that it is in Kierkegaard's way of appropriating Christianity that he transcends historical determination. Should we try to prove the immortality of the soul? This is a misunderstanding. "[I]mmortality, even proven, cannot be an object of knowledge, but . . . is a certain absolute relation of immanence to transcendence that cannot be established except in and through lived experience."[17] In various ways, Sartre argues that for Kierkegaard "the opposition of non-knowledge and knowledge is that of two ontological structures," two "orders of discourse," we might say, or two "language-games." Kierkegaard's linking of truth and subjectivity marks not just the locus of truth, but a certain status for subjectivity. Sartre shows how subjectivity is not just a special place but the very kind of achievement that we have called a folding back, or that Kierkegaard himself calls repetition. The way this achievement gets described makes it clear how it moves away from knowledge that a subject might possess toward a transformative achievement *of* a subject. There is a kind of inherent *difficulty* in the language Sartre uses here.

Let me give some more examples: This non-knowledge, he says, is "a decision of authenticity; it is the refusal of flight and the will to return to oneself" (236); "*knowledge* cannot take into account this obscure and inflexible *movement* by which scattered determinations are elevated to Being and reunited in a tension that confers on them . . . a synthetic meaning"; "subjectivity is temporalisation itself; it is *what happens to me*, that which cannot be except in happening. It is myself to the degree that I can be born only to adventure. . . ." The difficulty is that of trying to determine the radically new significance—what Sartre thinks in terms of "ontological structure"—brought about in and through what could be called a *transformative reflexive becoming*. The difficulty is not semantic so much as one of recognizing the existential/ontological/categorial significance of distinctions that can only be understood modally, not substantively.[18] Imagine trying to explain the significance of verbs in a language in which there were none, especially if you thought that our grasp of a whole manner of being hung on the outcome. Sartre shows that Kierkegaard's thinking is a struggle for recognition of what is structurally and existentially recessive, for a folding back through which the absolute, the transcendent appears within history, within time, within contingency. Sartre says this explicitly in different places:

Living, Kierkegaard lives the paradox in passion: he wants passionately to designate himself a transhistorical *absolute*; by humor and by irony he shows himself and hides at the same time. (239)

[T]he moment of subjective truth is a temporalised but transhistorical *absolute*. (237)

Subjectivity is *nothing* for objective knowledge . . . and yet the failure shows that subjectivity exists *absolutely*. (243)

In each case, the italicizing of "absolute" is mine. The word designates a freedom from the economy of objectifying, historicizing subordination, even if such freedom is won *through* this subordination. In fact it would not be inappropriate to compare here the dialectical logic by which the slave ultimately gets the better deal from the life and death struggle.[19] This "freedom" is not so much a "fact" in the world as a claim about the autonomy of a certain space of consideration and achievement. But this autonomy deserves comment. It is not that the subject is autonomous in the sense of being a substance that needs nothing else to be itself. Rather, even if we were to designate subjecthood an "openness to the other," and hence compromise its autonomy in advance, such an openness would be both this openness rather than that (and, as Heidegger would say, in each case "mine") and as an openness, it would not itself be determinate, but rather an openness to (ongoing, revisable) determination. To talk of an absolute here is to mark a logical/ontological distinction. If Sartre is right, we not only need to mark and remark the presence of the absolute in history, but we can do so in a way that does not compromise our status as historical beings (i.e., as formed by, and as deriving our identity through our involvement in history). Such an absolute can *only* be realized *through such an involvement*. Again, the absolute as Sartre unrolls it is modal, adverbial, found in a way of Being, and whatever advantages any more representational version might have, it runs the risk of being terribly misunderstood.[20] Sartre's essay "The Singular Universal" is a contribution to a conference entitled *The Living Kierkegaard*, and part of what is brilliant about his treatment is his exploitation of the way that through sacrifice (the Crucifixion would be an exemplary case) the dead can live on, and perhaps in this repetition "live" as they had never lived before. Of course, at the same time, they may be as dead as they always were when they were alive, but being objectifyingly misunderstood. What Sartre shows is that the mundane distinction between life and death needs to be replayed, redeployed within what we call life, and within what we call death. For the living can be dead, and the dead can live as never before. These reflections give a new twist to Plato's understanding of philosophy as a preparation for death, a twist presaged by Sartre's gloss (see above) on Kierkegaard's understanding of immortality in terms of inwardness. To understand what Kierkegaard was up to is not merely to do justice to Kierkegaard. It is to do justice to what Kierkegaard tried to do justice to—the way in which "the universal enters into history as the singular, to the extent that the singular installs itself there as universal." The individual can take up a relation to himself through which he maximizes the significance (universality) of his historical particularity.

Sartre is perhaps a predictable ally in the project of providing a dialectical reconstruction of Kierkegaard's Christian commitments. Unlike Kierkegaard and Heidegger (and even Hegel), Sartre does not find in Being-toward-death a source of transcendence.[21] Rather, it is the broader category of negation and non-Being that do the work for him. And if Sartre's positions (either in *Being and Nothingness* or in the *Critique of Dialectical Reason*) might be thought of as making an advance on Kierkegaard it must be in the way Sartre manages to maintain a logic of transcendence (via negation) while giving a powerful articulation to our contingent historical situatedness, showing in both his existentialist and "Marxist" phase that transcendence is not only compatible with situatedness but actually requires it, like swimming and water, even if the swimmer may experience the water as resistance. The situatedness of freedom is a condition of real freedom, not a limitation. But the implication of Sartre's analysis is that Kierkegaard's own response to Christianity *bears witness* to this connection, even if Kierkegaard's grasp of this dialectic is more formal than substantial.[22]

We know that Kierkegaard emphasized the importance of indirect communication[23] and carefully distinguished objective and subjective thinking. Sartre generalizes and radicalizes the implication of this when he says, "[T]he *theoretical* aspect of Kierkegaard's work is pure illusion." He continues:

> When we *encounter* his words, they suddenly invite another use of language, that is, of our own words. . . . They refer in his writings to what is named, or, according to his own declarations, to the "categories" of existence. But these categories are neither principles not concepts, nor the makings of concepts. They appear as lived relations to the totality, which one can reach by following the word along a regressive aim which leads back from the speech to the speaker. That means that not one of these combinations of words is *intelligible*, but that they constitute, by the very negation of every effort to know them, a reference to what grounds the effort.[24]

Sartre seems here to echo Wittgenstein's remark that our desire to speak when we can only speak nonsense nonetheless "points to something," and his talk of God as the "meaning of life, i.e., the meaning of the world," and of "the feeling of the world as a bounded whole [as] the mystical." This all suggests not strictly a negative theology, but rather a translating displacement of any objectifying discourse—religious or otherwise—into "lived relations to the totality," which sounds remarkably close to what I previously called, after Heidegger, ways of being-in-the-world. Sartre ends his essay with understandable reservations about Kierkegaard's relation to history (not unlike those we have already canvassed). But how are we to read the lessons he takes from Kierkegaard's Christianity? Sartre writes:

> In each of us he gives and refuses himself, as he did during his life. He is my adventure and remains, for the others, Kierkegaard, the Other, at the horizon—a witness for that Christian that faith is an ever-periled becoming, a witness for me that *becoming-an-atheist* is a long and difficult undertaking. . . .[25]

We might read this as drawing an analogy between becoming a Christian and becoming an atheist, but the stronger claim would be that because the only difference between them is at the "objective" level, they are *existentially equivalent*. Is this a Sartrean distortion of Kierkegaard's thinking, or faithful to its deepest impulses?

III

God as *wholly other*
—Derrida

I want to turn shortly to considering a number of ways in which we can read Kierkegaard as endorsing the various radical theses I have been drawing out. But before that, I would like to bring Derrida into this conversation. I have made a claim for existential equivalence between Kierkegaard's Christianity and Sartre's atheism. The parallel claim by Derrida would assert something like an *economic* equivalence. I would like to explore this alternative approach, and indeed explore the possibility of understanding existential and economic equivalence as themselves convergent claims.

The issue that we are concerning ourselves with in Kierkegaard—the status of religious language in his philosophical discourse—is tied up with various of Derrida's writings—on economy, on negative theology, on Heidegger and theology, on the gift, on death, and on Kierkegaard himself.[26] For convenience, I will concentrate on Derrida's *The Gift of Death*, in which most of these issues come to a head. The early Derrida was close to Nietzsche in thinking of God symptomatically as reflecting a desire for a fixed stabilizing point outside language—what Derrida dubbed a "transcendental signified." And Kierkegaard's appeal to interiority and subjectivity would surely fall to the same kind of critical pressure as did Husserl's appeal to a "sphere of ownness," to "solitary mental life," to "the absolute silence of self-relationship."[27] These surely would be clear-cut cases of the appeal to self-presence that Derrida had early diagnosed as the primary symptom of metaphysics. But things never were quite that simple. Derrida's treatment of Husserl could variously be seen as a deconstruction of phenomenology, or as a transformative renewal of phenomenology by a demonstration of the movement of difference that still haunts presence. And if one looks at the panoply of Kierkegaard's discursive displacements—indirect communication, use of pseudonyms, attempts to move away from "objective thinking," his embracing of paradox, etc.—it is not difficult to conclude that Kierkegaard, far from being a suitable case for deconstructive treatment, might himself be engaged in a parallel enterprise.[28]

The Gift of Death is divided into four parts. In the first two, Derrida discusses one of Jan Patočka's *Heretical Essays on the Philosophy of History:* "Is technological civilization a civilization in decline, and if so why?," in which Patočka plots the connection between religion and responsibility in terms of the appearance of a subject freed from the essential secrecy and the demonic of ancient orgiastic cults, and capable of freely relating to itself by relating to an infinite other. Here another kind of secrecy arises,

> or more precisely a mystery, the *mysterium tremendum:* the terrifying mystery, the dread, fear and trembling of the Christian in the experience of the sacrificial gift. This trembling seizes one at the moment of becoming a person, and the person can become what it is only in being paralyzed, in its very singularity by the gaze of God. Then it sees itself seen by the gaze of another, "a supreme, absolute and inaccessible being who holds us in his hand not by exterior but by interior force."[29]

Derrida draws out of Patočka the possibility (indeed necessity) of a history of secrecy, of a series of repressions of one secrecy by another, from Plato through Christianity, for which we need to develop a complex sense of economy and topology. Because what is repressed is also retained,

> [T]he logic of this conservative rupture resembles the *economy of a sacrifice* that keeps what it gives up. Sometimes it reminds one of the economy of sublation (*relève*) or *Aufhebung,* and at other times, less contradictory than it seems, of a logic of repression that still retains what is denied, surpassed, buried. Repression doesn't destroy, it displaces something from one place to another within the system. It is also a topological operation.[30]

This history of secrecy is also a history of responsibility, a genealogy of a subject and of a relation to an Other, a genealogy of what Kierkegaard will call subjectivity.[31] And the reference to the *mysterium tremendum* allows Derrida to set the stage for discussing the *trembling*[32] in Kierkegaard's *Fear and Trembling* as a reflection of a structure of exposure to the gaze of an Other whom one cannot see.[33] But first he inscribes trembling in a history of trauma and repetition that silently reminds us of Kierkegaard's all-too-human biography. Why trauma? Because there too we find the structure of a radical secrecy, in which the secret is hidden even from the subject to whom it "belongs." Derrida grasps that what makes us tremble is what "exceeds my seeing and knowing" and "concerns the innermost parts of me." And yet it is something we recognize, "a strange repetition that ties an irrefutable past (a shock that

has been felt . . .) to a future that cannot be anticipated." And the implication is that what is at stake is the vulnerability of my identity, my very being.
We may imagine that our very sense of ourselves as unified complete subjects
has been achieved in the face of clear evidence to the contrary—perhaps
what Wittgenstein called our "dependency." Derrida could surely not have
used the expression *tremblement de terre*—earthquake—as an example of a
trembling without recalling, and seeking to recall for us, Kierkegaard's own
description of his most traumatic personal event. As a young man, his father,
a severe and religious man, had confided in him that he had done something
shameful, and Kierkegaard had described the impact of this revelation as an
"earthquake," after which nothing would ever be the same. We know (it is
usually taken to be a separate event) that his father had cursed God as a
young shepherd boy on the Jutland heath, and came to see the many deaths
in his family as a sign that he had been cursed, and that Kierkegaard lived in
expectation of an even earlier death than actually befell him. We know, too,
that Kierkegaard described his own life as a "sacrifice"—a remark Derrida
strangely fails to mention—perhaps implying that he was having to pay for
the sins of his father. All of which suggests that our thinking of the connection between the self's relation to the Other, and the significance of God
may not be totally separate from the role of the father in constructing an
ideal of the self.

The word *earthquake* makes our assured distinction between the psychological and the religious *tremble*.[34] Although this is not a line that Derrida pursues, he does from the outset approach the question of God in Kierkegaard's
philosophical writings in terms of the structures and economies of thought in
which "he" is inscribed. If we have glossed trembling as a sign of ontological
vulnerability, there are more direct and immediate ways of noting its impact.
We may suppose that much of what makes us the kind of individuals we are
can be found in the sorts of reasons we give for the things we do, and our participation in a community of reason-giving. Derrida seems to be reporting
factually on God when he writes:

> God doesn't give his reasons, he acts as he intends, he doesn't have to give
> his reasons or share anything with us: neither his motivations, if he has any,
> nor his deliberations, nor his decisions.[35]

But he goes on:

> Otherwise he wouldn't be God, we wouldn't be dealing with the Other as
> God, or with God as *wholly other*. If the other were to share his reasons with
> us by explaining them to us, if he were to speak to us all the time, without
> any secrets, he wouldn't be the other.[36]

And this suggests the beginnings of a functional (or structural) understanding of the expression *God*, which intensifies throughout this volume,

even as, at times, it is explicitly problematized. And Derrida draws our attention to the parallel difficulties with straightforward reference embodied in Kierkegaard's repeated use of pseudonyms—here Johannes de Silentio. He comments:

> This pseudonym keeps silent, it expresses the silence that is kept. Like all pseudonyms, it seems destined to keep secret the real name as patronym, that is, the name of the father of the work, in fact the name of the father of the father of the work.[37] This pseudonym . . . reminds us that a meditation linking the question of secrecy to that of responsibility immediately raises the question of the name and of the signature.[38]

Derrida's point is to link the question of responsibility with that of the subject, and to suggest that revisions in our sense of the significance and scope of responsibility will be played out at the level of the subject's inscription in language—in the *name*, as well as in the modulation of his capacity to reveal himself in ordinary language.[39] In other words, Kierkegaard understands Abraham's "silence" (including his elliptical utterances) as marking a displacement of the framework of intelligibility and justification away from a public, universal standard toward a standard drawn from his relation to God, to the wholly other. But one of the more radical implications of Kierkegaard's problematizing of his own name, his own authorship, is that "God" too might come to be seen as a (public) name, that we might come to see that what is at stake in all this indirectness and secrecy is precisely not the discovery or affirmation of some new substantive truth, not a matter of fact, but something *essential* about the economy of responsibility.

What is the meaning of the *experience* of sacrifice? If Derrida is right, the significance of sacrifice, and of Abraham's preparedness to sacrifice Isaac, is that it marks an absolute limit to the ethics and the logic of calculation, in which obligations can be weighed and balanced against one another, in which my obligations can be limited and determined, etc. Sacrifice is an intrusion, an interruption of public intelligibility and acceptability, a repudiation of the ethical as the court of last appeal. As Derrida presents matters, what sacrifice teaches us is not itself the last word, but a vital component in "the aporia of responsibility," of any sense of responsibility that would acknowledge the irresponsibility involved in any determinable restriction of my responsibility.

> For responsibility . . . demands on the one hand an accounting, a general answering-for-oneself with respect to the general and before the generality, hence the idea of substitution, and on the other hand, uniqueness, absolute singularity, hence non-substitution, nonrepetition, silence and secrecy.[40]

The suggestion is that responsibility has a recursive power that breaks through any calculated settlement of my responsibilities. This is not an ethical claim, but a claim about the ethical. Silence then would be a mark of the incommensurability of this recursive responsibility with any specific conceptualization, or finite economizing of its content. And Derrida concludes that this *absolute* responsibility, as we might call it, "puts us in relation . . . with the absolute other, with the absolute singularity of the other, whose name here is God."[41]

> The other as absolute other, namely, God, must remain transcendent, hidden, secret, jealous of the love, requests, and commands that he gives and that he asks to be kept secret, Secrecy is essential to the exercise of this absolute responsibility as sacrificial responsibility.[42]

In each of these two formulations, Derrida invokes God in the shape of a *name*: "whose name here is God," "namely, God." Shortly afterward, he writes, "the absolute other: God, if you wish." Such a form of reference does not imply that "God" is *only* a name. We would have to be a lot clearer (or unclearer) about naming to be able to say that. But it puts us on notice to think that we may learn more about "God" (and names) if we approach the matter indirectly.[43] And Derrida is preparing the way for an interpretation of "God" as the marker of another ethical economy. Derrida's divergence from his earlier understanding of "God" as a transcendental signified, a projected (fictional?) external point of stabilization for language, not subject to the play of difference, etc., a Nietzschean demythologizing which would think of "God" as a metaphysical spare wheel, obfuscating at best, now becomes clear. For as he starts to cash out the broader significance of Kierkegaard's account of Abraham and Isaac in *Fear and Trembling*, it becomes clear that religious concepts can be seen as preserving us—we have yet to determine at what cost[44]—against an inane reductionism, in which our normal conceptualizable obligations have the last word. It is Derrida's claim that the horrific extreme of the Abraham story actually displays the structure of the most *everyday phenomena*: "Isn't this the most common thing?"

> As soon as I enter into a relation with the other, with the gaze, look, request, command or call of the other, I know that I can respond only by sacrificing ethics, that is, whatever requires me also to respond, in the same way, in the same instant, to all the others.[45]

Derrida's argument is that if every other is wholly other, an absolute other, then there is nothing that allows me to respond in this way selectively.

> I cannot respond to the call, the request, the obligation, or even the love of the other without sacrificing the other other, the other others, *Every other (one) is every (bit) other [tout autre est tout autre]*, everyone else is completely or wholly other.[46]

This teaches us something vital but disturbing:

> The simple concepts of alterity and of singularity constitute the concept of
> duty as much as that of responsibility. As a result, the concepts of respon-
> sibility, of decision, or of duty, are condemned a priori to paradox, scandal
> and aporia.[47]

Finally, in what amounts to a confessional mode, Derrida gives voice to
what amounts to the *experience* from which what he has been asserting seems
to flow:

> By preferring my work, simply by giving it my time and attention, by pre-
> ferring my activity as a citizen or as a professorial and professional philoso-
> pher, writing and speaking here in a public language, French in my case, I
> am perhaps fulfilling my duty. But I am sacrificing and betraying at every
> moment all my other obligations: my obligations to the other others whom
> I know or don't know, the billions of my fellows (without mentioning the
> animals that are even more other others than my fellows), my fellows who
> are dying of starvation or sickness . . . every one being sacrificed to every one
> in this land of Moriah that is our habitat every second or every day.[48]

Abraham's sacrifice of Isaac is, in other words, our everyday experience
writ large. But this reading is surely too hasty. The central move seems to be
to the generalization of my responsibility to the singular other, the other as
absolute other ("namely God") to every other. The argument must be that
the only significant criterion for inclusion is the otherness of the other, and
if anything that *increases* as knowledge, involvement, and acquaintance
recede. Charity may begin at home, but justice, duty, and obligation begin as
I close the gate behind me on the way out. The plausibility of this argument
rests on the appeal of its conclusion—which opens our eyes to many of the
invisible social and political horrors that surround us—and on the force of
the categorial distinctions (singular versus general, absolute versus negotiable) on which it rests. But the way in which these distinctions are deployed
bears closer scrutiny.

Derrida claims that I can only respond to the call of the other by "sacrificing" the generalizability of that response to all others, the ethical. I can see
three distinct ways of objecting to this claim.

1. If I am walking down the street and interrupt my daily round to go to
   help a man bleeding in a ditch I am not "sacrificing" all the others down
   other streets around the world. It may in some sense be a contingent fact
   that I am walking down *this* street, but such contingency is an essential
   condition of any life. Generalizability here does not add an impossible
   mountain of other analogous obligations, but that this is the way I (and
   indeed others) should always act. The good Samaritan was a man with

his own life *who went out of his way to help* someone he did not know and had never met, who was not part of his community, and from whom he might well expect no thanks.

2. The imperative here is to allow the interruption of one's determinate ethical space. It is not to acquire a new infinitely expanded ethical space. When we say things such as, "God is the name of the absolute other *as other*"[49] (my emphasis) the "*as* other" here does not mean "treated as belonging to some other category, that of the other," but rather, "as interrupting any positive ethical space one might set up." But as soon as Derrida talks about "my obligations to the other others whom I know or don't know, the billions of my fellows," he is starting to calculate excess, to add the others together. To say that God is the absolute other is to designate God as the iterable event of interruption. Overriding functions cannot be accumulated, and cannot be used to compound an indebtedness.

3. A shorter and tidier way of making a similar point would be to say that we are being asked to swallow a move from any to all, illustrated by the familiar but important objections to Descartes' method of doubt, which moves from the suggestion (true) that we might doubt any belief to the conclusion (false) that we could doubt every belief. If the grounds for doubt always include some beliefs not doubted, then we could doubt anything but not everything. Similarly, if any determination of our duties can be breached by an appeal we had not anticipated, this does not argue for an infinite expansion of our duties, but rather a permanent vigilance in avoiding complacency. Absolute openness is not just a scandal, paradox, etc. but a nonsense. The application of "absolute" to openness is dispositional; it takes the form of a readiness, a capacity, not a total inclusion.

There is yet another aspect to Derrida's argument which, in my view, requires the same sort of response. He writes:

> How would you ever justify the fact that you sacrifice all the cats in the world to the cat that you feed at home every morning for years . . . ?[50]

Derrida's point, here and elsewhere, is that singularities are not susceptible to ethical calculation, which requires the possibility of substitution. And if we tie justification to calculation, then we cannot justify our singular attachments. But we can explain how we come to have singular attachments—not least through chance, situation, etc.—in ways that, without calculation, distinguish my obligation to my cat from any relation I might have to unknown moggies in Madras. Implicit in this remark about cats and sacrifice is that there is no ethical difference between acts of commission and acts of omission. But this must be false. I fail in some sense to do vast numbers of things without even noticing (and to the extent that Derrida includes my obligations to unknown beings, I take it this category of omission gets included). It would make no sense simply to compare these omissions either with acts of willful neglect, or my carefully balanced decisions. What *is* true is that there are no a priori grounds for refusing to consider the ethical significance of an omission or a failure to act. The fact that such a refusal is always possible is an important part of our ethical life and discourse. Again, what would be an error as a positive claim hides a dispositional truth. And all the discussion of silence, the need for indirectness, the secret, etc., can, I believe, find its place here.

We have seen that Derrida from the first encourages us to think of God as a name, or as bound up with naming. But what has happened to "God" in the generalization we have just criticized? The justification for Derrida's generalizing reading of Kierkegaard's Abraham story is contained in this sentence: "If God is completely other, the figure or name of the wholly other, then every other (one) is every (bit) other. *Tout autre est tout autre*."[51] As Derrida acknowledges, "this formula disturbs Kierkegaard's discourse on one level while at the same time reinforcing its most extreme ramifications."[52] More explicitly,

> It implies that God, as the wholly other, is to be found everywhere there is something of the wholly other.[53]

It is hard to imagine that this is meant as anything other than a *translation*, a recommendation about how to read (and think). We might imagine it put: "Don't ask for God, ask for the wholly other."[54] Derrida recognizes the distinction between preserving a special reference (e.g., God) for "the infinite other," and allowing it to be distributed over "each man and woman." And he shows that while both Levinas and Kierkegaard seek to preserve this distinction, neither is able "to determine the limit between these two orders." Levinas would like there to be an analogy between the face of God and the face of the other, but analogy both distinguishes and elides, and we are left without a decision.

The issue of the status of God gets raised again, finally, in the course of Derrida's discussion of the secret. Abraham keeps silent, keeps his plans secret, from Isaac. He communes with God, but can tell no one else what he is doing, or why. And Derrida shows silence at work in that logic of the gift— turning the other cheek—repaying unkindness with love, that is the Christian message. There must be a secret: " and thy Father which seeth in secret . . . shall reward thee." And yet the left hand must not know what the right hand is doing, or else such a gift will become a strategy for achieving higher goals, such as salvation. And at the same time, Derrida is trying to get a handle on what Kierkegaard calls subjectivity, and its need for secrecy and indirect communication. What he proposes, and the exploitation of the complex structure of a gaze suggests a secret filiation with Sartre, is a dramatic translation of the language of God into that of a certain structure of secrecy.

We should stop thinking about God as someone, over there, way up there, transcendent . . . capable, more than any satellite orbiting in space, of seeing into the most secret of the most interior places. It is perhaps necessary, if we are to follow the traditional Judeo-Christian-Islamic injunction, but also at the risk of turning it against that tradition, to think of God and of the name of God without such idolatrous stereotyping or representation.[55]

How, then, are we to think of God, if not in this way? Derrida suggests this:

Then we might say: God is the name of the possibility I have of keeping a secret that is visible from the interior but not from the exterior. Once such a structure of conscience exists, of Being-with-oneself, of speaking, that is, of producing invisible sense, once I have within me, *thanks to the invisible word as such*, a witness that others cannot see, and who is *at the same time other than me and more intimate with me than myself*, once I can have a secret relationship with myself and not tell everything, once there is secrecy and secret witnessing within me, then what I call God exists, (there is) what I call God in me, (it happens that) I call myself God—a phrase that is difficult to distinguish from "God calls me," for it is on that condition that I can call myself or that I am called in secret. God is in me, he is the absolute "me" or "self," he is that structure of invisible interiority that is called, in Kierkegaard's sense subjectivity.[56]

Derrida goes on to link the history of God with the history of secrecy, which he describes as an economy.

I take this account to be continuous with Nietzsche's account of the growth of interiority through Christian asceticism, which, he declared, made man for the first time "interesting."[57] Derrida is claiming that if we understand the appeal of (and to) God as an economy—of gift, of silence, of visibility—then we can locate that economy in the structure of interiority that characterizes the modern subject as Kierkegaard has described it. Kierkegaard's gift to us, his self-sacrifice, is to have delineated so much of what Derrida is describing, to have risked (spiritual) death in the process. But how are we to link these remarks about secrecy and invisibility with our earlier critical assessment of Derrida's account of our absolute responsibility, where I argued that this absolute responsibility, this *ir*responsibility (from the point of view of ethics) is not an extension of the status of singularity to every other, but rather a willingness to have one's ethical arrangements challenged, an openness to interruption? Derrida distinguished two kinds of invisibility—the weak invisibility of what *can* in fact or in principle be made visible (buried treasure) and the strong invisibility of that which is of a different order (such as sound). If absolute responsibility is, as I have suggested, a kind of openness, receptivity to interruption, a *disposition*, then it is precisely invisible in the strong sense. For it will never *appear* as another responsibility, or realm of responsibilities, but only as a *way* of dealing with the first order boundaries of responsibility that one has set up for oneself. Its invisibility is of the same order as that of what Heidegger calls the withdrawal of Being.

IV

God is that all things are possible . . .
—Kierkegaard

So far we have argued (along with Wittgenstein) that religious thought, at least in its bare outlines, is a way of giving voice to different possibilities of being-in-the-world, (with Sartre) that Kierkegaard's religiosity may well not merely be useful for but be existentially equivalent to an enlightened atheism, and (with Derrida) that what we call God may be inseparable either from an openness to the other or from the structure of subjectivity. But so far we have proceeded indirectly, looking at the way certain central figures have come to terms with Kierkegaard. What of Kierkegaard himself?

Of course, one of the ironies of this question is that the first thing we know about Kierkegaard is that his authorship is a sustained putting in question of just this "Kierkegaard himself." But the question also allows us to cut to the core of the question of the meaning of God for Kierkegaard. If we look, for example, at his account of the self at the beginning of *The Sickness Unto Death* we discover an argument to the effect that we need to suppose that the self is constituted in a relation to God in order to be able to account for the range of kinds of despair we are capable of feeling.

> If a human self had itself established itself, then there could be only one form [of despair]: not to will to be oneself, to will to do away with oneself, but there could not be the form: in despair to will to be oneself.[58]

So, the direct answer to what Kierkegaard "himself" thought, if we allowed ourselves to suppose for the moment that Anti-Climacus is speaking for Kierkegaard, is that it is precisely to the question of what it is to be oneself that God supplies an answer. Anti-Climacus says that man cannot be self-constituted or there would be no question of "in despair to will to be oneself"—only of willing to do away with oneself. Rather, we are selves precisely to the extent that we relate ourselves to "the Power that established us." And, yes, Kierkegaard does not here *say* God, but a "Power." This seems to acknowledge that the question of whether we should give the name God to such a power is a separate issue. And that is because the argument is formal—if valid, it establishes the necessity of a relation to something other than ourselves, in relation to which we truly become ourselves. But it would seem to be an open question whether such a function could be served by a different formulation of the Other—perhaps "other people," "that which I cannot comprehend," etc. Is the argument valid? It is a kind of transcendental argument, one that begins with the way things seem (that there are different forms of despair), that then proceeds to account for these different forms. Now, it could be argued that it is not valid, that the fact that I may despairingly carry on willing to be myself does not show that I am self-constituted, that I actually have a constitutive relation to another being, a Power, but that I *believe I have*, or perhaps better (because mere belief could itself so easily fall to despair), that the structure of my selfhood seems to reflect such a heteronomous relation (perhaps what Wittgenstein called *dependence*). If we thought that the argument was to prove my actual dependence on an actually distinct being, then it would seem there are at least missing premises.

But if it would be sufficient to demonstrate a certain dependent structure of subjectivity, then the argument would be valid. The principle of charity would suggest that this latter interpretation might be preferred, which would bring Kierkegaard's view on the status of God into line with that we have gleaned from Derrida.

The interpretation of responsibility—contra Derrida—as an openness to the transformation of the boundaries of one's assumed responsibilities, which, if connected to God, would make God a modal or dispositional property of the self, would seem to be well confirmed by Kierkegaard's formulation of the difference between objectivity and subjectivity. In his *Concluding Unscientific Postscript* he wrote famously:

> Objectively the emphasis is on *what* is said; subjectively the emphasis is on *how* it is said.[59]

And by "how it is said," he means not style, but

> the relation of the existing person, in his very existence, to what is said. . . . At its maximum, this "how" is the passion of the infinite . . . [which] is precisely subjectivity.[60]

And Kierkegaard explicitly draws the implication from these two remarks for our thinking about God. Conceived of as an objective question, the existence of God is a misunderstanding. Why?

> [S]ubjectively, [what is reflected on is] that the individual relates himself to a something *in such a way* that his relation is in truth a God-relation . . . the objective way . . . is not achieved in all eternity, because God is a subject, and hence only for subjectivity in inwardness.[61]

Here, Kierkegaard makes it clear first that God is a quality (a mode) of a relationship, and not a thing, and secondly, God is a subject, and not a thing. God existing as a subject is, again, glossed as a dimension of subjectivity.

This puts in perspective the nominalistic remarks he made in his *Philosophical Fragments*, where Kierkegaard, like Wittgenstein and Derrida, traces the emergence of the word *God*.

> But what is this unknown something with which the Reason collides when
> inspired by its paradoxical passion, with the result of unsettling even man's
> knowledge of himself? It is the Unknown. It is not a human being, in so far
> as we know what man is; nor is it any other known thing. So let us call this
> unknown something: God. It is nothing more than a name we assign to it.[62]

In the very Kantian language of Reason running up against limits,
Kierkegaard insists, however, that such an account does not satisfy the
demands of passion.

Kierkegaard compares one who "lives in an idolatrous land but prays
with all the passion of infinity," who, he says, "prays in truth to God," and
one who "prays in untruth to the true God, and is therefore in truth wor-
shiping an idol."[63] As a final piece of evidence for Kierkegaard's modal displacement of God, consider his treatment of the question of immortality. It is
not susceptible of objective proof, but has to do with the passion of the infinite. Socrates might sound like a doubter when he asks "*if* there is an immortality," but,

> He stakes his whole life on this "if"; he dares to die, and with the passion of
> the infinite he has so ordered his whole life that it might be acceptable—*if*
> there is an immortality.[64]

In other words, Socrates, who lived as if there was immortality, who embodied in this way the passion of the infinite in his life, gave the highest significance there could be to immortality—an existential appropriation. Again,
this would testify to a modal displacement of the religious.[65] Similarly, when
Kierkegaard writes (in *Concluding Unscientific Postscript*) that "God is that all
things are possible and that all things are possible is God," we must interpret
this as the kind of belief that opens up a certain kind of life. It is not so much
a truth about some feature of the world, as a way of organizing one's Being in
the world. God is being glossed as a certain grounded hope.

If we consider too that the knight of faith is said continually to find the
infinite in the finite, we can see that Kierkegaard repeatedly emphasizes the
possibility of a transformation of the economy of subjectivity at the very
point at which God might be expected to enter the scene. Faith itself—
which could be glossed by what Derrida calls "the endurance of aporia"[66]—is
only simplistically understood as "belief in God."[67] What is crucial for
Kierkegaard is, for example, that there be a form of individuality—what we
have called singularity—which can reemerge *beyond universality*, that is,
beyond ethical generality. Finding the infinite in the finite might be thought
paradoxical, but the example Kierkegaard gives in *Fear and Trembling* does
admit of a certain coherence. Our knight dreams of the wonderful meal his
wife has prepared for him, but when he gets home, he finds meager fare.
Instead of being disappointed, he is content. The trick he has performed

involves being able to be *in* the world (with ordinary desires) but not *of* the world, that is, not tied to the satisfaction of those desires. Again, Kierkegaard is describing the religious life as a way of being-in-the-world.

But it could be argued that this whole vein of interpretation is in fact restricted to what Kierkegaard explicitly limits to religiousness A, a certain pathos of immanence, achievable, indeed, by paganism, and falling short of religiousness B, paradoxical religiousness, which he calls dialectical to the second degree.[68] Religiousness A is a step beyond "speculative philosophy" in that it understands truth inwardly, existentially. But Kierkegaard seems to suggest that it is limited precisely by its telos of successful enactment of the infinite, whereas paradoxical religiousness, dialectical in the second degree, perhaps embodies the anxious impossibility of such a resolution. It is not clear that Kierkegaard's account of this distinction is absolutely consistent. One might suppose that if paganism can achieve religiousness A, one could not be a Christian at this level. Kierkegaard is not clear:

> In my opinion, Religiousness A (within the boundaries of which I have my existence) is so strenuous for a human being that there is always a sufficient task in it. . . . My intention is to make it difficult to become a Christian, yet not more difficult than it is . . .[69]

I have never called Religiousness A Christian or Christianity.[70]

What lies behind the A/B distinction is, however, the very issue that has concerned us throughout this chapter. It is an achievement, says Kierkegaard, for us to have set aside our understanding of our relation to God as an external relation, and to have come to understand it as a dimension of our subjectivity, a relation we have to ourselves. But Kierkegaard comes to believe not merely that this does not distinguish Christianity from other religions (even passionate paganism)[71] but that we can understand the specificity of Christianity as embodying a new dialectic, one in which our relation to God becomes again a relation to something external, this time in a way distinct from the original naive sense. Clearly Kierkegaard is trying to cope here with the paradoxical historical reality of God made man in Christ. Religiousness B, paradoxical religiousness, seems intent on preventing us from succeeding in achieving even the complacency of successful embodiment of God in our lives. Kierkegaard seems to be concerned that God as a structure of subjectivity might involve a loss of paradox, a loss of dialectical development.

I would like to end by suggesting in summary fashion that religiousness B represents a misunderstanding on Kierkegaard's part of the implications already latent in his own account of subjectivity, a misunderstanding not dissimilar to Derrida's own development of a paradoxical (ir)responsibility. If the significance of "God" for subjectivity appears in "inwardness of passion," in my "God-relationship," my recognition of the other as other, etc., we can understand the life of Christ as the inaugural performance of this (self-) sac-rificial economy of life and the gift of death. He opened up a world, a way of Being, preserved by the scriptures, and by our reading of them. Christ may have shared with religiousness B the belief in his relation to an actual exter-nal Being (God), but our acknowledgment of his significance does not require that we share that view. The paradox might be reformulated as how a being who may have literally believed he was the son of God could inspire those who have internalized that understanding. Kierkegaard seems to sup-pose that without a new "outside," the dialectic (of doubt, of perplexity, or paradox) to be found in subjectivity will cease, that interiority breeds com-placency. But he has provided quite enough material for *difference* in subjec-tivity to keep good conscience at bay. If the self is a relation that relates itself to itself by the mediation of its relation to the infinite (to God, to its ultimate concerns), there is no reason to suppose that this self-relation will ever cease to be problematic.

To live in paradox is to be suspended in a space of contradiction. We may suppose that the "external" paradox of Christ, of God-made-man, is some-thing we lose sight of at our spiritual peril, but in fact we lose sight of its sig-nificance precisely to the extent that it continues to fascinate our sight, and has not become a challenge (and paradox) for our own lives. And if we were to dare to think that Christ never quite knew who he was or what he was for ("Father, father, why hast thou foresaken me?") we might come to see Christ as an exemplary instance of the gap between existence and knowledge.

We *are* invisible to ourselves—though there may be no one else who *does* see us. The *way we are* constantly outstrips any knowledge of who we are. In that gap alone, there is dialectical ferment enough. The parallel with what I have found to be the limitations of Derrida's reading is this: Derrida generates paradoxes by re-projecting proliferating positive obligations into the space of my habitual, even reflective, life, just as Kierkegaard opens up, like a new front, an external relation to God, just when we had learned to discard such externalist topologies. In both cases, we may wonder whether the very impulses that created difficulties in the first place are not reassert-ing themselves. It is our claim that the solution to the problems of religious discourse (and belief) are modal, the recognition that different orders of belief require different *modes* of application to our actions and attitudes, that "God" may best be understood as a disposition to open the space of one's ethical complacencies to being challenged, and that it is always a sign of the waning of insight to start up the engines of projection once again. There never was any other realm, but there certainly are radically different ways of inhabiting this one.

SIX

Dionysus in America

ETHOS BEYOND ETHICS

IT HAS BECOME CLEAR to me in one respect at least, that Nietzsche was wrong—in supposing that he would have to wait two hundred years for someone to be able to hear him, someone with ears behind ears, someone with whom he could . . . dance. That man has appeared, and along with a very select band—Heidegger, Deleuze, and Foucault—Charles Scott has found a way through the first aporia that confronts the reader of Nietzsche—that to follow Nietzsche would be to betray him.[1] "It is easy enough to find me," said Nietzsche, " the difficult thing is to know how to lose me." What is the secret here? The secret is that while the problems that Nietzsche dealt with, and the "doctrines" and concepts he invented or reworked—ascetic ideal, eternal return, ubermensch, affirmation, genealogy, ressentiment, will-to-power—can be analyzed, explained, even systematized, they each appear in Nietzsche's thought in the context of a *transformatory practice or performance*—the revaluation of all values, the overcoming of Platonism. And these problems and concepts are only betrayed by being drafted into a new postmetaphysical system. For they are each both symptoms, marks of a certain process of transformation, and embody what has been called a logic of *recoil*—they possess in themselves reflexive, dynamic, self-transformatory powers. The legacy of Nietzsche is that of a properly uncompletable project, the very character of which consists in its being changed, transformed, and one which even contains an account of why this must be. The ascetic ideal, for example, is both a part of the lineage that we must overcome if we are to recover from the sickness that it represents, and it is also part of that inheritance by which overcoming anything is possible. This paradoxical recoil can be both paralyzing, and in the right hands, enabling. Enabling, because the problems it articulates are not just the artificial products of philosophizing, they characterize the shape and the difficulties of our experience, our knowledge, and our worldly engagement.

We might, for example, suppose that the very idea of overcoming is the problem, and indeed Heidegger himself proposes that we cease all overcoming and let metaphysics be.[2] Heidegger's recommendation stems directly from the aporetics of overcoming, but it is not the only way forward. It may be that overcoming, with all its impurity and imperfections, with all its essential finitude, is the necessary shape of our responsibility. (Though I note that Scott ends up with a transformation of this proposition, arguing that interruption is the shape of our nonresponsibility. But surely this interruption is no mere pause or break, but another way of moving "forward" . . .)

The sense that paradox shapes our responsibility is alive and well in Scott's writing, indeed, essential to its life. And while I am sure he has his reasons for not making the comparison himself, I am very tempted to draw the parallel with the distinctively paradoxical Religiousness B that Kierkegaard describes in *Concluding Unscientific Postscript*, one that essentially refuses any synthesis of the temporal and the eternal, and which finds its responsibility in that refusal. As I confessed in the last chapter, it was a short essay by Sartre on Kierkegaard (1962) that reinforced my sense of the importance of Kierkegaard to the kind of project Scott is engaged in.[3] In "The Singular Universal," Sartre gives a stunning display of his own philosophical depths of response, and in a brilliant presentation of Kierkegaard's legacy he writes: "He is my adventure and remains, for the others, Kierkegaard, the Other, at the horizon—a witness for me that becoming-an-atheist is a long and difficult undertaking, an absolute relation with those two infinities, mankind and the universe."[4]

Kierkegaard, nonetheless, is blind to our history, and it is along these lines that Sartre interrupts and productively transforms Kierkegaard's understanding of our singularity.

It is in much the same vein that Nietzsche wrote that we have not got rid of God if we still believe in grammar. This precisely means that becoming-an-atheist is an infinite task, that the extirpation of foundational identity, unity, and otherworldly transcendence, all the alibis of ethical and existential complacency, is a task for a lifetime, and then some. And that it will be riddled with false dusks.

Derrida's sense that responsibility requires us to go through the undecidable, a going through that never ends, even if we are called on to act *now, today,* is a similar attempt at a kind of postmodern phronesis, one that is not itself without danger. These various efforts to extend and transform the shape of our responsibility seem, however, to take for granted some sort of subject that could take responsibility, or be responsible, even if not primarily understood as being held responsible. As I see it, Scott diagnoses even in this noncomplacent responsibility a danger of a new authenticity, a new coziness of self-relatedness. It is unclear, for example, whether the acknowledgment that obligation to the Other is infinite is not at least capable of functioning as a kind of hyperconfession, which would help one sleep better at night. Scott's

Nietzschean question is about the value of responsibility (see "Responsibility and Danger," Scott [1996]). For Nietzsche, we might recall, responsibility was a link in the chain that eventually led men to the scaffold. "Christianity is a hangman's metaphysics."[5] Why? Because free will allows for responsibility which leads to guilt which leads to punishment. To be responsible is to be accountable. And Foucault's genealogical studies of the responsible subject point in the same direction. Being a subject *of* and being subject *to* are two sides of the same being. Conscience and consciousness, as the French language suggests, are indeed linked.

On this reading, responsibility would be a value caught up in structures of power, coercion, and exclusion, values to which it may itself be blind. But the attitude of responsibility is also, if Nietzsche is right, a flight from the terrors, the impulses, the desires that can never cease to threaten our precious sense of ourselves as responsible subjects. To the extent that responsibility is linked to the ascetic ideal, it is a symptom of an affirmation of life—but on the part of a declining *form* of life. And every reworking or reinscription of responsibility only reaffirms that arrangement. It is through a reading of Heidegger's account of technology, and its excessiveness to all that is human, that Charles Scott concludes that the challenge and danger of technology may call for something other than a renewed humanism, perhaps a nonresponsibility which is not at all an irresponsibility. This "nonresponsibility" (like Merleau-Ponty's non-philosophy) suggests a certain play, a play receptive to what might have been excluded in the very formation of responsibility, at the boundary of responsibility.

It is tempting to speculate, however, on what is at stake in this rejection of irresponsibility. Does it not suggest that nonresponsibility is ultimately in the service of a deeper, broader, more open sense of responsibility? Could this ever really be avoided? Here, I could imagine starting another paper entitled: "A Humanism Beyond: or Beyond Humanism?" Is Scott really the scourge of humanism, or is he not helping us move to rejoin its broken project? I sometimes wonder whether (as Heidegger put it) *the furtherance of humanism itself* requires that it be overcome, that it become a form of overcoming. And I have an answer to the question I would anticipate from Scott, in response, as to my relation, my investment, in this interpretation.[6]

I was disturbed when I read the title of Scott's book: *On the Advantages and Disadvantages of Ethics and Politics.* It took me a moment to realize that what disturbed me was the absence of the two words that should have been there—*for Life.*[7] But these words are not so much absent as displaced—they reappear on the "title" essay within and are scattered throughout the book. Indeed, the book itself and his work as a whole could be titled *For Life.* "His hero, you know," another mutual friend confided in me, "is Zorba the Greek." And who would not be *for* life? The answer, surprisingly, and yet not so surprisingly, according to Nietzsche, is *most of us.* Life, or a certain possibility of life, terrifies us. To cope with this terror "we" first invent the tragic drama, and then we replace it with a rationalist philosophy. Philosophy then becomes a coping strategy by which we higher animals hide *from* ourselves what we are doing *to* ourselves. Philosophy is a symptom of that of which it would like to be the cure. Lacan called philosophy a discourse of mastery, but that mastery has its limits, limits that in an important sense it cannot master, but only mask. And this means that if our desire for a system "succeeds" it does so only aesthetically, by blinding us to its blind spot. Again, it is Nietzsche who impudently and impossibly, points to the spot, as the child points to the emperor's nakedness. And what is particularly important about the work of Nietzsche, Foucault, and Heidegger in this regard, the central figures (along perhaps with Derrida and Deleuze) in Scott's pantheon, is that for each of them, the plight of philosophy is not the abstract predicament of some theoretical discipline, but a vital point of interruption, of a possible break-in to ethical, political, "economic" cycles of reproduction and repetition. The move within philosophy from Kant to Nietzsche is the move to materialize and historicize the transcendental principles that for Kant are essentially and ahistorically human. The move from Nietzsche to Foucault is to expose the ascetic ideal, the ethical subject, in short, "man," to a wide-reaching genealogical tracking in which, horror of horrors, the transcendental exhibits what we could call a Moebius function, one that operates and develops in empirical history.[8] Strangely enough, and this is one of the most exciting consequences of this whole genealogical displacement of the transcendental, the experience of transcendence also gains a new significance, not as offering us access to an extraterrestrial reality, but precisely as opening us onto ecstasies of finitude. It is as if the intensities that had been displaced onto the otherworldly, where it seemed they might be better controlled, return as the shape, feel and texture of our own existence. As Scott wrote in "Wonder and Worship":

> When we experience the fragility of the context for our ultimate interests and answers—our world—and when we live this awareness that our world is imminently perishable, we find the intensity of our loves and beliefs strange.[9]

This can lead to cynicism, but cynicism would be a mistake. Rather we can instead experience

> surprise, hopefully delighted surprise, that the world and we are, and that that experience may quite legitimately intensify our appreciation of what we have, where we are, and who we are in this unexplainable and clearly fragile drop of light.[10]

There is intensity, then, though the experience of finitude. And this experience of the intensity of finitude is forcibly in play throughout Scott's writing. If there is a change, it is in the soberness and persistence by which he thinks both with and against the philosophers he returns to.

I would like to be able to take you to the *heart* of these challenging texts. And it is tempting to say, as Foucault went on to say of Deleuze, that there is no center "but always decenterings, series that register the halting passage from presence to absence, from excess to deficiency."[11] But I cannot deny that I am tempted by the occasional mirage of a center. We can find such an imaginary center occupying a critical role in the first chapters of both *The Question of Ethics* ("The Question Concerns Ethics") and *On the Advantages and Disadvantages of Ethics and Politics* ("Crossing the Ethical by the Nonethical").

In *The Question of Ethics*, Scott writes that

> [t]he reader will find that the question of ethics arises out of ethical concern as well as out of conflicts within structures of value, that ethical concern and suspicion of ethics qualify one another. The suspicion held by "the question of ethics" is that ethical concern has a pathogenic dimension and is composed of values that occasion human suffering in the pursuit of human well-being.[12]

Later, he speaks of "the difficult experience that our values and ideals—particularly our highest and strongest values and ideals—may . . . perpetuate their own worst enemies . . . may add destruction and conflict to the very lives that they would cultivate, upbuild and harmonize." And the question of ethics "allows us to participate with alertness in the self-overcoming of values and ideals that form our lives and are structured by often unattended and intense conflicts."[13]

As I say, these worries sometimes strike me as marking the center of Scott's thought. But I suspect that the center is rather a kind of molecule of connected centers. I shall try to sketch some of the other centers shortly. But I would like first to probe Scott's sense of the intrinsic dangers of the ethical stance.

It is a common observation that actions may have unintended consequences. We may admit that under some interpretations and on some occasions, our well-meaning acts may come unstuck. Pity can mask arrogant condescension. The starving third world children we save may grow up to wage bloody war with each other over a parched land.[14] What is distinctive about Scott's position here is that those ethical stances and attitudes belonging to a certain sense of self as a responsible moral agent are seen to have the seeds of their own reversal, or recoil, built into them. For Scott, the ethical moment is typically a moment of loss of self-questioning, a moment of fatal complacency, that reinforces our sense of the self as an identity, constituted by conditions that can now be left behind. Whether we understand values as objective, or duties and obligations as tied to a certain metaphysical selfhood, Scott sees the danger as ever present, as returning with every well-meaning attempt to eliminate it, or guard against it. Even questioning itself (as Derrida noted) and overcoming are subject to the same processes of reinscription and co-option. Scott is clearly taking to its limit (and beyond) a venerable tradition—which diagnoses in the best of human behavior—self-serving motives, self-deception, the dangers of good conscience, self-satisfaction, etc. The problem here, of course, and Scott is well aware of this but I am not sure he can escape it, is that every effort we make to extirpate good conscience can certainly come to *feel like* a way of achieving another good conscience. Scott's solution here, if it is a solution, is to try to engender a kind of response-ability or nonresponsibility to which the ethical subject traditionally understood would no longer be linked. But we cannot just say "there is an openness," "there is a reponse-ability." We will return to saying "I," but with a recursive decentering, a new restlessness.

The question that surely poses itself here is whether there is not another danger, symmetrical to the one that occupies him (of the ethical impulse, against its own apparent desire, wreaking pain and disaster)—namely, that this hermeneutics of suspicion can become so insistent as to take on, as it were, a life of its own. Scott reassures us "that ethical concern and suspicion of ethics" qualify one another. But sometimes one wonders whether the suspicion of ethics, wedded as it is to an unending genealogical investigation, does not suffer threats from both ends—first, that genealogy could become an end in itself, committed, for instance, to the truth of its results. Recall Foucault replying to an interviewer who accused him of positivism for believing that what his research was uncovering "actually happened": "In that case I am a happy positivist." It is no accident that he later concerned himself, as if in compensation, with practices of care of the self. From the other end, there is a danger, all too hard to name in this atmosphere, that the recoil of the ethical on itself will come to assume the status of a necessity, a kind of postdialectical logic, swamping the singular fragile goodness of an act of generosity or kindness. Another way of putting this would be to ask: Is it not possible that this "self-overcoming recoil" might, precisely in its formal force, recoil upon itself and come to see itself as participating too fully in the project of philosophical representation?[15]

If there is a molecular structure, or a cluster of fundamental concerns distributed throughout Scott's writings, within which his interest in genealogy, in the ascetic ideal, in transformation (or interruption), and in excess all move, then the second locus I would isolate for our examination is the significance given to what, after so much trouble with the word, we still call want to call *experience*.

"Wonder and Worship," for example, ends with a celebration of the connection between these two phenomena, which he puts like this:

> If I am right in saying that wonder makes both oneself and the other stand
> out with intense and attractive vividness, worship can be the occasion for

recalling such a state through re-enacted patterns of experience and for inclining one toward a style of life which gives a place of honor to the experience of wonder. When that occurs, worship has intensified one's experience of the value of life and his experience of the strangeness that there is life at all.[16]

Experience is not of an object (Scott describes wonder earlier as "the absence of both subject and object"), nor is it simply an undergoing in which the subject is transformatively enhanced. Already, in the experience of wonder, experience is the site of a displacement, an interruption. One of his key examples is that of the ruined temple, which reminds us of man's finitude.

More than a quarter of century later (in *The Time of Memory*) some of the same themes still pulse. Scott recalls standing "in the summery yard of my home . . . I remember that I was arrested by the experience, both surprised and captivated by it and surprised and captivated over being surprised and captivated by it . . . I remember that the image came back to me occasionally with happy puzzlement."[17]

Wonder and strangeness have been replaced by surprise, captivation and puzzlement. . . . And the experience of finitude has taken on the shape of memory of the past, in each case my past—and yet, importantly, a past presented through memories in which what is mine, and me, and what is not me or mine is itself put in question. And it is not just that there is work to be done in connecting *then* and *now*, which would itself force the recognition of the constructed nature of selfhood. No—it is not just that. The experiences Scott records are in-themselves experiences that do not lend themselves to univocal representation. For example,

> When I had the experience of standing in the yard and looking toward the alley, I felt very distinctly that I had already lost something that I could not gain back and that I could not catch up with something that was in front of me as well as behind me . . . like lost time.[18]

It is as if the loss of memory and the memory of loss are one and the same. The temptation to treat Scott's personal memories as idiosyncratic symptoms alights temporarily on my shoulder and then flies off. If we were to interrogate this strange memory, looking away from the house at the paths and shortcuts leading away from it, we might easily conclude: "This is uncanny," indeed literally so, *Unheimlich*. And we might then recall that in Freud's essay of this name he interprets this experience of the *Unheimlich* through the story of the Sandman and the loss of eyes, as fear of castration. What drives away the suspicion of mere idiosyncrasy in Scott's recollections is that his evocation of the central theme of loss, even when there may be nothing precisely lost, is arguably more fundamental than any particular way in which it may be figured, as in castration. It is quite possible to reread Freud in this light. And to read Scott's *The Time of Memory* as a powerful contribution to that rereading.

This book moves through various modes and dimensions of memories, myths and powers of transformation—from Mnemosyne and Lethe, to Apollo and Dionysus, to institutional memory, and finally to a generous, and quite properly critical engagement with Levinas. I cannot begin to summarize the book, but it would not be too misleading to say that it deals with various economies of memory, in which memories do not return us to any univocal or pure origin. But in the range and the variety of their lineage-constituting capacities, and their transformative powers, they irreversibly thicken our intimate bonds with what cannot be represented, with what will always retain a power to disrupt the self. Levinas, for Scott, ultimately experiences loss, and loss of meaning, in terms of a return to an infinite source of meaning. What is quite distinctive, indeed courageous, about Scott is the persistence, his merciless insistence on something like affirmation without a telos, a hospitality to what lurks at the boundaries of self. This hospitality is in no way structured by an infinite obligation to the other person, indeed it is a welcome to "oneself" presupposed by each and every real capacity for welcoming the Other.

There is a quite extraordinary faith that what Sartre described as the project of "becoming-an-atheist" can deliver, if not meaning, then intensity, that the *via negativa* is in some curious sense, productive, even if what it produces is only a capacity to go on, to plunge once more into the darkness with passion. *Da capo.*

Perhaps I could draw Scott back to Kierkegaard briefly once more, to where Kierkegaard reminds us of Lessing's choice between Truth, on the one hand, or the perpetual striving after truth on the other. Scott would have to take the second option. But I think he would then divide it once again, insisting that alongside this striving, we strive against our temptation to arrive, knowing that this desire seduces us each time to the death of desire. There are those who allow that identity cannot stand apart from time, but think that justice can be done to this insight by insisting that identity be temporally constituted. There are others who notice that this process is not without its victims, but accept that the constitution of meaning (in, e.g., narrative intelligibility) has its price like anything else. And there are yet others who find in the fact of our lineages both as individuals and as cultures, the source of the field of unsynthesizable *trouble* for which, if we were honest and courageous, we would give up everything. This is a striving for truth that must never quite arrive.

In constructing my labyrinthine molecule of Scott-ish passions and centers, I have mentioned the perversity of ethics and the intensity of experience. It may not be quite of the same order, but I do want to hold up to the light a third, pervasive dimension of Scott's work by asking, "Why does he write such good books?"

To read Scott is to witness what Kierkegaard called an emancipatory performance. Kierkegaard insisted this take place via a double reflection, one that passes through both the conceptual grasp of the object and a subjective engagement. Scott's engagement is not so much subjective as with the project of ruthlessly breaking down, transforming, and interrupting the envelope of subjectivity. To witness this performance is to begin to know how it might be to feel, to think, to live differently. There is sometimes a roughness, a Whitmanesque lack of polish in his prose, which nonetheless drives forward alertly acknowledging what matters, responding in all directions, drawing together, but not too together, a range of references, discourses, considerations, constantly opening up connections where philosophy had closed them down. He is, as Foucault put it ("What is an author?"),[19] the inventor of a discursive practice. The recognition of memory, of memories, presents a quite proper challenge to "grammar," as Nietzsche called it. At times, Scott explicitly alludes to this aspect of his practice.

> I am struggling with words and phrases that can perceive and remember memory in its temporality, as it were, and I am repeatedly driven in this perception and memory to metaphors of metaphors, vague approximations, subjunctive moods, and highly qualified substantives. [But he has not, at least here, gone overboard. . . .] There are enough losses and memorial presentations that occur through the uses and features of available grammars, manners of expression and indication to make unnecessary, in this essay, a further display of something like shadowless "space" that is unfixed, devoid of mass, impersonal and capable of endless transformation.

Scott has a unique voice, and a singular sensibility. He is, I believe, pursuing a fine line along a rocky and treacherous path, one that seems at times impossible to navigate. There is a huge affirmation in his writing and yet it travels through darkness, and would even repudiate the term *affirmation*. But how else to understand the quite extraordinary stern passion in his prose, a passion directed against the satisfaction of so many of philosophy's stock desires. And there is a lusty synthetic capacity—of linkage, connectedness, the relentless pursuit of an unattainable goal, one that nonetheless refuses synthesis. Finally, it is hard not to see the whole project as having a real palpable coherence, permeated throughout by an ethical drive, an ethics beyond ethics, an emancipation of the flesh that refuses all sense of an original, natural integration.

I recently came across a wonderful opening to another book, Aldo Leopold's *A Sand County Almanac*, which struck me as a wondrously appropriate way of getting perhaps to the heart of Charles Scott's work:

> There are some who can live without wild things, and some who cannot. These essays [and books] are the delights and dilemmas of one who cannot.[20]

"BEING TRUE TO THE EARTH," OR, THE STARS CAN WAIT

> The eternal silence of these infinite spaces terrifies me.
> —Pascal, *Pensées*

> Stars, stars! / And all eyes else dead coals
> —Shakespeare, *The Winter's Tale*

There are those who cannot read Levinas, those for whom the tone and texture of his thinking just sticks in the throat, and will not be swallowed.[21] The distaste begins at the point at which it is claimed that the subject is hollowed out, vacated by the need, the fragility, the mortality of the other. To such a reader there seems to be an unthematized affective premise, one that Nietzsche long ago diagnosed with exquisite clarity, one to which a very particular and tragic history has made Levinas particularly vulnerable. On this view, Levinasian ethics is a philosophy of guilt, and guilt is neither necessary nor desirable as a response to horror, despair, or otherwise inexplicable survival.

This is the essence of Charles Scott's response to Levinas.[22] Levinas's position gets its plausibility from exploiting the logic of alterity, the Otherness that resides in the Same, but this guilt-driven ethical overlay occludes a relation to another other. It hides a relationship to a more primitive other, to something radically nonhuman, which nonetheless contributes to the very substance of our being, a relation captured best perhaps by Pascal's reference to "the eternal silence of these infinite spaces." Scott makes a great deal of our material kinship with what seems utterly distant and alien, the minerals shared by eyes and stars. I will argue, however, that we are being offered a false choice. Not only do we not need to choose between inhuman starlight and the ethically interpreted face of the other, neither of these alternatives survives scrutiny. Scott helps liberate us from a claustrophobically ethical sense of our relation to the other, but his cosmic alternative needs phenomenological fleshing out. Materiality has many forms and levels other than the mineral. Scott has lost sight of something important—that it is through our eyes that a world is opened to us, and in a way that our other senses can only dream of. We can speak and write of the stars only because we can see them. And our utter dependence on the Great Star (Sun) for warmth is something a knowing vision can only begin to imagine.

Do our eyes have a special kinship with the stars? If so, the kinship is entirely man-made. The minerals from which my eyes are made come from outer space only to the extent that this earth itself is from outer space. But that is not an elsewhere; it is an ancient *here*. And there is nothing special about my eyes in this respect. My fingertips too—my tongue, my stomach, and the dirt between my toes all have this mineralogical dependency.

We have to ask what is at stake here in the image or the metaphor of the mineral, and the minerality of our eyes. The mineral is perhaps the ulti-

mate humbling displacement of our problematic humanity. Such a displacement proceeds in a cascade. We are not just subjects, our subjectivity is in
thrall to the Other. We are not just human, we share much of what makes
us human with all other mammals. We are not just mammals, we are living
beings and it is as such that we strive to survive, flourish, and reproduce. We
are not just living beings, our organic existence rests on the inorganic properties of its constituent parts. Somewhere here we will find minerals. But if
we proceed down this chain of being, we will surely pass through the mineral to the atomic, the subatomic, and on to primitive fields of force in
which the cold clarity of inorganic structure was only a waystation. And in
returning to energy fields, we return to primitive scenes of motion, which
put the stony silence of the mineral to shame. I worry, in short, about what
seems to be the specific willfulness of this geneominerology. One good reason for not treating the pursuit of constituent elements as illuminating or
chastening is that there is a certain arbitrariness about the stopping point in
the journey. Humans are not giant columns of quartz, not rocky promonto-
ries. When our bodies are burnt, we "return to" ash and steam, it's true—
minerals that would fertilize a basil plant.[23] But when we are eaten by a tiger
or by worms we "return to" amino acids and proteins. Scott acknowledges
our distant kinship with other living beings in his references to fungi and
protozoa, but only in connection with our common receptivity to light. And
yet does not our common dependency, not on starlight, but on the light and
the heat of the sun offer an even more effective displacement of the subject-
centered privilege of the eyes, eyes that are blinded by looking straight into
the sun? What then is at stake in this mineralogy?

I cannot help thinking here of the conclusion of Foucault's *Archaeology
of Knowledge* in which he "sympathizes" in a somewhat brutal way ("I understand the unease of all such people") with those who

> have found it difficult enough to recognize that their history, their econom-
> ics, their social practices, the language that they speak, the mythology of
> their ancestors, even the stories that they were told in their childhood, are
> governed by rules that are not all given to their consciousness.[24]

Foucault says he is "abolishing all interiority in that exterior that is so indifferent to my life, and so neutral that it makes no distinction between my life
and my death."[25]

The paradox in all this is that both Scott's pursuit of the mineral and the
light beyond (and yet within) the human, and Foucault's pursuit of this neutral exteriority, in spite of the pain it causes him and others, are *passions*, and
in each case reflect what Nietzsche would call a will to truth. It is hard not
to ask what is served by this will.

Scott's brush with science, especially with magnitudes, densities, dis-
tances of unimaginable vastness is inherently problematic. His argument is

that the unimaginable quantitative vastness of the universe, when coupled with our mineralogical kinship with the stars, suggests a second distance, "a distance from ourselves and our customs and our communities of endeavor and knowledge."[26]

I suggest, however, that the true lesson of cosmic scale is the poverty of those senses of self and those forms of community that fail to maintain an openness to it, that either exclude this exteriority or incorporate it all too well.

Consider the parallel in Nietzsche's writings: In his early essay on truth (1872): Nietzsche writes:

> Once upon a time in some out of the way corner of the universe which is dispersed into numberless twinkling solar systems there was a star on which clever beasts invented knowing. . . . After nature had drawn a few breaths, the star cooled and congealed, and the clever beasts had to die.[27]

With this kind of God's-eye-view account, Nietzsche attempts the very same "explosion of anthropomorphic images" as Scott attempts mineralogically. Scott, after Deleuze, I would guess, counts on having skirted the obvious response to these kinds of moves. However large the cosmos is, however dense the matter from an imploded star, such scale, such quantity, etc., is utterly devoid of significance unless it is significant to some such creature as man. That some piece of immense rock is spinning billions of light years away has no significance whatsoever unless it is significant to the same sort of creature that cares to put on matching socks in the morning. Nietzsche in effect gets caught in his own net only a few pages later when he writes:

> [E]verything marvelous about the laws of nature, everything that quite astonishes us therein and seems to demand our explanation, everything that might lead us to distrust idealism: all this is completely and solely contained within the mathematical strictness and inviolability of our representations of time and space. . . . We produce these representations in and from ourselves with the same necessity with which the spider spins. . . . All that conforms to law, which impresses us so much in the movement of the stars, and in chemical processes, coincides at bottom with those properties which we bring to things.[28]

It would be a mistake to dismiss the force of these remarks by saying that this was an early essay, and Nietzsche was still flirting with idealism. And it would be a mistake to suppose that the force of these remarks is limited to scientific laws. The experience of wonder, awe, horror, and insomnia . . . are all experiences that, even as they displace and undermine a narrow sense of subject, reestablish it in a properly troubled form. Scott argues that the ratio of difference between vision and person is greater than between self and other.[29] But not all ratios have *ratio*. We may look at the stars, and marvel, but the stars, for all their immensity, are utterly blind, and cannot see us. Even their blinking is an illusion. It is, I am sure, equally an illusion that all this is here "for us."[30] It is the same puffed-up arrogance to suppose that we are the center of the universe. Our capacity to open a world may not be unique. But we have so far seen nothing extraterrestrial that comes close. It is not that man is the center of the cosmos, but that with man, or perhaps life in general, we do find, for the first time, the birth of orientation, the inauguration of the possibility of perspective, or truth (and lie, fiction, etc.).

Scott is quite right to stress that the radical dependency of our subjecthood is misunderstood when construed under the sign of guilt. But the minerality of the eyes seems, to me at least, to take us in the wrong direction in looking for more fruitful ways of correcting our anthropocentrism. We should be suspicious of the sidereal, galactic imagination. To be true to the earth is to be slow to turn away from the black holes it already offers us. (And strange to tell, the very word *mineral* is derived from the word mine in the sense of holes dug by men in the earth.)

Interrupting the holiness of the Levinasian face, Scott notices the hair growing from a nostril, the pimple, the scar, the large chin. The face is or has a materiality. If it says, "thou shalt not kill," it is because it is deeply mortal. Scott sees in the face of the other not just my obligation, but also my, our, materiality. But this materiality is not the only or even the most fruitful way of interrupting the transcendence of the face. For the eyes are the sites of the emergence of the most material of relations—the devouring gaze, the petrifying stare, the pleading look, the endearing glance. The eyes are the vehicles of relations of force, of power, of intimacy, invitation, or destruction, the most material relations you could want, and ones in which my subjecthood is radically put in question.

To be seen in war can mean to be killed, to be betrayed. To be seen on the road can mean not to be killed. To see our prey or the object of our desire may mean that we will not starve, that we will be sated. Seeing and being seen are mortal events.

Consider too the different modalities of our "being seen"—by lovers, by enemies, by strangers, by those in need, by those engaged in secret activity, by children, by animals—and in each case in a variety of situations and circumstances. Vicki Hearne (in *Adam's Task*)[31] has a whole chapter on cats, which centers on the observation that they are always looking at us. And compare Derrida's discussion of being seen by a cat.[32] In each case there is a very distinct kind of materiality involved, one in which I am grasped, totalized, albeit imperfectly, within a field of concern. If I become aware that I have been seen by the other, my whole being, as Sartre so brilliantly described it, can be recrystallized. But if I look at the eyes of the other, what do I see? If I look into the eyes of my beloved, I may "see" her love for me, her response to my love for her (I may actually see the dilation of her pupils). If I look at her eyes, I may notice their color, the extraordinary texture, the minute blood vessels . . . all these material features have become visible to *my* eyes considered as organs of sense. If I look into the eyes of my cat, eyes that look like fine glass marbles riven with fat dark slits, I find myself staring into a terrestrial black hole, in which I can find no orientation, no clue, no bearing.[33] Then I look into a mirror, and I find myself flickering back and forth between minutely observing the textures and colors, realizing that what I am looking at is actually doing the looking. Here, we do not have borrowed minerals, but rather interlaced structures whose materiality is of a different order. An order that, equally, has nothing essential to do with guilt. What I am suggesting here is that the structures of orientation, world opening, or object devouring which the eyes make possible are misunderstood when drawn up into an idealistic schema. Rather, they are bound up with the very materiality that could liberate us from such an idealism.

But this raises the further question of whether Scott's account of Levinas in this respect is fair or complete. He attributes to him fundamental "feelings of mourning, exile, and persecution," a sense of "continuous guilt," and a heavy serious, obsessional quality to his writing. I have to admit I have at times had a similar response. But I wonder whether one might not redirect Scott's remarks in the direction of a question about the development of Levinas's work, or the compatibility of claims he makes at different times, or in different books. I am thinking particularly of Levinas's descriptions of the night and of the materiality of modern art in *Existence and Existents*, and again in *Time and the Other*. It is very difficult to attribute idealism to Levinas here as he seems to be explicitly struggling against it. And if we were to distinguish between material and cosmic exteriority and the alterity of the Other, Levinas seems here to be on Scott's side, focused on exteriority.

For Levinas, the experience of the night, especially insomnia, is the experience of an impersonal vigilance that witnesses the ebbing away of consciousness, the extinction of my subjectivity. For Levinas, my very formation as a subject is not just guiltily hollowed out by another human. It is itself the legacy of the destruction of an impersonal being.

> The *il y a* encompasses consciousness . . . the consciousness of a thinking subject, with its capacity for evanescence, sleep and unconsciousness, is precisely the breakup of the insomnia of anonymous being . . . to take refuge in oneself so as to withdraw from being . . .

What is Levinas describing here? He is describing the experience of the night in which "The 'I' is itself submerged by the night, invaded, depersonalized, stifled by it." He speaks of the horror of the night, "the silence and horror of the shades," a horror in which the determinacy of things is dissolved into "a swarming of points" without perspective. It is not, as with Heidegger, that Being slips away to reveal the Nothing, but that Being is inescapable. "Darkness," he says, "reduces [the things of the day] to undetermined anonymous being, which sweats in them."

In these early passages, Levinas is in touch with something that surely does with darkness just what Scott tries to do with the role of light, especially starlight, in vision. What Scott says of light—"a pre-perceptive dimension of vision and in vision, which composes an enactment of our bodies and indicates severe limits to the personal and so-called human aspects of our lives"[34]—is precisely what is accomplished by Levinas's account of the *il y a,* darkness, etc.

My second example of where Levinas seems to me importantly to escape Scott's determination of him as "dependent on a fundamentally idealistic account of human experience"[35] comes from his approving account of the deliverances of modern art and painting, which he sees dedicated to presenting the brute materiality of things. Let me focus on two aspects of Levinas's remarks here:

    a. The meaning of the liberties a painter takes with nature are not correctly appreciated when they are taken to proceed from the creative imagination or from the subjectivity of the artist. The subjectivity could be sincere only if it no longer claims to be vision. Paradoxically . . . painting is a struggle with sight.[36]

Here, the look presents a fractured world. Compare this with Scott's claim that "light proceeds from matter"[37] and that eyesight depends on minerals created by stellar implosions. Which is more disclosive of *effective* otherness? Perhaps we need to ask what is meant by "materiality" such that it can interrupt our subjective formations. This takes us to the second aspect of Levinas's discussion of contemporary art: the materiality of being, which is a direct consequence of the breakdown of the totalized visual field:

    b. [T]hings break away and are cast toward us like chunks that have weight in themselves. . . . They are naked elements, simple and absolute, swellings or abscesses of being. . . . Here is a notion of materiality which no longer has anything in common with matter as opposed to thought and mind which fed classical materialism. . . . Here materiality is thickness, coarseness, massivity, wretchedness. . . . Behind the luminosity of forms, by which being already relates to our "inside," matter is the very fact of the *il y a.*[38]

This account, indebted perhaps to Sartre's counterposing of phenomenology to what he termed digestive idealism,[39] presents us with the kind of visceral materiality that really does get under our skin. Can the minerality of starlight really compete here?

It might be said that this materiality is far from a challenge to our subjectivity, our anthropomorphic tendencies. The vulgar adjectives of this materiality are stuffed with human concern, as we brace ourselves for the impact of these thing creatures breaking through the palisades of idealism.

But this is a condition we never leave behind. We are always writing *against* the hubris of this and that form of humanism, and *for* a certain possibility of renewal of our capacity for response, opening ourselves up to what fear, anxiety, horror, weariness, and the delights of everydayness keep closing off to us.

So far, we have followed at least the broad strokes of Scott's way of setting up the problem, pursuing the suggestion that we might be implicated in a certain sidereal exteriority before and in distinction from our relation to the other person. In this last part of my response, I want to question the distinction that we have so far accepted between our relation to the stars and to the other. Might it not be that at the level of the significance of our experiences, the two are intimately connected? Here, I take myself to be offering another strategy with which to circumvent Levinas's guilt-soaked grasp of my relation to the Other.

Scott is right to be dismayed by the way in which Levinas, in his response to Philippe Nemo's question about how thinking begins, moves all too quickly from a reference to traumatic events to reading books and to the Bible. Scott is understandably dismayed to hear nothing about "war experiences, psychological traumas, or political crises." Levinas affirms that thinking probably begins with "traumas or gropings to which one does not even know how to give a verbal form, a separation, a violent scene." The move to reading books is what allows these "initial shocks" to take on a symbolic articulation. Scott's objection, if we can call it that, is that the experience of trauma, far from being helpfully illuminated by Levinas's religious commitments, has been hijacked by them. Subjectivity is only hostage to the Other because of the original impossible obligations of the people of God. Now, it may be that Scott is right about the schema of interpretation that Levinas is deploying here. But as he goes on to suggest, what Levinas is actually dealing with is not just our relation to the Most High, but the interruption, perhaps necessary interruption, of our sensuous, even carnal, life by the suffering of the other. Rudolf Bernet puts this well:

> My enjoyment is vulnerable because it is exposed to the risk of being disturbed or interrupted by the event of meeting with the suffering of the other. For a subject in the midst of enjoyment, such a meeting is equivalent to a trauma, one which Levinas does not hesitate to paint in the most dramatic of colours, speaking of the "bread torn from my mouth," of "haemorrhage," etc.[40]

Scott wants to be able to "avoid feelings of catastrophe or of absolute responsibility," "to enjoy the efforts to provide for the day's dwelling places . . . to come back home refreshed and enjoy a dinner with people we love"[41] without sounding like Marie Antoinette.[42]

I am not convinced that going by way of the stars is the answer. Rather, I propose that we detach the intimate connection of subjecthood with trauma from its ethical horizon.

This does not mean detaching it wholly from the relation to the other. Bernet puts it like this:

> It is true that the subject can be traumatized by the unleashing of the forces of nature that it believed it held under its domination so as to better enjoy them. But this does not take away from the impossibility of ignoring that which in those events refers to the other.[43]

Understanding the intimate connection between subjectivity and trauma—a connection that spawns the strange logic in which the subject is both threatened by and created by trauma—we come to see that some of the work of troubling subjecthood that induces Scott to reach for the stars has already been done in the traumatic genealogy of what it is to be a subject at all. I must admit that I understand the primacy of the ethical in Levinas, and the structure of obligation in which he inscribes it, as a very specific and ultimately pathological *effect* of trauma, much as it would be to empty one's house of all valuables after a burglary. In this, I suspect, Scott and I may be in lonely agreement. I would propose, on another occasion, to revisit the sites of violence, separation, loss, invasion, that subjects traverse in their formation, in a way less stifled by the ethical atmosphere that Scott cannot breathe.[44] Some of these sites are universal—birth and weaning, for example—some tragically singular, such as child abuse, shell shock, and the suicide of a loved one. And I see no reason not to suppose that each, importantly, allows for both affirmative and resentful ways of going on.

I propose this way forward because it seems to me that the debt that our eyes have to starry minerals is powerfully overshadowed by the impact on our young eyes of very terrestrial things we should never have seen, or a beauty we can never forget.

The scene Scott sets for us is one in which ethical anguish is banished from the *heimlich*, from the intimacy of the home, in which the cosmic compact between our eyes and the stars is a private illumination. I have throughout proposed that the black holes that deepen, trouble, and ultimately restore to us a subjectivity "changed utterly" are more terrestrial and human than Scott's startrek would suggest. I conclude with a brief sojourn to a quite other scene, one set for us by Freud in his essay on the Uncanny, the *Unheimlich*, one in which the passage between the eyes and the heavens is negotiated very differently.

From the outset, we begin to suspect that we have not entirely left trauma behind. Freud defines the uncanny as "that class of the terrifying which leads back to something long known to us, once very familiar." Freud adopts Jentsch's example of the structure of the feeling of the uncanny— "doubts whether an apparently animate being is really alive [or conversely]"—with artificial dolls and automata as examples. It is perhaps more than curious that a blurring of the line between animal and mineral, and between human and inhuman, is just what is in play in both Scott and Foucault, but I will not pursue this here. Freud fastens on Hoffman's story "The Sandman," and I will focus on the eponymous episode:

> In spite of his present happiness, [the student Nathaniel] cannot banish the memories associated with the mysterious and terrifying death of the father he loved. On certain evenings his mother used to send the children to bed early, warning them that "the Sandman was coming"; and sure enough Nathaniel would not fail to hear the heavy tread of a visitor with whom his father would then be occupied that evening. When questioned about the Sand-Man . . . his nurse [said]: "He is a wicked man who comes when children won't go to bed, and throws handfuls of sand in their eyes so that they jump out of their heads all bleeding. Then he puts the eyes in a sack and carries them off to the moon to feed his children. They sit up there in their nest, and their beaks are hooked like owl's beaks, and they use them to peck up naughty boys' and girls' eyes with."[45]

I have elsewhere picked a bone with Freud over his insistence that this story is clearly about the fear of castration, and I will not repeat this here.[46] What this story brings out is the way in which the night is not just studded with stars, nor the horror of the indeterminacy and irremissibility of being, it is a scene of at least an imagined trauma connected with the eyes. What Freud omits to remind us is that the children are being told to close their eyes, to go to sleep. And the implicit threat is that if they do not submit to this parental regulation of their senses, even of their state of consciousness, the organ in question will be gouged out and become a mere thing, even an edible thing. Here, the mineral in the eyes is no benign constitutive element but handfuls of sand—not stardust, but a blinding trauma administered by an evil other. To Scott's figure of the distant star corresponds that of the moon and an uncanny lunar dining scene. Recall also Oedipus, who loses his sight not from sunglare, or starlight, but by his own hand, bearing witness to the tragic blindness of his life. My point, very simply, is that we do not have to choose between the inhumanity of starlight and the suffocating atmosphere of Levinas's guilt-gorged grasp of the infinity of the Other. And it would be a mistake to be driven to embrace either an icy minerality or a sealed domestic intimacy just to escape from the traumatic proliferations of survivor guilt.

When Scott says that Levinas's position depends on his idealist premises, I find this a helpful way to articulate something of my own difficulties with Levinas. But when Scott puts modern numbers to what Pascal called "infinite spaces," I want to reply with the ancient observation that while we can see the stars, the stars cannot see us. And I want to say this without being labeled an idealist. It is no accident that Scott focuses on the eyes, for they are surely the site from which idealism is launched. Scott aims to disrupt the privilege of sight by inaugurating a reverse dependency, a mineralogical dependency of the eyes on the stars that, by being able to see, they seem to dominate. It was in this same spirit, as we have seen, that Nietzsche began his early (1872) essay on Truth, where, among "numberless twinkling solar systems, there was a star upon which clever beasts invented knowing."[47] Nietzsche comments on "how aimless and arbitrary the human intellect looks within nature." He compares us to the gnat that is just as likely to think of itself as the flying center of the universe. "The proudest of men, the philosopher, supposes that he sees on all sides the eyes of the universe telescopically focused upon his action and thought."

It is curious that the object of Nietzsche's attack here, the privilege attributed to objective knowledge, is not far from being repeated in Levinas's attempts to displace the primacy of ontology—by contrasting totality to infinity. Scott's distinctive position rests on the idea that a kind of cosmic hubris still resounds in Levinas's ethics of otherness, in virtue of its being circumscribed within the realm of the human. What if being human involved a relation to what is inhuman, prehuman, nonhuman—even mineral? A kind of exteriority, not captured by alterity? Perhaps even veiled by it?

Scott's mineralogical meditations are quite as much as anything an attempt to get us to accept a shift in our words and images.[48] And there is huge untapped scope for exploring the role of the inhuman in the human. But as a matter of probability, it seems a whole lot less likely that much illumination will come from noticing common constituent elements, when everything points to the importance of relations, and to complexity in the arrangements of parts, rather than in the constituent elements. Scott's enchantment with the stellar might perhaps be appropriately chastened by Nietzsche himself:

> All that we actually know about these laws of nature is what we ourselves bring to them—space and time. . . . But everything marvelous about the laws of nature, everything that quite astonishes us therein and seems to demand our explanation, everything that might lead us to distrust idealism—all this is completely and solely contained within the mathematical strictness and inviolability of our representations of space and time. . . . [W]e produce these representations in and from ourselves with the same necessity with which the spider spins . . .[49]

PART III

Ethics and Politics
after Deconstruction

SEVEN

Notes toward a Deconstructive Phenomenology

<hr>

> What is phenomenology? It may seem strange that this question has still to be asked a century after the first works of Husserl. The fact remains that it has by no means been answered.
>
> —Merleau-Ponty

ARE MATTERS ANY clearer today? Are we *really* in a position to make sense of an expression such as "deconstructive phenomenology"? Surely this *contradictio in adjecto* is cousin to "round square," or "dancing fish."

Derrida has often been attacked by phenomenologists for the failures of his "critique," and it was only with caution and with some suspicion that his work was discussed in the main phenomenologically oriented societies.[1] Nonetheless, I would like here to try to draw on the work of Derrida, Levinas, Blanchot, and others not to bury or praise phenomenology but to address the theme of phenomenology's renewal.

First, what should we think of this theme: Renewing Phenomenology?[2] Some immediate responses:

1. Phenomenology has always been *about* renewal—of philosophy itself, of culture, of the philosophical attitude.[3]
2. As a self-confessed "perpetual beginner," Husserl saw phenomenology as requiring a continual renewal of its own project.[4]
3. Husserl's own career—moving through various phases of phenomenology—*demonstrated* the dynamic, self-transformative potential of phenomenology.
4. Phenomenology as a movement, is one of self-renewal—with existential (Sartre),[5] hermeneutical (Ricoeur),[6] transcendental (Husserl),[7] and other dimensions or developments or versions of "phenomenology."

And "renewal" is itself a concept of central thematic concern to phenomenology, a concept on the cusp of time and history, experience and transcendence. To the extent that phenomenology is about reactivation, going "back to the things themselves," phenomenology is precisely the overcoming of the distinction between the old and the "new," and thus a meditation on the very idea of "renewal."

If we apply some of these considerations to phenomenology, we would come to see that it is only by reactivation, contestation, and starting again that phenomenology can be itself. It can only stay the same by repetitions that allow deviation, take risks, and repudiate strict identity.[8] Non-philosophers and, surprisingly, some philosophers have a tendency to treat critique, even change, as destructive, when it is actually the force that keeps whatever *is* alive. Heidegger and Derrida have had to rescue destruction and deconstruction respectively from the charge of negativity. As Derrida put it, "[D]econstruction . . . is not negative. Destabilization is required for 'progress' as well."[9] Sartre had to defend existentialism in similar terms.[10] And this same issue is at stake in the charge that Socrates *corrupted* the youth. Actually what is needed is precisely a phenomenological attitude toward "destruction"—a suspension of our natural attitudes. What philosophers seek to destroy is not the world, nor our capacity for creative response to it, but dead and moribund forms of our relationship to the world.

I cannot here attempt a synoptic account of "phenomenology" today, or of what "deconstructive phenomenology" might be, or might look like. Rather, I shall "assemble some reminders," some notes toward our continuing through phenomenology a critical engagement with the matter of philosophy. Some of what I say could have been said in the early '70s, when "deconstruction" was first launched, some not. But what was or could have been said then could not have been repeated *now* until today!

There are a number of dimensions to phenomenology of particular and lasting importance:

1. Its critique of all positivity (naturalism, psychologism, *Weltanschauung theorie*)—on the grounds of its (essential) naivety, its confusion of "fact" and "essence," its theoretical and reflective poverty, its incapacity to think anything like the transcendental.
2. Its problematizing or "suspension" of the natural attitude. In one sense this is common to all philosophy; what is important here is not one version of this move rather than others, but phenomenology's recognition of its continuing necessity (it is the name of a problem, not of a solution).
3. The recognition of something like intentionality—or nonnatural relations to the world (see Heidegger on "intentionality" in his editor's preface to Husserl's *Phenomenology of Internal Time Consciousness* [1910],[11] see Levinas's essay "Beyond Intentionality").[12] We may legitimately ask whether "intentionality" is not more important as a function (opening

up alternatives to causality) than as a quasi-psychological attitude. (See chapter 9, "What is Eco-Phenomenology?") This would explain how intentionality can appear not merely as "consciousness of . . ." but also in linguistic forms, such as intentional verbs.

4. The recognition of the necessity of concepts such as "horizon," "context," and "world" which will link together structures of meaning, experience, and "being-in-the-world."

5. The philosophical renewal to be found in a return to "experience"—that experience supplies *something like* a preconceptual ground[13] that includes suffering, need, mood, the play of the active and the passive, graspings and undergoings, the constitution and undoing of identity, etc.[14]

Let us now remind ourselves of some of the wealth of ways of taking up, relating to phenomenology that the twentieth century has witnessed:

1. Heidegger took care to appropriate "phenomenology" in his own way— at the very point at which he departed from Husserl's understanding ("letting what shows itself in itself be seen as it is in itself")[15]—and set the scene for a certain subsequent thematization of receptivity in *Gelassenheit*—letting beings be.

2. Merleau-Ponty and Sartre both saw existential phenomenology as heir to the legacy—and did not, for example, see the impossibility of a complete reduction as an impediment, but, quite as much, as something essential to thematize and internal to the life of philosophy itself.

3. Levinas clearly sees himself as some sort of phenomenologist, or at least as treating phenomenology as a jumping-off point.[16] He writes explicitly of the phenomenology of eros,[17] and the "Other" appears precisely as a limit of intentionality.

4. Derrida's work not only began in intimate discussion with Husserl,[18] he described *Speech and Phenomena* as his most philosophical work, and insisted that it was necessary to go through transcendental phenomenology to avoid vulgar realism, etc.[19]

5. It may also be worth reporting that when Jean-Luc Marion was once asked how he would describe the kind of work he and others like him were doing, he is reported to have answered: "We are phenomenologists."[20]

Although it is something of a heuristic fiction, the strongest form of phenomenology (though for that reason perhaps the most vulnerable) is what Husserl called transcendental phenomenology,[21] which verges on idealism. I now suggest some of the challenges to which transcendental phenomenology has had to respond and which have shaped something of the legacy we have begun to trace. Such challenges continue today. I group these challenges under three headings: language, loss, and responsibility.

Despite the example of Frege, the general drift of the twentieth century's "linguistic turn" was away from Platonism and idealism toward a more social, contextual, materialistic account of language, and more generally toward language and away from spirit, consciousness, and experience. We might characterize phenomenology in a neo-Kantian way as a move from a naive to a reflective attitude, in which we focus not on what is there, but on how it is given, and our own constitutive activity. But this account is then vulnerable to the recognition (a) that this activity is not primarily personal but public—that the individual's relation to symbolic and cultural formations is more passive or receptive than simply active, and (b) that we cannot think of consciousness without understanding its symbolic/linguistic structuring. Derrida's readings of Husserl are not, however, just "critiques."[22] What is so fascinating about them is that he brings out tensions latent within Husserl's own work, of which, in many ways, Husserl was well aware. The need for geometrical truths (and hence science in general) to be *written* to achieve the ideality proper to it, which makes it a science, is exactly the dilemma Husserl begins with. And the double sense of perception on which Derrida plays (as both immediate, confined to the present, and as including retentions) is exactly where Husserl hopes he can hold things together. Basically, Derrida tracks down Husserl to an expressive model of the relation between meaning and language, and argues that there is a backdoor of linguistic constitution—a world of difference that makes presence possible—that Husserl can only point to, but not himself thematize. And in the course of doing so, Derrida draws on the phenomenon of "hearing oneself speak," acknowledging, even stressing, its seductive allure. Is Derrida then really a phenomenologist in disguise? It would not be misleading to say that the thematics of showing are not being contested by Derrida, but being extended. And the same could be said of the whole move from one sense of "experience" to another, where what is shown, displayed, or performed are the aporetics of experience. But this showing is specifically a linguistic undergoing. Heidegger anticipated this kind of relation when he said that he was not trying to offer a new theory of language but to bring about a new experience with language, a new relation to language.[23]

Derrida is quite as focused on the constitution of meaning as was Husserl. All his references to the text and to textuality are evidence not of a break but a continuation. What are we to make of the trouble Derrida had with the claim that "there's nothing outside the text"?[24] We need only think of the reduction as Husserl practiced it (in *Ideas*, for example, he says that "[a]ll reality exists through 'the dispensing of meaning'"[25]). Husserl comes within a hair's breadth of idealism, protected only by a *methodological* self-understanding. But the thrust of Derrida's claim is, if anything, in the opposite direction. We have already alluded to Derrida's famous remark about the need to go through the transcendental to avoid empiricist naiveties, and it is significant with what success Gasché could pick up on the expression "quasi-transcendental."[26] Ultimately, Derrida finds in language the same protection against positivist reduction for which Husserl devised phenomenology.

The linguistic turn "within" phenomenology is well illustrated by the turn to hermeneutics of another of Husserl's heirs: Paul Ricoeur. It is Ricoeur's view that the aporias of time cannot be resolved within a phenomenology that, like Husserl's, fails to draw on the synthetic resources of language. The reduction to inner time-consciousness does not help. It is, he claims, through *narrative* that the aporias of time are at least resolved, if not (formally) solved.[27] However, in fact it does not so much even resolve these aporias as allow us to formulate them, and dramatize them, more effectively. My identity is contested through competing narratives, and balanced between narratives I construct and those from elsewhere to which I am subjected. Before Derrida, and providing another (ambiguous) foil for his thought, we find Heidegger's own recognition of the impossibility of demarcating language either as an instrument of man, or as some sort of region of the world. His concern with the world-opening power of poetry, with the way in which language sustains and infuses our very being in the world, is a tacit repudiation of the model by which subjects constitute the world by their own "acts."[28] Language forces us to a recognition of a certain dimension or moment of passivity, community, and the limits of even transcendental psychology. And yet, we recall, Heidegger continues to focus on the importance of a new *relation to*, or *experience with* language, in which the echo of intentionality is unmistakable.

The second challenge to traditional phenomenology can be focused on the sense of loss. "Loss" may seem a strange word to use here. I have in mind various versions of the advent of irrecuperable negation in Blanchot's writing of disaster,[29] in Levinas's adumbration of the infinite other,[30] of Husserl's thinking of the possibility of the end of all meaning,[31] and of Derrida's ruminations on sacrifice and gift, and on the messianic *a-venir* ("to come").[32] These economies of nonrecuperation, nonpresence, disrupt any final resolution of meaning or identity. But what is extraordinary is that deconstruction has come to recognize them under the heading of experience. Derrida's development on this score has an uncanny parallel to that of Husserl quoted above. In 1967, he could write:

> As for the concept of experience it belongs to the history of metaphysics, and we can only use it under erasure. "Experience" has always designated the relationship with a presence.[33]

Whereas the late Derrida talks apparently freely about "an interminable experience," "the [impossible] experience of death," "the experience of the non-passage," "the experience of mourning," and even "the experience of what is called deconstruction."[34] Here, we may say we have a "moment of decision" (but not, I think, one of madness)—which may take each of us in different ways, and may take a lot more than a moment. If phenomenology could be thought to have as its focus not consciousness, not perception, but experience,[35] we might come to see that all these features and factors that have been thought to breed a problematic "presence" can return as the *wealth* of experience. Phenomenology would then find itself in a kind of partnership with genealogy, with psychoanalysis, indeed with various political struggles, in ways that we can glimpse but have as yet no rules for. This whole prospect will clearly rest on the historic fate of a word such as experience, which has already been lined up on various sides. Blanchot and Agamben, for example, write about the impossibility of experience,[36] while Derrida writes more about the experience of impossibility, of aporia.[37]

Finally, philosophy faces the disturbing power of one of its fundamental concepts—that of responsibility. This last trait is even more a cluster of questions than the other two. From the beginning, before it was Derrida's word, it was Husserl's. Responsibility, for Husserl, meant living and thinking within the possibilities of reactivation, even if his idea of a community of scholars living in "the unity of a common responsibility," contributing to "a radically new humanity made capable of an absolute responsibility to itself on the basis of absolute theoretical insights," is now honored only in the breach.[38]

Heidegger's meditations on the task of thinking at the end of philosophy, on the plight of the West, on the call, the appeal, are moving in the same element. Heidegger's destruction of the tradition, of ontology, is in the service of what is first a program of renewal. Later, less of a program. Derrida comments:

> Now we must ourselves be responsible for this disclosure of the modern tra-
> dition. We bear the responsibility for this heritage, right along with the cap-
> italizing meaning that we have of it. We did not choose this responsibility,
> it imposes itself upon us, and in an even more imperative way, in that it is,
> as other, and from the other, the language of our language.[39]

The filiation is clear. Derrida is taking responsibility for responsibility as Husserl had originally laid it out, rethinking reactivation in terms of language rather than intuition, rethinking language in terms of the trace, chance, the proper name, signature, rather than in Heidegger's more poetized ontological way, and insisting on the original displacement wrought by the other. He conceives the other, beyond Levinas, as both the dimension of initial and permanent ruination of all presence, and as not confinable to the other man.[40] Being responsible for responsibility, reactivation—it is in such expressions that the importance for deconstruction of the phenomenological tradition in its broadest sense appears.

Responsibility, then, becomes a permanent capacity for reopening any and all of the complacencies into which we have fallen, every form of good conscience.[41] It means a deeply self-subversive willingness even to suspend the *epoché*, to lay ourselves open to the sufferings of others, to the pressures and exigencies of the world, without which, as Derrida put it once, a conference would just become "another one of those events where, in good company, one strings together a few talks or speeches on some general subject."[42] We cannot any longer be philosophers without being in-the-world, exposed to mortal concerns, concerns that displace the safeties and assurances of any managed context, attempting as best we can to respond to these concerns, not least in our thinking. My sense is that it is something like a deconstructive phenomenology that will best allow us to formulate and appropriate the risks and opportunities of that recursive possibility of exposure.[43] And in this way, phenomenology will live on.

EIGHT

Responsibility Reinscribed
(and How)

SINCE THE MID-1980s, much of Derrida's work has been devoted to thinking through the ethical dimension of deconstruction in terms of justice or, more frequently, responsibility.[1] Responsibility has been thought of as a responsiveness or openness to what does not admit of straightforward decision, to what exceeds conceptualization. If deconstruction *is* responsibility (or justice), the urgency of *this* moment can be found in particular topics, issues, and situations but also in the continuing response to the call of philosophy itself, reactivating perhaps a certain tradition of philosophy as responsibility. Not everyone will agree that the fate of philosophy and our own capacity for philosophizing is bound up with that of deconstruction. But the ethical and political dimension that responsibility Derrida gives to deconstruction answers at least those critics who have thought it alien to such concerns.

In the previous chapter, "Notes toward a Deconstructive Phenomenology," we outlined the emergence of the centrality of responsibility to phenomenology in its broadest sense through Husserl (responsibility as living and thinking within the possibilities of reactivation), through Heidegger (relocating that reactivation through responsiveness to language), and through Derrida (openness to an otherness that ruins all presence). We have described Derrida as "taking responsibility for responsibility." But if for Husserl the implication is that language must observe a certain fidelity to intuition, and for Heidegger that we must observe a certain fidelity to language, for Derrida the reinscription of responsibility bears all the difficulty of his own complex relation to language, and not just to language "as such" but to the language of philosophical inquiry. In particular this issue of responsibility raises its head in evaluating those moments when philosophers, in response to the urgency of the times, transpose their philosophical discourse into a political context. Potentially at least, there is a tension between the need for a "response," and the "ability" to respond (in a discourse whose parameters of significance may have been exceeded). Consider, for example, Heidegger's now-infamous "Rectoral Address." Our first dismay is at what he is saying, our second at his saying it. But perhaps the lingering worry is about his willingness to use for overtly political purposes a language supposedly honed for the project of reinterpreting the texts of the tradition. *The Other Heading* raises this same question about Derrida. When he writes, "[I]t is necessary to make ourselves the guardians of an idea of Europe . . ." it is not difficult to feel a certain astonishment. But what Derrida has done is to enter the realm of public discourse by converting the old principle of writing under erasure into an insistence on bringing to the surface the aporetic structure of central philosophical concepts. Instead of new words, or old words with displaced meanings, Derrida works to develop the contradictory implications of concepts central to the tradition. Responsibility is one of these concepts, and like "justice," it is privileged in being able to guide our very reception of it. When Derrida writes, "Now, we must ourselves be responsible for this discourse of the modern tradition," he is of course putting a weight on a word that is part of the modern tradition. When he writes, "[W]e bear the responsibility for this heritage," his words are inseparable from the tradition itself. Responsibility is obligation, burden, duty, etc. No words are forbidden, if ever they were. Indeed, if anything, Derrida is increasingly willing to draw the most traditional words within his embrace, because it is the disturbing embrace of ex-appropriation, of dislocation. For each word he chooses, deconstruction will be its undoing, and its restoration as a word with which to think. The word *responsibility* is a case in point; there could be no more potent entrance into ethical and political discourse.

Elsewhere, I discuss in this context some of the ambivalences surrounding Derrida's recognition of the limitations of both Levinas's and Heidegger's restriction of the Other to the human Other.[2] Here, I would like to pursue some of the categorial and methodological difficulties that surround Derrida's resurrection of responsibility.

In "Eating Well,"[3] Derrida tells us that "responsibility is excessive or it is not a responsibility."[4] In *The Gift of Death* he will draw the consequence that I can never justify the fact that special obligations (to my friends, my pets, my children) are not equally extended to all other beings.[5] I argue that this understanding of the implication of "excessive" is mistaken. Derrida successfully transforms responsibility from being an attribute of a subject to being an openness that makes being a subject possible. But the price of this achievement is the disabling of any quantitative characterizations of our responsibility. "Excessive," in other words, is a term that signals the need for a category shift. It inscribes at one level considerations that cannot be satisfactorily dealt with or recognized at that level.[6] I shall illustrate this structure of argument and the issues it raises by a brief excursus into early Heidegger reception.

In his inaugural address, "What is Metaphysics?" (1929)[7] Heidegger deploys the expression "Nothing" (*das Nichts*) as a way of pointing to a dimension of concern beyond that of "beings," one in which the English "no-thing" is arguably an improvement over the German. Wider appreciation of Heidegger got off to a mixed start with Ryle's review (1929) of *Being and Time*.[8] Ryle is full of praise for Heidegger, while fearing that his presuppositions will steer him onto the rocks. Twenty years later, having become famous for his Oxford lectures on "Austrian railway stations" (Bolzano, Brentano et al.), Ryle launched the concept of the "category mistake" in his *Concept of Mind* (1949).[9] The most immediate application of this phrase was to diagnose the error of dualism, of supposing that in addition to the Body, we need to posit a complementary entity, the "ghost in the machine"—the Mind. And it is not too difficult to see this book as a logically cleaned-up, and partial, transformation of *Being and Time*. Where Heidegger displaces substance altogether by talking about different modes of Being, and replaces what for phenomenologists is essential to the mental—intentionality—with Being-in-the-world, Ryle understands the mind as an illegitimate hypostatization of certain kinds of predicates—a category mistake.[10]

Carnap, in his essay "The Overcoming of Metaphysics through Logical Analysis of Language" (1931),[11] had accused Heidegger's 1929 discussion of Nothing of being full of "metaphysical pseudostatements" and being in "violation of logical syntax." "Nothing" is being treated, illicitly, as a thing. How else could Heidegger arrive at the folly of "Das Nichts nichtet" (Nothing noths)? Carnap's essay, however, raises serious questions of intellectual responsibility. For the whole point of Heidegger's essay is to elucidate the potential of the experience of "Nothing" for giving us access to the Being of beings. That Nothing is not a thing, but an experience giving us access to things *as such*—the central thesis of Heidegger's lecture—seems to have wholly escaped Carnap. It may perhaps have offended Carnap that Heidegger insists that there must be a higher court than logical consistency, that the sense of such logical operators as "not" must be more than merely formal. And PC Carnap's firing squad mentality, his righteous sense that there is a proper form of language for philosophy, rings hollow in the light of the well-rehearsed logical holes in positivism itself.

However, while Heidegger may be pushing for a certain derivativeness of formal logic, there is no mistaking the kind of weight he attaches to the distinction between Being and beings—the ontological difference. Heidegger writes, for example, that "[f]or human existence the nothing makes possible the openness of beings as such." For example, through anxiety, in which we come "face to face with the totality of beings as it slips away," we are lifted out of our everyday being alongside things in the world to being aware *that* there is a world, *that* our everyday engagement with it can become thematic, need not be taken for granted. The movement from being *alongside* things to being aware *that* there are things, and *that* there is a world, gets its force not from any repudiation of logic but from the way it grounds a logical distinction (say between a relation and a proposition) in an existential transformation, or, to put it in a less question-begging way, because of the way in which it allows us to see logic and experience as mutually informing. I may be listening to a lark singing without being aware of the bird *as* a lark, without being aware *that* the bird is a lark. That change of awareness counts as a qualitative transformation and not just (say) a modification of intensity, by embodying a logical/grammatical distinction. If we articulate this awareness, we end up with an assertion, a proposition, a claim, and it is no accident both that these have a distinct logical status (truth-bearers) and that they are human practices.

If Ryle felt that the development of phenomenology in Heidegger's hands courted disaster, it was, I suspect, because he did not share Heidegger's ambition, one inherited from Husserl, to ground formal categories in experiential ones. One obvious expression of this is Heidegger's substitution of the term *existentials* for many of those essential features of Dasein's Being that would otherwise have been called "categories."[12] Ryle continues to believe in the primacy of grammar.

How can we distinguish the position of the phenomenologist from that of the logician? The implication of the respective roles played, for example, by Husserl's sharp distinction between Fact and Essence[13] and by Heidegger's insistence on the distinction between Being and beings—the ontological difference—is that categorial distinctions[14] are both unavoidable and fundamental. This does not mean that what philosophers would like to be able to keep separate can in fact be so kept. Heidegger struggles mightily to sustain the ontological difference against the threat of an entanglement of levels. Categorial distinctions are not just claimed to be fundamental; such claims are fundamental to the distinctness and power of the thought in which they occur. And understanding and communicating the categorial status of claims being made is a central concern of philosophy.

Is there any principled explanation for the entanglement of levels? A clue may be provided by a strange phenomenon, one that may not be limited to philosophy, but seems at first blush characteristic of it—*the double inscription of key concepts*. In addition to Derrida's account of responsibility, I offer as examples the account given by Kant of causality, Nietzsche of truth, and Sartre of freedom. One way or another, all philosophers who aim at scope and depth[15] generate some version of the distinction between empirical and transcendental concepts, that is, between concepts already functioning pre-philosophically in everyday life, and concepts introduced or reworked by philosophy in order to ground, regulate, or account for the operation of those everyday concepts. It is perhaps hard to imagine philosophizing without something approaching technical concepts. And yet concepts that function at both levels are particularly powerful both for structural/ systematic reasons—where this double inscription seems to weld the levels together—and for making philosophical pronouncements on the wider stage, where the link between an empirical concept and some deeper level gives it a special power. Kant's account of causality functions in the first way, appearing both at the level of an empirical concept and also as the glue that conjoins the empirical and the transcendental. Indeed, without transcendental causation the whole structure would collapse. Nietzsche's account of truth rubs our nose in this double inscription. "Truth," he says, "is a lie." He appeals to a more sophisticated account of truth (and its opposite) in denouncing our ordinary understanding and/or valuation of truth. And yet, of course, he draws on our pre-philosophical attachment to the value of truth in condemning it as a lie. We approach Derrida's discussion of responsibility even more closely with Sartre's discussion of freedom.[16] Sartre claims that "[m]an . . . is wholly and forever free or he is not free at all"[17]—a remark remarkably similar to Derrida's claim about the excessive nature of responsibility—and elsewhere Sartre writes not that man is free but that "man is freedom." These two hyperbolic claims about freedom come to the same thing. To say that we are "wholly and forever" free is not to deny the existence of prisons or paralysis but to try to connect the way we think about empirical freedom with a deeper claim about what it is to be human. And to say that "man is freedom" is to emphasize that freedom is not simply a property of human beings ("man is free") but a fundamental and essentially illuminating condition. To shift our sense of freedom from being a property to being a fundamental condition is to propose a change in the categorial status of "freedom." And yet, just as Nietzsche does with truth, he draws on the value we already attach to freedom in its everyday sense to infuse this "transcendental" claim with significance. A critical response to Sartre would be to say that this deep phenomenon to which he is alluding—sometimes described in terms of negation, or the power to nihilate—is not freedom, but the (or a central) condition for freedom. His reply would be that we do not understand (empirical) freedom adequately unless we understand what its various instances share. What they share is not merely some common structural feature or quality, but a characteristic infusion with consciousness.

The immediate consequence of this move is to destabilize our habitual capacity to distinguish between everyday cases of freedom and its opposite. And the consequence of that destabilization is to open us up to probing questions to do with self-evaluation and self-understanding, questions that Sartre himself often puts in terms of responsibility. Nietzsche described Christianity as "a hangman's metaphysics." (It was in a rather different sense that Marcuse said that for Sartre man was free even at the hands of the executioner!) The same logic applies to Sartre. The hyperbole of freedom leads to a hyperbole of responsibility. We become responsible, accountable if only to ourselves, for choices we never even knew we had made, as if the logician's definition of freedom—that we could have done otherwise—had taken root in the soul. It is this double inscription of freedom, freedom as practical and as ontological, that gives rise to the sense that Sartre's is a philosophy of freedom. The danger of course is that the link between ontological freedom and those values and concerns we ordinarily associate with freedom might become weakened or severed. We might then agree that Sartre had successfully begun to describe the conditions for freedom, but that much more needed to be said even to complete that level of description. He himself makes just such a move in his *Critique of Dialectical Reason* (1960). In the meantime, there is no doubt that Sartre had achieved the goal of disturbing our complacency about the limits of our responsibility ("We are all responsible for the war"). The haunting possibility of bad faith that serves as the instrument of (self-) critical vigilance rests on the double inscription of freedom, on a certain mobility back and forth from its ontological to its existential significance.

Early in *Of Grammatology* (1967) Derrida declares as his main goal that of *faire trembler* (disturbing, shaking up) the value of presence. If I am right, the function of remarks of the sort we have quoted from Sartre and Derrida in which an absolute claim is made about an apparently empirical concept, is to insist on a change in the categorial status for the concept in question. It is comparable to putting your foot hard down on the accelerator, which in a car with automatic transmission will effect a change to a lower gear. In the case of "There never was any 'perception,'"[18] what looks like a strong empirical claim is, of course, a claim about the illegitimacy of "perception" functioning as a philosopheme, of our supposing that there could be experience not already entangled with language and with judgment.

In his "Afterword: Toward an Ethics of Discussion" (in *Limited Inc*)[19] Derrida elucidatingly reformulates his "notorious" claim *"Il n'y a pas de hors-texte"* as the claim that "there is nothing outside context," adding that "[this] formula would doubtless have been less shocking, but [would not] have provided more to think about." There are those who think that these claims are not synonymous, but they do share the same property we have diagnosed. They serve not to tell us some general inductively arrived at truth about what there is, but to announce, and to proclaim the legitimacy of a theory of meaning and truth, and a corollary "method" of interpreting philosophical (and other) texts. Derrida's claim that responsibility is excessive or not a responsibility sounds like a claim about the scope of (my) responsibility. I suggest that it is the claim "that responsibility is excessive or not a responsibility" that is excessive. It does have an important category-shifting significance of the sort that we have already diagnosed, but Derrida is led astray by Levinas in thinking that I have very large actual responsibilities, perhaps so large as to be unfulfillable. This claim is the consequence of taking too literally a productive "category mistake," properly and successfully deployed in other ways.

Levinas's philosophy works on the double inscription of the ethical. What is called the "ethics" of the face-to-face relation is strictly speaking not ethics at all, but a proto-ethics.[20] And proto-ethics is not a kind of ethics, but rather the laying out, opening up, of a dimension of relatedness that makes the ethical possible. That Levinas falls foul of this confusion appears in his interview "The Paradox of Morality"[21] when he says that "when we sit down at the table in the morning and drink coffee, we kill an Ethiopian who doesn't have any coffee."[22] This is meant to elucidate the breadth of scope of "Thou shalt not kill." But it is not just false, but incoherent. Which Ethiopian do I thereby kill? Would it really be morally equivalent to kill an Ethiopian and forego the coffee? And why an Ethiopian rather than some other starving child? If I cannot determine which one, do I kill everyone who doesn't have any coffee? What has having coffee got to do with the matter? If an Ethiopian has harvested it for export, might it not be the wages from that activity that keep him alive, not the coffee? These are not the questions of a heartless soul. What is at issue here is recovering the insight from under the incoherent exaggeration, recovering what I might call the modal propriety of the claim. Often, but not always, when I do something for my own benefit, I could instead be doing something that would benefit someone else more needy than I. But it is ethical incontinence to suppose that what follows from this is that I always should so act. That would involve me in the same kind of distance from the care of my self, a neutralizing abstraction from my own situatedness, that characterizes certain kinds of hysterical utilitarianism. Levinas is confusing the fact that there are no a priori limits to my ethical exposure to the other, the powerful grain of truth here, with the claim of infinite obligation or responsibility, one which would convert my drinking a coffee into an act of indiscriminate murder.

There are other important claims being advanced here implicitly—for which there is a modally correct and a hopelessly overblown interpretation. Compare for example: (1) a failure to prevent a wrong (e.g., save a life) is indistinguishable from committing that wrong (e.g., murder), with (2) *there are circumstances in which* a failure to prevent a wrong *may be* indistinguishable from committing that wrong. The first formulation must be flawed for reasons of quantification. If ten children are drowning in front of me, I cannot be said to have murdered the ones I am unable to save, even though, had I abandoned others, I could have saved them. My claim that "there are no a priori limits to my exposure to the other" does not mean that I cannot justify my morning coffee. There may be no absolute justifications, but whoever thought justification required absolutes?

An account of my "exposure" to the other is proto-ethics, an account of how the ethical comes into being. It is, consequently, no accident that "Eating Well," in which Derrida's discusses responsibility extensively, is subtitled ". . . or the Calculation of the Subject." Derrida's category-shifting argument is designed to show that we think of responsibility too late if we think of it as the property of a "subject." Subjects are already lost to calculation (values, rights, determinable responsibilities). That is how the concept of "subject" functions. But such an account cannot enjoin particular responses; it rather points to the space of my response-ability. In Levinas's writing, killing is doubly inscribed, meaning both the taking of life and any violence to the other that repudiates or blocks my response to his needs, or deafens me to his or her call. But "the other" cannot mean "all others" in some additive, or even distributive sense, such that I have impossible-to-fulfill obligations to every other person[23] in the cosmos. Which is why Derrida's allusions to "my obligations to the other others whom I don't know, the billions of my fellows (. . . and animals)"[24] seem to me misplaced. I am not a divine being, or even a health-care organization, but a mortal humbly drinking a cup of coffee, aware of the fragility of every sense I might have of "what my situation is" or "what my responsibilities are." But equally aware that to respond or act at all I cannot cease to be finite, situated, to have my own needs and limitations, etc. Double inscription is both powerful and dangerous. There is real dramatic intensification when we think of drinking coffee as killing. But it would be a terrible mistake to think of killing someone as comparable to drinking a cup of coffee. It is true that the potential for active and passive violence in our everyday life is real enough, and easily lost sight of. What is not true is that finding my place in the sun *need* block the light from anyone else. Levinas is somewhat recklessly universalizing zero-sum models. It could be said that the Ethiopian reference reminds us of the implications of global capitalism for broadening our sense of the context of significance of our actions. To buy an ivory pendant, knowing what we know, is (surely) to support elephant poaching. It is more true than ever that no man is an island. But there are notoriously many principled options here, and it is not clear whether being a careful, ethically informed consumer is not more of a recipe for a beautiful soul than a practical contribution to social transformation. Inconclusive arguments about boycotting the products of exploitative labor conditions show us precisely why our exposure to the other is not some huge, excessive obligation, but rather a complex openness to requests, demands, pleas that call not just for an acknowledgment of my obligations, but for scrutiny, for negotiation, for interpretation, and, ultimately, for recognizing both opportunities and limitations.

In conclusion, I would like to put a little pressure on the assumptions with which I have been operating. My sympathetic allusions to Ryle's idea of a "category mistake," a concept that one could almost as easily draw from Kant's distinction between the empirical and the transcendental, rest on the utility, perhaps unavoidability, of recognizing that key philosophical claims are always of a categorial nature, or something closely analogous. This caveat is meant to include claims about the *limits* of categorial or conceptual thought, such as that couched by Derrida in terms of an opposition between the excessive and the calculable. It is hard to imagine continuing to think without taking for granted, most of the time, that working distinctions between different levels and different categories can actually be sustained. It is not clear, however, whether the idea of double inscription presupposes this or flouts it. Double inscription occurs when key concepts function at two distinct levels for structural/systematic purposes.[25] That we frequently come across this structure in the most powerful philosophical writings does not, however, make it unproblematic. And I have tried in Derrida's case to separate out responsibility as a kind of constitutive openness to the other, and any attempt to dramatize the supposed resultant scope and scale of our obligations to others. There are, however, reasons to think that distinctions between levels are quite as imperfect as they are necessary. We may oppose appearance to reality as two different levels, and yet we know that appearances are part of the real. We oppose ordinary language to philosophical language and yet we know that the sense of the latter would dry up unless it was continually fed by the former. Following Heidegger, we oppose the ontic to the ontological, and yet this distinction is sustained by a being whose (ontic) condition is to be ontological—Dasein. The structure that best illustrates this combination of opposition and continuity is the Moebius strip—at every point two radically discrete sides, but only one surface. Would taking this lesson to heart teach us anything about responsibility?

Derrida contrasts responsibility as calculable with responsibility as excessive. The way he elaborates on the excessive (references to the billions of my fellows, etc.) suggest an ill-advised quantitative interpretation, one that nonetheless rightly explodes any deal by which I have given myself a good conscience.[26] This quantitative interpretation allows Derrida to avoid the charge that Hegel laid at Kant's ethics, of being merely formal. But there are two better ways of thinking of the interpenetration of responsibility as openness to the other, and such specific responsibilities as I may acknowledge. The first I have already adumbrated: My *exposure* to the other means that there are no a priori limits to my responsibilities. But there are limits; I cannot save all the drowning children. The second way of grasping the interconnectedness of these two levels is no less significant here for having a broader application. Responsibility as openness to the other can function adverbially as a modal operator in *the way we deal with and understand* such finite responsibilities as we do take on:[27] willingly accepting consequential or corollary responsibilities, and acknowledging responsibilities we would never have chosen.

Finally, however, the ultimate reworking of the sense of responsibility is to say that philosophy is itself responsibility (cf. "deconstruction *is* justice").[28] The fact that philosophy is a response (to pain, to dis-ease, to wonder, to anxiety, to confusion) is a truth it is particularly important not to lose sight of. Responsibility is a certain kind of attentiveness and fidelity of response.

Importantly, it suggests a displacement of the primacy of the subject and the will, that philosophy is quite as much grounded in what befalls us, in our situatedness, our exposure, as in our powers of positing. And one way of understanding the opposition between responsibility as calculation and as excess is to think of excess as a kind of unlimited recursivity, or movement between our concepts and the experiences to which they are tied, a movement akin to what Merleau-Ponty called hyper-reflection.[29] If philosophy as responsibility is the willingness to live in, to endure the uncertainties and aporias that accompany our capacity for conceptualization, we might come to think that Keats put it quite well when he coined the phrase "negative capability."

NINE

What Is Ecophenomenology?

THE NEED FOR A RAPPROCHEMENT WITH NATURALISM

PHENOMENOLOGY WAS BORN out of resistance to the threat of naturalism. But if phenomenology is to be able to think about Nature, it must either rescue Nature itself from naturalism, or work out a new relationship to what it had perceived as the danger of naturalism. Or both.

The resistance to naturalism is a principled resistance, in various senses. If naturalism means that phenomena are fundamentally governed by causal laws, with the possible addition of functional explanations, and relations of succession, conjunction, and concatenation, resistance takes the form of limiting the scope of such phenomena, or showing that even in those domains in which naturalism might seem wholly appropriate—the realm of what is obviously Nature—naturalism is fatally flawed as a standpoint.

For example, to the extent that perception brings us into intimate relation with the manifold things of this world, and definitively breaks through any sense of phenomenology as an otherworldly idealism, it also becomes clear that phenomenology and naturalism could not simply agree to a territorial division. A phenomenology of perception quickly discovers that it is only as spatially and temporally embodied subjects that seeing takes place. Through seeing (and hearing and touching) we differentiate the world into discrete bodies, including ourselves, bodies that occupy distinct places at particular times, and in the case of animate bodies, they are bodies endowed with a mobility that reflects their needs and desires. These are not just natural facts about the world, but fundamental dimensions of the world, dimensions that structure the very possibility of factuality. And bodies certainly structure perception, insofar as perception is essentially perspectival, bound to surfaces of visibility, limited by obstruction, and tied powerfully to our embodiment—our typically having two eyes, two ears, two hands, and muscles that allow us to move in various dimensions. And that embodiment appears in more complex ways, in our having various somatic and social desires that shape and direct perception, and in the temporal syntheses in which it is engaged. Many of these structures of bodily finitude are invariant for any living creature, and could be said to *constitute* perception, rather than qualify it. If something like this is true, a certain phenomenology, at least, is both inseparable from our involvement in the world as natural beings, and points to aspects of that involvement that do not seem to be captured by naturalism. Does this mean that we have managed to carve out a space for phenomenology within nature, reinforcing the divorce of intentionality from causality? The key to our position here is that there are dimensions essential to perception that reflect non-accidental aspects of our natural existence. This means that intentionality is *structured*, in a way that *fills out* what is specific about perceptual consciousness, rather than interrupting or contesting the intentional stance. But does this structuration reinforce the distinctness of intentionality (from naturalism) or does it offer a bridge across which a certain conversation could begin?

One might suppose that what phenomenology points to fundamentally is another level of causality, one that is presupposed by the operative causality of everyday phenomena. That other level would be describable through an evolutionary naturalism, one that would explain, for example, how living creatures have acquired the functionally integrated and environmentally responsive bodies that they do indeed possess, and perhaps explain how it is that complex individual living beings developed in the first place, for example, through the incorporation into a single "body" of what began as a group of simpler symbiotically related organisms.[1] Would such an account of a deep causality make phenomenology redundant, or would it actually facilitate an engagement between phenomenology and naturalism?

It may not strictly be required by my project of a certain reconciliation between naturalism and phenomenology, but it would be fair to say that I am operating here with a certain residual realism, one that resists the idea both that it is pretty much up to "us" how we organize the world, and that even what we take the boundaries of the self to be is somewhat arbitrary. While I am as ready as anyone—and more than most—to acknowledge instabilities, the other in the same, difference lurking in the heart of identity, I am unable to let go of the unifying power of the organism even as it contains and balances my competing drives and is vulnerable to the malfunctioning of its cells. The privilege of the organism in thinking identity (notwithstanding Deleuze), is, curiously, not in the fantasies of integration that it offers us, but the drama of the ongoing struggle for unity.

If ecophenomenology can give us better access to nature than that represented by the naturalism that phenomenology was created to resist, by supplementing intentionality structurally with non- or pre-intentional characteristics of nature, would not ecophenomenology be the future of a phenomenology, one that has purged itself of its traumatic gestation in opposition to nature?

Phenomenology could be said to concern itself with what appears in its appearing. But what is at stake here? What is at stake is a recovery of a relation to "things themselves,"[2] one that is covered over by all manner of objectifying illusions—of habit, reflection, naturalism, commodification—whose shared *modus operandi* is the occlusion of the activity of time in an apparently always-already-achieved presence.

Phenomenology opposes itself, then, to a certain kind of naive naturalism, and to a broader sense of the natural through which the products of human engagement lose any trace of that production. But to recover an engagement with the *sache selbst* is not at all to return to some pure presence, it is rather to return to a world in which the relation between present experience and the complexity of what is being experienced has always been deeply complex and stratified. Ecophenomenology is the pursuit of the relationalities of worldly engagement, both human and those of other creatures.[3]

By focusing now on two rich dimensions of such engagement, I would like to develop a sense of a middle ground of relationality, a space neither governed by simple causality, nor by simple intentionality, and suggest that in this space phenomenology can recover from the trauma of its birth in opposition to naturalism. These two dimensions we could call the plexity[4] of time and the boundaries of thinghood.

THE PLEXITY OF TIME

Even though the value of presence has often occluded what is at stake, rather than helped us explore it, it has properly drawn our attention to the centrality of time to experience.[5] While time is central to my sense of phenomenology as essentially oriented to relationality, our experience of time, and the temporality of our experience, can function both as an obstacle to this orientation and also as its central plank. If we think of time as a series of discrete presents, or simply "live in the present," relational complexity is dead. And yet, there is no richer dimension of relationality than time. On the basis of our experience of time and the temporality of our experience, we grasp the continuous identities of things, the coordination of their processual and pulsing rhythms, and many virtual and imaginative ways in which even in the instant we enter a connectedness that transcends the moment. And every form of connection is put into play and contested by the powers of interruption, interference, and breakdown. Phenomenology is indeed descriptive in the sense of trying to get clear about the structures of these relations and disruptions, but, heedless of Hegel's warning, such descriptions are also edifying, in alerting us to the illusions of immediacy, and in showing us how deep temporal complexity is articulated, and how it changes the way we see. For the moment, we can distinguish four strands of the plexity of time: the invisibility of time, the celebration of finitude, the coordination of rhythms, and the interruption and breakdown of temporal horizons.

TIME AS INVISIBLE

It is a commonplace to identify the eternal with the unchanging, and time with change, which would put time and eternity at odds with each other. A clue to how misleading this is can be found in the relation between the visible and the invisible. We typically think of the relation between the visible and the invisible in, broadly speaking, spatial terms. The invisible is either hidden by the visible, or occupies some other ethereal realm. But if by the invisible we mean what does not give itself to a certain kind of immediacy then we may find the invisible curiously closer to hand than we thought. If, for example, the invisible is to be contrasted with a sense of visibility to which the mere illuminated availability of the thing in front of us is sufficient, then we may find the invisible to be a clue not just to a secret or hidden realm, but to a more subtle grasp of visibility itself.[6] And for this, we need to move not to another deeper or more rarefied space, but to time.

Suppose I look out the window—what do I see? A tree. There it is. It is there in front of me, as visible as I could want. But what do I see when I see a tree, what does seeing it consist in? If I were an ant climbing up the tree, in some sense I would be able to "see" the tree. We might argue about whether the ant can really see the tree if it can only see a part of the tree at any one time or if it does not know what a tree "is." It is clear that what "we" call seeing can be compromised, or at least questioned, by certain kinds of conceptual or perspectival "limitations." If this is so, then seeing a tree cannot just consist in its being there, in the light, and my having my eyes open. ("Intuitions without concepts are blind," as Kant put it.)[7] But there is a less obvious dimension in which seeing is compromised—that of time. We know that we cannot "hear" music at an instant, but that hearing requires participation in a certain temporality. We have to undergo an experience in time. It does not take long to hear "that there is music playing in the house," but to hear the music "as such," to hear what is being played, to hear the piece itself— these each require our temporal engagement. Now, of course it is possible that from only three bars I can immediately identify the piece, even have an image of the score flash into mind. If this happens, I will have come to recognize the true temporal extendedness of the object in a snatch, or glimpse. The moment will capture something importantly nonmomentary. In this, and in many cases where there is in fact no score to be found, the temporal pattern recognized in the moment is one that is essentially repeatable, however distinctive this particular occasion may be. By analogy, I am suggesting that the life of the tree, the living tree, the tree of which we glimpse only a limb here, a trunk there, or views from various angles, this temporally extended persisting, growing tree, is invisible. Sometimes we try to capture this extended visibility with the word *watch*, as in "last night I watched the match." In watching there is the suggestion of a certain synthetic activity that addresses significantly extended features in the object. Even there, we seem to run against the grain when we try to think of something that essentially unfolds in time as "visible." Something that merely perdures is visible because time does not operate as a dimension of essential unfolding or articulation. So one moment can easily represent any other. But something that grows, develops, transforms itself cannot as easily represent that aspect of itself in any one moment. Think of those photographs of sporting victory that capture the "moment" of accomplishment. The raised arms, the open mouth, the wild eyes mark the moment at which a certain significance has arisen in the course of events.[8] The sign here, the mark of significant accomplishment, transition, or depth, precisely attempts to mark the relation between one particular moment and the temporal horizon of its significance. The sign renders the invisible visible. But it also renders the invisible *as such* invisible, precisely by providing a substitute for it. It is here, for example, that we find the paradoxical success of narrative.

There is an invisible in the heart of the visible to the extent that the essential temporal articulatedness of things is not itself obviously presented in their immediate temporary appearance. And if, furthermore, the eventuating ground of things is not itself present, visible, available to us, whether we think of this as an eruptive event (Heidegger), or the product of a contingent conjunction of forces (Foucault). It may, or may not, have ever once been visible. The question here is what can be seen, and this does not admit of a general answer. There are many ways in which "They have eyes but they can not see . . ."

What phenomenology does is to activate and reactivate the complex articulations and relations of things, restoring through description, through dramatization, a participatory engagement (bodily, imaginative, etc.) with things. A turn to the articulatedness of things, and to their eventuating groundedness, is a return to the conditions of human fulfillment, and connectedness, but also to the sources of renewal, transformation, and resistance.

The Celebration of Finitude

The fact that time resides as the invisible in the visible opens us to a transformed relation to time. To show this, it would be hard to improve on remarks made in the course of Leishman's commentary on the first of Rilke's *Duino Elegies:*

> The ideal of complete and undivided consciousness, where will and capability, thought and action, vision and realization are one, is the highest Man can form, and yet so impossible is it for Man to realize this ideal, to become like the Angels, that it is rather a rebuke than an inspiration. What, then, remains for Man? Perhaps, in Pater's phrase, to give the highest possible significance to his moments as they pass; to be continually prepared for those

moments when eternity is perceived behind the flux of time, those moments when "the light of sense/ goes out, but with a flash that has revealed/ the invisible world."[9]

It may seem strange that I would give a platform to what sounds like neo-Platonism. But for us humans the consequence of the impossibility of the angelic is the transformation of the most ordinary, whether we see this as an opportunity, or as Leishman does, as an obligation: "[T]he price of these moments of insight is a constant attentiveness and loyalty to all things and relationships, even the humblest and least spectacular, that immediately surround us."[10]

This sense of the infinite in the finite, which is precisely not a spiritual dilution but an intensification of the concrete, can take a number of forms. Repetition, and the awareness of repetition, can be taken to the extreme of intensity that we find in Nietzsche's eternal recurrence. Here, connectedness between individual events generates a kind of depth to every moment through which its very singularity is heightened. The intensity of the loving gaze, or the kiss (see above), is essentially connected with the suspicion of the merely sequential passage of time, and the capacity to dwell in a presence amplified by retention and anticipation. Finally, we can come to experience the passage of time as such a constancy that time itself becomes the best candidate for the permanent, what does not change.

If I am right, these various approaches to the infinite in the finite involve a kind of prerepresentational part/whole relation in which the parts are seen to bear within themselves the imprint of the whole, not as burden, but as an intensification. Such a relation captures the kind of complexity with which ecophenomenology would treat time.

Coordination of Rhythms

To the extent that things bear and embody rhythms, pulses of temporal development, they form part of a manifold and stratified field in which these rhythms interact, interpenetrate, interfere with one another, become locally coordinated, and so on. Fireflies come to flash synchronously at the end of an evening, while cicadas carefully space (or time) the periodicities of their emergence from hibernation so as not to overlap and compete. The point here is that through rhythm and periodicity time acquires sufficient autonomous efficacy to generate its own relational differentiation. This example illustrates well the significance of a middle ground. For the coordination of rhythms does not appear here as the result of the synthetic or constitutive activity of any kind of subject, nor any simple causal mechanism. Clearly, there are evolutionary processes behind cicada periodicity. And competitive advantage is doubtless tied up with causal mechanisms such as the effect of lack of food on survival rates. What is salient here is that such mechanisms seem to be subservient to the advantages accruing from the eventual rhythmic coordination and differentiation

THE INTERRUPTION AND BREAKDOWN OF TEMPORAL HORIZONS

Lastly, while these first three aspects of temporality build on, if they do not simply respect, the horizonalities of time within which things live, move, and have their being, time is, importantly, not just about grasping the invisible continuities lurking below the surface of the visible. It is equally about interruption, breakdown, discontinuity—about the arrival of the unexpected, about the unintended consequence, about the ghosts from another time that still haunt us, about *Nachträglichkeit*, about blindness about the past, about the failure to move forward, about dreaming of impossible futures, etc. And it is especially in its pursuit of this last of these four aspects of time that ecophenomenology preserves us against a premature holism, an overenthusiastic drive to integration. The multiply fractured wholes with which we are acquainted include within them many perfectly completed developments, many acorns that turn into oak trees, and many images, desires, and fantasies of wholeness. Anything, taken singly, can be broken or unexpected or fractured. But not everything can suffer this fate. *We need a model of the whole as something that will inevitably escape our model of it.* Indeed, it could be said that when it comes to nature, time as physis, as eruptive event, escapes representation long before it is party to expectations that are not met. It escapes representation by being its presupposition. While I have focused on what we could call temporal relatedness and its breakdowns, it is quite true that there is a kind of primary invisibility in the very upthrust of time as event.

These four strands—the invisibility of time, the celebration of finitude, the coordination of rhythms, and the interruption and breakdown of temporal horizons—offer us, I am suggesting, not just analytical pointers as to how we might think about time, but ways of enriching our temporal experience. This account occupies what I have called a middle ground overlapping the space of intentionality, avoiding both the language of causality and that of ecstatic intentionality. While an ecophenomenology could profitably pursue the theoretical elaborations each of them would make explicit, I will not do this here. The fundamental focus of these remarks has been on their contribution to an enhanced attentiveness to the complexity of natural phenomena, and the ease with which that is hidden from view by our ordinary experience.[11]

THE BOUNDARIES OF THINGHOOD

It is possible to imagine a world without things, or at least a cosmos of gaseous swirlings and passing clouds. It may be that what we imagine is not possible, that for there to be swirlings, there have to be the cosmic equivalents of coffee cups or bathtubs to contain the swirlings. Nonetheless, we seem to be able to imagine a thingless world. But it is not our world. We could of course imagine a viewpoint on our world in which what we now experience as things would be so speeded up that these things would appear as processes. Extinct volcanoes would be momentary pauses of an ongoing activity, as when a swimmer turns round at the end of the pool. Individual animate organisms would be seen as part of a wider flux of chemical exchanges. Things as we know them would disappear. And as this speeding up would enable us to see things, to make connections, that were not previously available, who is to say that it would be a distortion? Do we have any basis for saying that seeing things at this or that speed is more accurate? Well, perhaps we do. If we imagine everything so speeded up that it happened in an instant, it would be impossible to make distinctions at all. It is hard not to see that as an information-deficient environment. And at the opposite extreme, we can imagine such a slow perspective that rivers did not detectably flow, and rays of light seemed to linger forever in the sun's starting blocks. Such perspectives would be distorting because the phenomena of relative change and relative stability would not be available. And as these imaginative experiments are conducted with the memory of such a distinction being indispensable, it is hard not to see these other extreme views as deeply deficient. It might be said that the very slow view really does teach us something deep—that nothing really changes. But that is much less deep a conclusion from a world in which change is not apparent anyway, than from a world of which we might say that *plus ça change, plus c'est la même chose*. All this is to encourage us to suppose that not only would it be difficult for us to make sense of a world of total flux, but that if such a view were to rest on the idea that the temporal frame from which things are viewed is entirely up to us, the flux view is simply a mistake. To make this point the other way round—on the total flux view, there would be nothing very special about May 18, 1980, the day on which Mount St. Helens erupted, compared to the day before, or the day after. On the "ordinary" view—which we are defending, there really are events as well as processes, births, deaths, and catastrophes, as well as continuities. And these concepts are of an ontological order, not just epistemological. That does not mean that we may fail to notice them, or to care much. When we crush cicadas under our feet, we may not register the crunch, and if we do, we may think of it as part of a wider "process" in which only a small percentage of these creatures survive to maturity. But we do know, and most, if pressed, would acknowledge, that there are individual cicadas, and that crushing them ends their lives, even as it allows that cicada's body to reenter the food cycle by providing nutrients for nematodes.[12]

So, things may come and go. But for them to come and go, they have to be real while they are here, or else they could neither come nor go. Buses come and go, but it would be a strange passenger that refused to get on the bus on the grounds that "buses come and go." Or even more deeply, that this bus will eventually be scrapped. The mechanic working on the bus knows that although the parts will eventually wear out, the connection between the parts is real enough that if one part fails, the bus may not run, and if it is replaced, it will. The surgeon knows the same about his patient. And the poet knows the same about the word she ponders. If she gets that word right, the poem will fly.

Permanence, then, is no test for reality, and many ways in which we think about internal complexity, the part/whole relation, and functional integrity would be impossible unless we admitted the existence of things. It could be replied that these considerations are no less fictional than the original belief in things, and that, of course, once we make one error, others will follow. Of course I do not *really* doubt the existence of things, or worry that you need this demonstrated. Nonetheless, good stuff happens when we try to explain why we take *things* seriously. References to mechanics, surgeons, and poets are to people concerned with maintaining, or creating, complex things, things that can break, or break down, or falter, or fail to be realized. Here we have distinguished between machines, organisms, and works of art. Mount St. Helens was a very large lump of rock held together by intermolecular forces and by gravity (and torn apart by pressure from molten magma). A rock is not a machine or an organism. But even a rock has a certain organized integrity. David did not throw sand in Goliath's eyes; he threw a rock at his forehead. And the rock arrived at his forehead all at the same time, causing serious damage to the skull's capacity to protect the brain, bringing about the collapse of the whole Goliath.

It might be said that nothing of much importance could be true of all these things, from giants to mountains, from buses to poems. Perhaps the differences between them will turn out to be even more interesting, but the point of identifying them all as *things* is to draw attention to something they share, which I have called organized integrity.[13] Obviously, this comes in many shapes. Rock composed by aggregation has a less "organized" integrity than rock that, under compression, has formed a large crystal, where the parts have come together in a way that reflects a pattern of organization (as in a snowflake). And to capture the kind of integrity we find in living organisms, we need to speak of self-organization and (dynamically) of growth, self-maintenance, self-protection, and reproduction. Between rocks and rockfish, there are of course many other kinds of organized complexity—such as machines, stock markets, weather systems, and plants. My point in offering here a reprise of the great chain of being is to bring to the fore the idea that things, and the organized integrity that they manifest, come in many forms. And that their unity depends, typically, on the relationships between their parts. Now, this relationship may be as sensitive to disruption as you like, or as resistant to disruption. A watch mechanism is given a case to keep out dirt that would disrupt its workings in a split second. Gyroscopically driven mechanical systems have the power to maintain their balance in the face of external agitation. What we commonly take to be typical of living systems, however, and some other animal collectivities and human creations, is that they each actively maintain some boundary with what lies "outside" them. Such boundaries are, in part, the products of the very processes that maintain them. Boundaries are the waystations between insides and outsides, the sites of negotiation, of transformation, of sustenance, and of protection. Boundaries are real, and yet they are often recessive and ambiguous. Boundaries are not at first things, but they arise in and for certain things, and they may even turn into things. (Think of the Berlin Wall, think of the line we must not cross in a relationship.) But for our purposes, what is especially important is that boundaries are the sites of a special kind of phenomena—limina—and a whole new opening for phenomenology.[14]

We have arrived at this point, the threshold of a new/old continent, by highlighting the reality of things, over against continuous flux, and their possession of a certain organized integrity. We moved on to claim that it is an initially distinctive feature of living things that they maintain this integrity by creating boundaries, which are sites of management of inside-outside relations. This story we are telling is not a biological story. Indeed, to repeat some of the Husserlian hubris, it is engaged in what I would call tentative legislation for any subsequent science. The hubris derives from the thought that there are categories and concepts importantly at work in any science that are not its distinctive property, but also that sciences themselves operate as boundary-generating systems. If so, individual sciences are not in the best position to talk about science as such. At least part of the role traditionally played by metaphysics[15] is here played by ecophenomenology's concern with the fabric of time and with the events that occur at boundaries—phenomena that are not the proper purview of any one science. Such a liminology would deal not only with the maintenance of boundaries within individual organisms, but the ways in which the shape and location of boundaries is transformed during growth, adaptation, and the struggle to survive. It would deal with how the breaching of these boundaries is coordinated in the interest of higher groupings (families, organizations, sex, war), with symbiotic and productive relations of dependency between species, and with the psychic formations necessary both for the maintenance, mobilization, and transformation of such boundaries. All this is not the subject matter of one science, but thinking through these liminological events is something that an ecophenomenology could protect and encourage.

What would liminology concern itself with? The imperative of boundary maintenance leads to such phenomena as dependency, cooperation, symbiosis, and synergy. But also rupture, catastrophe, and transformation. All of these are, in an important sense, natural phenomena, phenomena that appear at many different levels in nature. But equally, they also suggest something of a concrete logic for nature. And not just what we usually include in "nature."

BETWEEN INTENTIONALITY AND CAUSALITY

The shape of the gap between naturalism and phenomenology depends on how one thinks of nature. The fundamental principle of phenomenology, that of intentionality, specifically names consciousness as the central actor: "All consciousness is consciousness of something." This is not just a claim about consciousness, but a claim about the kind of relation that consciousness brings into being, which we could call a nonnatural relation. I may be an embodied being, and the object of my awareness may be a tiger or a mountain. But the relation between us—seeing, fearing, hoping, admiring—is not a causal relation, nor a physical relation, but an intentional one. When I admire the mountain, the mountain is not affected, and even if rays of light passing from the mountain to me are necessary for this admiration to take place, the admiration is something of a different order. I may be dreaming, say, of an imaginary golden mountain, making a causal account of the relation even harder to sustain. And yet the absence of proximate cause does not refute causality. Think of finding a giant rock halfway down a valley. Or seashells in a farmer's field. If we associate causality with determinacy, with linearity, and with a certain kind of automatism it is important to understand intentionality as opposed to causality. But if the realm of causality were to be expanded in a way that overcomes these prejudices, what then?

One obvious way of beginning to bridge the gap between intentionality and causality would be to introduce the idea of information. When I admire the mountain from my window, I add nothing to it, and take nothing away. My relation to the mountain may develop—I may decide to climb it. It might kill me through exposure or avalanche. But here at the window, causality is at a minimum. What I receive is information about the mountain, directly from the mountain, in a way directly caused by the actual shape of the mountain. But I receive this as an information processor, not as an impact of matter on matter. Does this help us to naturalize intentionality? Only a little. When a boot makes an imprint on soft ground, we may say that there is a direct causal dimension—the squishing of clay—but there is an informational dimension, reflected in the precise shape of the imprint. And yet information can be registered, without it "registering" with the clay. What then is distinctive about human consciousness? The sight of the mountain is information "for" me. Whereas we would say that the imprint of the boot is not information "for" the clay. Two kinds of reasons could be given here. First, that the clay has no brain, no capacity for symbolic decoding, not even a nervous system. We are tempted, then, to say that because the clay cannot think, cannot reflectively process information, that even if there is something more than mere causality operating, it does not add up, say, to the impact of a footprint on a Robinson Crusoe.[16] And secondly, the clay has no interests, no relation to the world such that what happens out there could matter to it.

This second deficiency, the absence of what Ricoeur would call an intentional arc, does not reduce intentionality to causality, but if we accept that this connection to practical agency is central to intentional meaning, it does locate intentionality within an interactive nexus from which causal powers cannot be separated. If I "see" a fruit as succulently delicious, this is intrinsically connected, however many times removed, with my enjoyment of fruit, my capacity to eat, etc. The fact that I am now allergic to fruit, or that I cannot afford this particular item of fruit, is neither here nor there. The point is that I am the kind of being that eats sweet things, and the structure of my desire reflects that. The same can be said of erotic intentionality and all its transformations and displacements. If this is so, intentionality is firmly lodged within my bodily existence, within the natural world.

It remains to ask how the relation of "ofness" or "aboutness" can be understood naturalistically. We could say this: that intentionality is naturalistically embedded, but is itself an indirect natural relation. It is indirect because it is mediated by such functions as imagination, transformation, delay, and memory, which are often, but misleadingly, associated with interiority. The frame within which the intentional functions is a complex nonreductive natural setting, in which humans' needs, desires, fears, and hopes reflect different levels of their relation to a natural world. What we call consciousness is perhaps only derivatively (but importantly) able to be broken down into consciousness of this or that. Or to put this claim another way, all specifically directed intentional consciousness draws on the manifoldness of our sensory and cognitive capacities. Con-sciousness is a networked awareness, a with-knowing, a knowing that even as it is separated into different modalities, draws on those others. (Something similar could be said about the relation between individual awareness and the connection this establishes or sustains with others. Through con-sciousness we not only register the significance of things for us, but also connect things together with other things.) Our being able to focus on one particular domain or object may well depend on our other capacities, with these capacities being ultimately integrated in our embodied existence. And we must not forget our capacity for productive transformation of the intentional order—our capacity for becoming aware of our own awareness, taking our activity as an object of a second order awareness. I would make two comments here: First, the dependence of focused attention on other nonfocal awarenesses is illustrated in our capacity to see objects as solid, round, etc. These latter properties are arguably (as both Berkeley and Merleau-Ponty have argued) dependent on our capacities for tactile manipulation, which is imaginatively but only tacitly implicated in our vision. We may only be able to see what we do see because we can also touch. Secondly, our capacity for self-consciousness rests firmly on this capacity for demarcating a bounded field, even when that is our own awareness. We can only speculate that there is some cognitive crossover from our more primitive capacity to register and defend our own bodily boundaries and systemic integrity, operations that only continue in consciousness what begins at much more primitive levels of life.

In this section I have tried to indicate various ways in which thinking about consciousness would take us into thinking about our interrelated capacities to understand things within fields of relevance (horizons), to bring to bear on one modality of awareness interpretative powers drawn from other dimensions (such as the tactile in the visual), and to reconstitute our awareness as the object of a second order awareness. I have suggested that in these and other ways, consciousness is tied up with the construction, displacement, and transformation of fields of significance, and of significance as a field-phenomenon. Merleau-Ponty helps us think through the connection between such phenomena and the idea of a body schema. And I would suggest a more primitive basis for the idea of a body schema in our fundamental need to manage body boundaries. These sorts of connections illustrate how much a certain naturalization of consciousness would require, at the same time, an expansion of our sense of the natural. That is at least illustrated by (if not grounded on) the existence of things with various degrees of cohesive integrity, which leads, eventually, to ways of managing boundaries. These ways of managing boundaries are natural phenomena that spill over into what we normally think of as distinct questions of meaning, identity, value, etc.

DEEP ECOLOGY

A friend sent me a paper in the late 1970s in which he first connected Heidegger to deep ecology, and then charged ecological thinking in general with fascistic tendencies. I do not propose to deal with the politically troubling aspects of *his* argument. But the central worry about ecological thinking, especially its deep version, is worth dissecting.[17] I want to argue that the dividing line between benign and pernicious appropriations of the ecological perspective has to do with these liminological issues of boundary management which ecophenomenology is in a position to address.

I will draw lightly on Arne Naess and George Sessions's "eight points," presented as an outline of deep ecology.[18] Deep ecology is deep in part because of the imperatives it generates from certain claims it makes about the relations between humans and the rest of nature, some of which are already evaluations. The fundamental claims here are that nonhuman life has an intrinsic value independent of its value for humans, that biological diversity promotes the quality of both human and nonhuman life, and that much of the current shape and scale of human interference in nature is both contrary to the recognition of these values and unsustainable. The fascistic implications thought to arise from these claims would include the claim that one could justify active human population reduction to accommodate the needs

of other species, and that, more broadly, the rights of individual humans are
to be subordinated to those of the species. More generally still, the deep-ecol-
ogy perspective is presenting itself as a kind of meta-legislator of value, dis-
solving within itself every other dimension or consideration.

The plausibility of such draconian conclusions arises from the understandable belief that if the alternative is an irreversible destruction of nature,
or an unstoppable escalation in human population growth, that is, some sort
of catastrophe, then almost any measures might be justified in an emergency.
When the house is on fire, you don't reason with the child who wants to fin-
ish his Nintendo game; you grab the child and run. (And explain later.) But
if the house is merely smoking, or there are reports of its smoking, the situation is less clear. Deep ecology is a crystallized vision of the desperate state we
are in. But the need for radical remedies is a reflection of the totalizing
aspects of the diagnosis. What I want to suggest, however, is that so-called
deep ecology is the product of an *uncontrolled* application of the methodological virtues inherent in the ecological perspective. The central virtue is the
recognition of the constitutive quality of relationality: Things are what they
are by virtue of their relations to other things. What look like external relations are, if not internal, at least constitutive. Living things eat each other,
breathe and drink the elements, live in communities, while inanimate things
have properties that depend on the properties of other things. Limestone
cliffs would not last long in acid rain. Everywhere, it is the interplay of relative forces that produces results, not the absolute forces themselves. What the
ecological perspective teaches us is that things with no obvious point to their
existence play a role in the life cycles of other beings. It teaches us that the
survival of a particular species may depend on the preservation of an environment with very specific features. And it teaches us that the life, death, and
flourishing of things is tied up with other factors, conditions, and creatures in
ways for which we typically do not have a map, and under variability toler-
ances we do not know. We can study these things, of course. But as much as
ecology is a science, it is also a counsel of caution, precisely because it deals
with the interaction of widely disparate kinds of things. In this way, environmentalism quite properly gives a renewed material plausibility to religious
warnings against hubris.

Here, we need to contrast a precise science with a field science. A precise
science fundamentally idealizes its objects, and in so doing, it can develop
highly sophisticated theoretical structures—most notably in mathematics. A
field science deals with the interaction of many quite different sorts of things,
allowing no consistent method of idealization, and inhibiting complex axio-
logical development. Ecology is just such a science. And if we extend "science" more broadly, the same must be said of geography, history, and anthro-
pology. In between, we find physics, chemistry, and biology, and all those
sciences that profit from controlling conditions in laboratories. It is a com-

monplace of physics that a universe in which there are only two bodies exhibits much less mathematical complexity than that of a universe with three bodies. And once a fourth body is added, all hell breaks loose. Real-life biological environments contain not just huge numbers of bodies, but bodies of very different sorts, each of which manages, through various different procedures, its own relation to that environment, or to its own niche in that environment. It is curious to realize that although we could not mathematically, or in any other way, really give adequate representation to the complete workings of such a complex system, nonetheless such "systems" do "work." This is not such a mystery, of course. Representation often plays only a small part in the way of the world.[19] But of course another reason why such complex systems work is that we usually do not have any precise sense of what it is for them not to work, what outcomes would be failures. Does the outbreak of myxomytosis in Anglesey rabbits signal a failure of the system after foxes have been eradicated, or does it mark a successful transformation of the system? Deep ecology would say that while there may be difficult cases, there are also clear ones: that we know what a dead lake means, and that photographs from space argue that the earth, itself on the Gaia view a living being, is dying.

The fundamental thrust of phenomenology is its nonreductive orientation to phenomena. That is what is meant by "Back to the things themselves!" To the extent that deep ecology would permit or encourage the reduction of "things" to the function or role that they play in some higher organization, deep ecology would be opposed to and opposed by phenomenology. I suspect that the ecological perspective more broadly does indeed harbor a tension between finding in "relatedness" a basis of a higher-order synthesis, and recognizing that the kind of relatedness in question will constantly and awkwardly interrupt such syntheses. Take a group of people in a room. We may listen in on their voices and say, "That must be the French soccer team," recognizing them under a collective identity. We may, on the other hand, remember that each of these people has a distinct outlook on the world, that they cannot be collectivized or serialized without an objectifying loss. When we watch them playing on the field, we may conclude that to understand "what is happening," we need a perspective in which we move between these two viewpoints, just as the players themselves, each separately, move in and out of various forms of collective or subgroup consciousness. (One player may be aware of what an opposing player is doing, and have a good understanding of where his teammate is moving up to. Another may have a sense of the strategic opportunities created by the different styles of play of each team.) What is clear here can be seen writ large in a living environment in which a multitude of creatures compete and cooperate, eat and feed each other, and whose awareness of one another's presence or existence will vary and fluctuate. If every living being not does merely have a relation to its outside, to what is other than itself, but is constantly managing that relationship economically (risking death for food, balancing individual advantage with collective prosperity, etc.), then however much it may be possible, for certain purposes, to treat such an environment collectively, that treatment will be constantly open to disruption from the intransigence of its parts. Important as it is to see things in relation to one another, and tempting as it then is to see these spaces, fields, playgrounds of life, as wholes, that wholeness is dependent on the continuing coordination of parts that have albeit residual independent interests. At the same time these "things" we call environments or niches are themselves subject to what we might, after Derrida, call the law of context. And context is an iterative and porous notion. While all meaning (every creature) is contextual (exists in relation to a sustaining field), no context is fully saturated, closed, or determinate. Context is porous for the scientist in that his model of the environment will always be vulnerable to the incursion of "other factors."[20] But it is porous in itself, "on the ground," too, in that unusual or unexpected events may always come into play. And it is porous for living creatures in the sense that the whole way in which their embodiment anticipates the "world out there" may turn out not to protect it from injury or death.

THE ENDS OF NATURE

It would be a brave scientist who would admit to being an Aristotelian today. The idea that things have an inherent *telos* seems halfway to a primitive animism. But discarding a poor metaphysics may fail to do justice to valuable intuitions. An inherent purpose is a hard thing to find when dissecting a frog; it does not appear alongside heart, legs, sinews, etc. But nor does agility, noxious taste, and camouflaged coloration. That a living organism exhibits a set of integrated functions organized around certain ends—survival and reproduction—would be harder to deny. It is not so much that the frog *has* reproduction as its end. Rather, the frog—and every other living being—could better be said to *embody* that end. Frogs may be said to serve other ends, such as food for the French, or for grass snakes, or keeping down the population of water spiders. But these are extrinsic ends. To say that a frog has reproduction as its end is not to suggest that these are independently definable ends which frogs serve. It is simply to say that the whole of froggy being is organized in such a way that it maximizes the possibility of its reproduction, species survival. Within that umbrella, we understand its individual activities—jumping in the air, to catch a fly, to eat, and to grow. Reproduction supplies a hierarchical framework of interpretive intelligibility. Purposiveness is not a part of a frog, but a many-leveled characteristic of its behavior, which ultimately makes it the kind of being it is. At some levels, the frog clearly has purposes in the plural. Whatever it thinks it is doing, it is actually sitting on the leaf soaking up the sun or hunting flies. Its behavior is purposive in the sense that there are ends toward which its behavior is adapted and directed. We may balk at saying that survival and reproduction are higher order purposes. It might be said, instead, that they are just outcomes of the successful pursuit of other smaller-scale ends, outcomes that have further consequences. The extreme view here would be to say that a living organism was just a temporarily successful collection of mechanisms that, operating in proximity, tend to perpetuate themselves—that there really is just mechanism here.[21] In my view, the ways in which brains, and to some extent nerve ganglia, coordinate and even in various ways represent the whole of a creature to itself (body schemata), the emergence of immune systems, levels of organized defense for the whole organism, suggest that this view of a creature simply as a successful collection of parts won't fly. These three features—hierarchical organization of functions, internal "representation" of the whole, and systemic defense mechanisms operating singly and together—provide a basis for saying that a living creature is not just a collection of parts, but functions, importantly, as a whole. But living creatures, then, *are* ends, they do not have ends. And of course, this analysis would make it hard to attribute to a rock the desire to fall to earth. The elimination of a rock's intrinsic terraphilia should still allow us to acknowledge, however, the feature we noted above when discussing the rock with which David smote Goliath—that, perhaps only for a moment, the rock is an aggregated unity, which can be thrown all at once, or admired on a desk. Other rocks can be sat on, climbed, worshipped, protected against quarrying, etc. There are obvious many ways in which human purposes can enter into the definition of integrity. But the rock that David threw did not get its integrity from David or Goliath. Rather, David made use of the rock's own integrity by picking it up, placing it in a sling, etc.

It would be a foolish not just a brave scientist who declared himself to be an Aristotelian. But just as politics is too important to be left to generals, so nature is too important to be left to the natural sciences. There are considerations cutting across the different sciences that can be productively contemplated together. The particular considerations I am raising here have to do with the way in which various kinds of things maintain their integrity, manage boundaries, and relate to their surroundings. Each of these considerations raises ecological (and eco-nomic) issues, and is best approached through a certain kind of phenomenology.

I recalled earlier the centrality of the distinction between Fact and Essence for Husserl. Yet it was Merleau-Ponty who insisted that we understand essence not in a Platonic way, and not as an objectified representation, but rather more something like a structure of our Being-in-the-world. As Merleau-Ponty put it: "[E]ssence here is not the end, but a means. [It is] *our effective involvement in the world that has to be understood and made amenable to conceptualization.*"[22]

PHENOMENOLOGY: AN OPEN FUTURE

I have discussed the attractions and dangers of deep ecology, as a case study of how sensitivity to relationality and interconnectedness can turn into an over-rigid holism. The charge of fascism against deep ecology is understandable, if problematic. The central question has to do with the way in which *closure* operates within deep ecology. And this issue permeates so many contemporary disciplinary debates. The question of closure is the question of economy. In the way that I am construing it, ecophenomenology is an important part of our vigilance against a certain kind of closure. The insistence on taking urgent measures such as drastic human population reduction to save the planet offers a dramatic case study of the economy of boundary management.

For one of the key questions faced here is the kind of logic we apply to our thinking about the boundary. In so many areas, what we could call *emergency conditions* demand that we decide yes or no, friend or foe, inside or outside the tent, etc.[23] The reptilian brain is in charge. I assume it is this logic that operates when T-cells in the blood go on patrol, looking for "foreign" material, where there really is an on-off, either/or switch. This mechanism turns out to be too crude when the body's immune system somehow comes to recognize parts of itself as "foreign," and attacks them. Or when it is persuaded not to attack invading cells that mimic the body's own. But this crudeness may be precisely what is normally needed. In contrast to this binary logic, there are more complex responses. "He is not my first choice, but he is someone I can work with." "I'm not really hungry, but you might be able to tempt me." Many boundary disputes get "resolved" by power-sharing agreements, mutual access, dual sovereignty, taking turns, symbolic contests, etc. There are issues about how we will fairly arrive at a yes/no decision (contests in which all parties accept the rules), as well as about how to how to resolve disputes in which there is no fully satisfactory answer. And it may be that the norm is that these different logics are always both in play. If Mexico and the United States ever agree to an open border (rather than more heavily defending the border), it might well be that this openness becomes possible precisely as Mexico and the United States become *separately* stronger, politically and economically. The property lines between houses in American suburbs are often marked very loosely on the ground. But this may reflect the fact that everyone has very accurate maps (and there is a highly developed legal system), so that if necessary, a legal determination can always be made. Where the yes/no border logic is dominant, it often reflects an underdeveloped capacity for thinking, that is, for negotiating complexity, or the recognition that there are forces that would disempower those who think in such a way. Extremists drive even the moderates from the middle ground. What this shows is that a binary logic can operate between binary logic and negotiative thinking. Gresham's law (bad money drives out good) may apply to intellectual life too. Phenomenology is a site of resistance to such tendencies. Are we then operating on an oppositional relation to binary thinking? Finally, no. There really are emergencies when there is no time for subtlety, where you have to decide—friend or foe. Phenomenology is a resource for the phronesis necessary to distinguish these cases from others.

How does this relate to the question of closure and openness with which we began this section? The strength of deep ecology lies in its taking Hegel's dictum seriously—that the truth lies in the whole. Truth here need not take the form of one comprehensive statement or vision. Even our grasp of individual truths is sharpened when we understand their limitations, conditions, etc. What is distinctive about deep ecology is its sense that the earth really is a strongly interconnected whole, one in which humans currently play an important part. The problem is that we play that part largely in ignorance of the aggregative effects of our acting. We are pissing in the reservoir then wondering why the water tastes funny. Deep ecologists are understandably worried about the gap between the collective consequences of our individual actions on the rest of the biosphere, and our grasp, whether individual or collective, of the impact we are making. Questions of totality figure in this diagnosis at many levels:

1. We each experience only a part of the earth—our own backyard plus trips, tours, vacations, movies, traveler's tales. If my tree is dying, I notice. But the earth slowly dying is not obvious, not something I can see at a glance out of my window. Time, as we have seen, is often invisible. There is a gap between what I can see and what may really be happening. The glance is ripe for education.[24] Even the possibility of this gap may be something I am unaware of.

2. When I consider *my own* impact on the earth, I believe I would find it hard, even if I tried, with my friends, to do *irrecoverable* harm. And to the extent that our consciousnesses of the significance of human action are resolutely individualistic, the collective impact of humans on the earth will fall beneath our radar screens. "Perhaps something should be done, but there is little I can do." Here, there is a gap between an individualistic moral sensibility and the aggregated impact of human activity.[25]

3. The deep ecologist not only believes that the earth is an interconnected whole, in which everything affects everything else. He believes that on his model of that interconnectedness, various disaster scenarios loom, and at the very least a series of uncontrollable, irreversible, and undesired outcomes.[26]

4. These consequences will occur unless very dramatic changes are made very soon. Either masses of people will come to their senses and demand this through normal democratic procedures. Or we need to suspend democratic institutions altogether.[27]

An ecophenomenological critique of deep ecology would attempt to open up options within its closed economy. The argument that there are circumstances in which democratic societies might suspend democracy is not as totalitarian as it might seem. Every state has emergency powers—to deal with riots, natural disasters, and threats from foreign powers. And of course, democratic institutions can operate as elected dictatorships between elections. Emergency measures, yes/no logics, do make sense where questions of life and death are concerned. The question of whether *the earth is a living being*, however, is not a fact of nature, but inseparable from the very questions about self-preservation, boundary maintenance, and nutrition that lurk at the borders of living things and other natural phenomena, and complex systems.

CONCLUSION

What, then, is ecophenomenology? I have argued that ecophenomenology, in which are folded both an ecological phenomenology and a phenomenological ecology, offers us a way of developing a middle ground between phenomenology and naturalism, between intentionality and causality. I claim that our grasp of Nature is significantly altered by thinking through four strands of time's plexity—the invisibility of time, the celebration of finitude, the coordination of rhythms, and the interruption and breakdown of temporal horizons. And also by a meditation on the role of boundaries in constituting the varieties of thinghood. Ecophenomenology takes up in a tentative and exploratory way the traditional phenomenological claim to be able to legislate for the sciences, or at least to think across the boundaries that seem to divide them. In this way, it opens up and develops an access to the Nature and the natural that is independent both of the conceptuality of the natural sciences and of traditional metaphysics.

TEN

Globalization and Freedom

[T]his society is irrational as a whole. Its productivity is destructive of the free development of human needs and faculties, its peace maintained by the constant threat of war, its growth dependent on the repression of the real possibilities for pacifying the struggle for existence—individual national, and international.

—Marcuse

Not only must one not renounce the emancipatory desire, it is necessary to insist on it more than ever, it seems. . . . This is the condition of a re-politicization, perhaps of an other concept of the political.

—Derrida

WHAT IS CALLED "globalization" is the site of a profound struggle over the meaning and value of freedom. There are those who argue for globalization in terms of the benefits of free trade, giving poor people in remote places access to world markets for their goods. And there are those who argue that globalization exposes all those it touches to the coercive effects of profit-seeking capital flows, creating new dependencies and enslavement. Whether we assume that economic freedom lies at the heart of personal, cultural, and political freedom, or whether we think of globalization as independently impacting these broader freedoms, for example, through cultural dissemination, or information flow, it is clear that there is no consensus on whether globalization promotes or inhibits freedom.

It might be thought that the key to resolving these issues lay simply in clarifying our terms. Perhaps if we distinguished economic freedom from (say) political freedom, we might be able to agree that globalization tends to serve one end and not the other. But are these so easily kept apart? And, even more critically, are we as clear as we need to be about the continuing viability of the very idea of freedom? If we take our cue from a certain tradition of caution about metaphysical language, a caution captured by Heidegger when he said that "all fundamental words have been used up,"[1] and by Derrida's attempts at a postmetaphysical closure, would not "freedom" go the same way as "subject," "identity," "self," or "God"? Would we not have to keep a rigorous distance from its residual humanism? Is there not a crisis in the concept and value of "freedom," quite as much as a crisis about freedom "itself"?[2]

THE FRAGILITY OF FREEDOM: DERRIDA AND MARCUSE

Marx's heirs are many, and Derrida's *Specters of Marx* is heir not just to Marx, but to Freud and Heidegger.[3] In this confluence, Derrida could also be said to echo an earlier triangular synthesis published some thirty years before, Marcuse's *One Dimensional Man*.[4] Marcuse may not be actively haunting Derrida, and Marcuse's central concern, which we could call the fragility of freedom, is one whose role in deconstruction remains to be determined. It is quite clear, however, that the value and significance of freedom is critical to discussions of globalization, even as it appears in those discussions in a paradoxical guise. And while it is not a concept central to *Specters of Marx,* and while indeed we might think it even threatened by Derrida's distancing himself from any teleological conception of history (SM, 74), Derrida insists on emancipatory desire as "the condition of a re-politicization" (SM, 75).

Is Marcuse still relevant to contemporary questions about freedom, culture, and globalization? In his affirmation of a radical freedom, Marcuse (like Sartre) seems committed to a critical humanism, vulnerable to deconstruction:

[T]he whole appears to be the very embodiment of Reason. And yet this society is irrational as a whole. Its productivity is destructive of the free development of human needs and faculties, its peace maintained by the constant threat of war, its growth dependent on the repression of the real possibilities for pacifying the struggle for existence—individual national, and international.[5]

And yet we may wonder how far Derrida is from this. Derrida's *Specters of Marx* could be seen as a preemptive strike, a diagnosis and protest *avant la lettre*, against the U.S. *National Security Strategy* document[6] issued on September 17, 2002, a document that reanimates the spectral vision that fueled the McCarthyism of the 1950s (reds under the beds) and projects it onto the global scene as a theater of threat from shadowy enemies against which unending preemptive war provides the only security. This document spells out precisely, in case we had missed it, how, as Derrida put it (SM, 1993) this "new 'world order'" seeks to install "an unprecedented form of hegemony." And it is indeed "a novel form of war" . . . but interestingly, it is not this time "a great 'conjuration' against Marxism." What Derrida called "the manic, jubilatory, and incantatory form" of this "dominating discourse," the form "that Freud assigned to the so-called twilight phase of mourning" is still there. So is the "long live capitalism, long live the market, and here's to . . . economic and political liberalism."[7] But 9/11 has allowed a spectral displacement, from Marxism to Islamic terrorism. And perhaps this is even an improved enemy, a supercharged phantom. In addition to ideological hostility, the new phantoms, hard to locate in their Afghan caves, or with their many doubles in Iraq, now represent fear mixed to a more potently explosive formula—ideology, yes, but also religion and race.

But did not Marcuse rest his hope on certain concrete angels—displacements of a disappointing proletariat—students, blacks, the third world—angels who are now so late in arriving that it should be clear they are not coming? Interestingly, Marcuse himself acknowledges that this is indeed *hope* and not any kind of historical necessity:

> *One Dimensional Man* will vacillate throughout between two contradictory hypotheses: (1) that advanced industrial society is capable of containing qualitative change for the foreseeable future; (2) that forces and tendencies exist which may break this containment and explode the society. I do not think that a clear answer can be given. . . . The first tendency is dominant, and whatever preconditions for a reversal may exist are being used to prevent it.[8]

In this formulation we find a succinct version of the logic that Derrida will seek to displace. Where Marcuse sees the explosion of inside by outside as necessary but subject to anticipatory co-option, and hence uncertain, Derrida will treat as a misunderstanding the idea of choosing between inside and outside as the source of transformation.

In fact, one could claim that for all their philosophical distance there is a real convergence here. Marcuse's own sense of the ironic containment of change itself destabilizes the inside/outside relation. And were Marcuse to have concluded that the cavalry was not coming, might he too not have signed up to Derrida's "messianic without messianism," or hope without hope? If we enlarge the space just opened up—Marcuse's contradictory concepts, his ambivalent strategies, and Derrida's aporetic possibilities—we find the broad arena of a displaced inheritance in which deconstruction responds to Marx; if focusing on class struggle is too reductive, or too dated, recognizing that we operate within a space of (convoluted) contrariety is indispensable.

I attempt here to schematize this space in a very preliminary way in terms of (1) the logic of destruction, (2) the logic of contradiction, (3) the logic of aporia. Thinking through these various dimensions calls for a *phronesis* of contrariety;[9] the interwoven workings of these logics define for us the challenge of globalization.

A PHRONESIS OF CONTRARIETY

If Marx stood Hegel on his head, we in our time are perhaps standing Marx on his side—displacing, transforming, and ramifying his ideas. I argue in this section that while there may be no overall logic of history, there are indeed a multiplicity of "logics" that capture the kinds of connections we find ourselves part of, the dilemmas we face, and with and against which we can work. Globalization itself cannot be understood without disentangling the logics that inhabit it, drive it, and undermine its promise. Instead of a single historical teleology, we now face—more broadly—the proliferation of contrariety (complexity, contradiction). I want to argue that this is now the dominant dimension of our engagement with the world, and that what it requires of us is a new kind of phronesis, or practical wisdom.

Globalization seems to intensify contrariety. Why? Globalization is understood here in terms of:

1. A process of accelerated global communication of information and exchange of goods in a new world order that both sustains these possibilities and exploits them;[10]
2. The global logic of deterritorialization, in which any interiority is vulnerable to dehiscence—penetration and distribution of its "assets";
3. The double effect of material closure. There is no more *outside* and no more interiority;[11]
4. The destabilization of fundamental material homeostatic processes (impacting weather, life, evolution).

Globalization intensifies contradictions of all sorts. For a start, it forcibly restructures the ways in which we inhabit space and time. The much-vaunted closure of metaphysics perhaps reflects the closure of our experience of the world, and its possibilities.

Consider the way we deploy the inside/outside relation when we think on a large scale. The world used to contain its own outside, whether as a beyond for explorers, or as a space where waste could be disposed of. Now there is no outside, no space for expansion, no more *terra nullius*,[12] no *Lebensraum*, no slack, no "out," or "away" as when we throw something "out" or "away." We are living on a Moebius strip, in which the symbolic other side is actually the same surface, and we will meet it again round the corner. Yet so much of our making sense, let alone the intelligibility of our actions, still rests on being able to export, exclude, externalize what we do not want to consider. When that externality is no longer available, we are in trouble. Many said that the end of the cold war, for example, would bring a peace dividend. Instead, it directed unwanted attention back toward intractable social problems such as poverty, disease, and unemployment, for which the only solution seems to be to bury our collective head in the sand, to create new structures of enmity, or otherness, to expel contradiction and recrystallize the world into foolish binary simplifications. It is symptomatic, too, in this same vein, that there are some who support space exploration on the grounds that we may soon have to leave planet Earth.[13] But might not our apparent need for an outside[14] reflect a failure to accept our global finitude, and our own failure to devise modes of behavior appropriate to it? In this light we can connect topologically the symbolic traumas of 9/11, and the loss of the Columbia space shuttle on reentry, with the new Anti-Missile Defense proposals (son of Star Wars), and even the announcement of a new mission to Mars (Feb. 2004), a dramatic misdirection of a flailing hope for something better. The specter of terrorism is that global interconnectedness might not all be positive, that it might not be able to be organized entirely on our own terms. "One world" cuts two ways. These topological problems are particularly tough for countries with experience of empire, whose identity and self-understanding is tied up with the management of the extraction of resources (human or material) from there to here. It is perhaps no accident that current U.S. policymakers are the sons of European immigrants who were themselves often escaping (religious) persecution—"solving" a problem by leaving it behind. The problem of race in America, for white supremacists, must be that in this case the management of this relation to the other went horribly "wrong." The experience of global finitude is (negatively) the recognition that the patterns of problem solving we have become used to externalizing—finding ways "out"—are increasingly less plausible. We may be tempted to move from space to time, to project or await "other" futures, however implausible.

But time is itself caught up in this globalizing closure. We are coming to realize that we can no longer rely on the reversibility of our actions, that time is not just a playground for experimentation, that we cannot assume that the damage technology wreaks can be fixed technologically. Nature is becoming part of history in the sense that we are making irreversible impacts on the very processes that sustain its course. This is a dramatic shift from nature playing the role of reliable constant backdrop, the home to which boys could return after their games. This irreversibility impacts not only nature, but also our sense of ourselves and our powers. Times are out of joint. Temporalities once laminated together are peeling apart in an accelerated "uneven development." For example, we are acquiring powers (military, biological, media manipulation) that surge ahead of the social practices and institutions needed to regulate them. And with large-scale species extinction, the all-too-human time of technology-driven environmental transformation is cutting sharply into evolutionary development. Irreversibility, de-coupling, uneven development. . . . A poignant example of the latter, which poses the greatest difficulty, is that potentially disastrous environmental change may not be obvious until it is too late to change it. The "always already" can be the "sometimes too late"! This is precisely the claim being made about global warming. To the extent that the political processes that might affect such change are driven by immediate considerations, we may well be losing the war between short-term advantage and long-term survival.[15] Topology and temporal considerations combine perhaps in heightening the danger of dialectical naivety. When Kant said there was nothing quite as good as a good will, he was pointing to our inability to control or determine the consequences of our actions. But this is no defense against being blind to the obvious and predictable "blowback" that certain actions call forth.[16] The refusal to consider such consequences makes sense when the future is elsewhere, a world away. But in a finite world, many more futures will catch up with us, and the luxury of kicking the ball into the long grass is no longer available. This temporal externalization—dumping waste in the river of time—makes sense under more expansive conditions. But makes less and less sense as the world gets smaller.

If these claims are plausible, it suggests that there is no longer any proper outside, reworking with more historical and material specificity something of the logic of Derrida's "There is nothing outside the text."[17] Similar consequences follow for the idea of interiority. One can show quite formally the impossibility of a pure interiority and hence its inability to serve as a metaphysical ground. What is arguably historically distinct about globalization in its current form is that it actively targets interiorities for de-territorialization, dehiscence, asset stripping, total mobilization of any resources that may be locked up in an archaic interior. In some sense, of course, we may see such a process as "disclosive" of the truth about identity—that all boundaries, all identities, are carved in shifting sand, dictated not by some deep essentialism but by the plays of forces that constitute them and to which they have been subjected. But it is one thing to acknowledge this truth, and quite another to promote the active implementation of such dissolutions.[18] It was this that led Marcuse to diagnose consumerism as a plague on human agency, because it infects and destroys the "interiority" needed for political resistance. The broader impact of economic globalization is to render any precapitalist formation vulnerable to market penetration. Market economics are, importantly, amoral. They may at times and in certain places, "lift all boats,"[19] but there is no necessity here at all. Family life, the health, security, or longevity of individuals may or may not give a competitive advantage. The law of profit is as unsentimental as the arithmetic with which one can count the dead and injured on a battlefield.

The breakdown of our traditional capacities to reduce complexity by externalization, and (in the West) of our ability to draw on (and as philosophers and activists, to appeal to) the resources for resistance made available by a certain interiority, suggests a crisis in the imaginary. If individual and collective thought and action is shaped fundamentally by the ways in which we deploy the categories of inside and outside, same and other, friend and enemy, identity and difference, then globalization is at the very least a privileged site for struggle over this imaginary. Moreover, the struggle against war is the struggle against the regressive deployment of the simplest modes of this imaginary.[20] I understand Derrida's development of the logic of the spectral as a strategy of resistance operating in just such a space, one that even puts into question the very category of the imaginary.

I have proposed a phronesis of contrariety, to meet the challenges thrown up by the ways in which globalization disturbs us at what Kant would call the "aesthetic" level—our social schematizations of space and time. At the "analytic" level, there are further important differentiations to be made. I have tried to give voice in a perhaps naive way to what are, I believe, irreducibly distinct modes of "contrariety." By "contrariety" I am trying to capture the whole range of what one could call the constitutive impediments to "progress." And yes, I do believe in progress, at the very least in the sense that a recognition of these structural impediments would indeed be—progress.

I distinguish three different modes of contrariety:

1. Natural resistance, counterreaction. Classic formulations of this principle would be Newton's Third Law of Motion—For every action there is an equal and opposite reaction—and Sartre's coefficient of adversity— "Les choses sont contre nous." We tend to think of the contrariness of nature as appropriately responded to by further human control. Critical environmental questions arise at the point at which reaching for more control is seen to be hubris.

2. Dialectical opposition, where a reflective grasp has an effect on the process itself. An example—the resistance that comes from trying to apply a scheme that will supposedly benefit those whom it affects, when they resist its introduction (such as the coercive democratization of Iraq). The contradictions of implementation, which appear when a complex reality ruins a reductive model of development (as often happens in the impact of free trade policies), borrow from both natural resistance and dialectical opposition.

3. Aporetic breakdown, where an operation breaks down under its own logic. Consider Kant's arguments against lying, trying to acquire all the money in the world (how could it then be worth anything?), and Derrida's account of the logic of the gift. More solemnly, we have to include here the possibility of gaming any system by manipulating its ground

rules for private gain *in such a way as to undermine the very legitimacy of the system.* Gaming democracy (buying votes by advertising) is clear enough. Gaming globalization is hard on its heels.

These distinctions are meant to be heuristic. In concrete cases they are often mixed together.

A new phronesis of practical engagement in the world has to find ways of addressing these contrarieties, and not see them as forbidding action but as profoundly informing it. This whole analysis could perhaps be poured into the space marked by Derrida's "indécidable." The necessity of marking this space in this way is tied to the vital importance of avoiding regressive short-circuiting reversions to primitive imaginary schemas. The logic of the ghost is perhaps the introduction into the imaginary of what I have called the phronesis of contrariety.

All three of these modalities of contrariety are frame-dependent. That is to say—they each appear within a definite nexus of human concepts and concerns. If the first (resistance) seems to occur within nature, and hence outside any frame, in fact, it is just when nature is "responding" to our attempts at domination that a "logic" often emerges. A classic case here would be the development of antibiotic resistance. We can expect that the conquest of some diseases will be less of a decisive victory and more of an endless struggle. Frame dependency is necessary for any "logic" at all to operate. The connection between these logics, and species of contrariety on the one hand and frames on the other, is this: Frames are not just voluntary interpretive schemes.[21] To the extent that they supply the recurrent shapes of our engagement in the world, the paradoxes, failures, obstacles, ironies, and tragedies generated by the logics that inhabit them are *real.* Moreover, as we shall see, it is often the very operation of these very frames that generates "external" resistance, opposition, blowback, as the "real" bites back. Critics of globalization make much of such phenomena. Free trade could be described as our contemporary frame of frames, and I will explore shortly why it can be expected to break down.

In the meantime, it is worth perhaps pointing out how this language of frames captures not just Marcuse's uncertainty, but also Derrida's account of a weak messianism, a messianism without religion, the possibility of an impossibility, and why this account is genuinely complementary to a more orthodox Marxist critique. Awaiting the *arrivant,* the impossible possibility, is founded on the recognition that possibility/ impossibility/ necessity are Janus-headed creatures that purport to speak about the real, but do so always within the space of a frame, often invisible. This language is infected by a paradox— that some such frames are unavoidable for the deployment of these modal expressions—but this frame dependency undermines the manifest meaning of these expressions. If the frame were to change, the impossible might become possible. Typically, we suppose this means: If *per impossibile* the frame were to change. . . . But this "impossible" may just reflect the particular sense of the boundary between possible and impossible laid down by the frame we hold near and dear. We emphasize here ways in which the pursuit of the impossible projects transformations in the frameworks that restrictively define the possible. On this reading, the impossible is a candidate for actualization. Surely the "messianic" dimension that Derrida often invokes in *Specters of Marx*, a messianicity without messianism, would want to steer clear of such positivity? But the status of the "impossible" is not reducible to those concrete occasions on which what it projects is actually realized. It is a repeated reaching-out-beyond that stands apart from any actual success or failure.

When Abraham has faith that his son will be returned to him, or the knight believes, against all reason, that he will get back the woman he loves,[22] we can suppose that "God" functions in these remarks as a marker of the limits of human understanding. The god who moves in mysterious ways, who surpasses all understanding, marks the limit, the unanticipatable limit, of our powers of anticipation.[23] Human hubris is both the overestimation of one's powers and the underestimation of the possible.

Despite its bad press, the value of every philosophical idealism, or every trace of idealism in philosophy, is that it traces the boundaries of the thinkable, what we take *for good reason* to be possible. While Marx gave concrete content to Hegel's idealizations, the task Marx has bequeathed to us, perhaps, is to explore the traces of logic/structural necessity that still drive Marx's thinking. Marx inherits from Hegel the sense of a logic of history, that class struggle, or the logic of capital, would of necessity, lead to the progressive emiseration[24] of the poor, to revolution, to the withering away of the state, the impossibility of socialism in one country.[25] We have had revolutions and yet we have seen both the dramatic strengthening of state apparatus, and the emergence of post-state capitalistic structures—multinational corporations, and weak, failed, or marginal states. We have witnessed not international socialism, but rather global capitalism and "free trade." We have witnessed explosions in ethnic violence and fragmentation and a revival of cultural defensiveness and religious fundamentalism. Our claim is not that Marx correctly predicted this or that, but that what Derrida said once about phenomenology it is quite as true of Marx and Marxism: There is all the difference in the world between a position that falls short of [phenomenology] and one that goes through it.

Precisely why free trade is problematic both for economic and political freedom I will address shortly.[26] I want first to try to explain why it is such an attractive idea, and how its problems can best be addressed in terms of a phronesis of contrariety. The proponents of the connection between free trade, broader human freedoms, and development are legion and go back some way. Before Fukuyama[27] there was Milton Friedman[28] and before him

Adam Smith. More recently we have the U.S. National Defense Strategy document in which it is the central pre-positioned ideological plank. The fundamental idea is that access to global trading markets will allow rich and poor alike to flourish. Its attractiveness rests on the fact that it is a win-win model, the tide that raises all boats. The only losers would be those who choose not to participate. It also brings people into contact with each other more than ever, increasing interdependency and making conflict less likely. The more we bring down tariff barriers, the less "friction" there will be, and the more easily the game will be played.

The analogy to playing a game is also seductive. Once you know the rules, you can concentrate on playing your role without distraction. Work can be more focused, quality will go up, etc. Anyone who has ever been absorbed in a game in which the messy world has been replaced by a set of rules and a board or playing field or screen (or page), will understand the attraction of this idea. When we write books, the confidence that we can get them published is highly motivating. If, in order to get published, one had to find a tree no one wanted, cut it down, soak the wood pulp, etc., the practical threshold to being a writer would be prohibitively high. But the games from which such a seductive picture is drawn are in fact underpinned by background conditions. We may play football before dinner, but football does not feed us. We agree to abide by the rules because we can "afford" to lose. We enter wholeheartedly into a game precisely because we do not fully identify ourselves with our role in the game. We *choose* to play the game; we know we *could* in principle tear up the page, walk off the pitch, tip up the board, turn off the screen. The attractions of game playing, however realistic, rest on a certain detachment from real life. But these attractions do not carry over to the game of life where that separation is not assured. In a wealthy culture, the availability of low-wage employment for many (not for all), and of easily available credit, are indeed the kinds of safety net that allow risk taking. In cultures without these safety nets, market economics can be lethal. There is a reason for this. It may seem as if free trade is an activity enabling individuals to prosper, and it clearly can. But this is an accidental by-product of the operation of markets, driven by the iron law of profit. What drives investment flows offers no security to individuals or groups. We imagine a frictionless world in which, say, desperate need would translate into rock-bottom wages, new investment opportunities, and hence some sort of equilibration. Not only is the world never frictionless, nor the playing field "level," we now know that markets are not just the neutral space in which players compete, they are managed, manipulated, and distorted for profit. Markets are themselves "gamed."[29] This is, if you like, an aporetic consequence of the game logic of the free market, one in which the system, taken to its extreme, implodes on itself. The possibility of such aporetic consequences is not unrelated to the fact that corporations can buy or rent the "states" that would otherwise be regulating them. Many small states have smaller GDPs than the annual profits of large companies.[30]

Let us now pursue more directly the problematic consequences of the free trade frame.

DEVELOPMENT AND FREEDOM

It is sometimes suggested that the very value of radical freedom is some sort of residue of bourgeois humanism, or Western metaphysics. Levinas once argued that Western intellectuals can be blind to the fact that the problem of hunger may be more pressing than the problem of freedom. Would global responsibility then be hampered by the projection of "Western" ideals? There are also strong arguments affirmatively connecting freedom with development. Freedom is somehow both embodied in and promoted by the opening of markets to free trade.[31] Marcuse's articulation of the fragility of radical freedom, the paradoxes and aporias it faces, helps us address both of these issues, and shows how they are connected.

First, the metaphysical argument for linking development and freedom. The fundamental objection here is that the Enlightenment model of freedom rests on the idea of a subject whose autonomy consists in a certain independence of sustaining conditions, one that approximates as far as possible a substance "that needs nothing in order to be itself."[32] What is wrong with this idea of freedom is not, however, that it is connected with a certain autonomy, but that it understands autonomy as unconditioned. If instead we understand autonomy as itself assured only by broad participation with others in assuring the conditions necessary for security and flourishing, if, in other words, we see autonomy as resting on a positive heteronomy, then we would have exorcised the specter of metaphysical humanism from the value of freedom. Freedom does not require a hysterical denial of dependency; in fact, it flourishes only when the conditions on which it depends are affirmed and cultivated. And there is every reason to value an individual freedom once its heteronymous conditions have been recognized as in prior need of satisfaction.

Individual freedom taken as the *ground* in no further need of elaboration will generate "contradictions," but these can in principle be defused or short-circuited once a certain heteronymous conditionality is acknowledged. Thus, we tend to think of human rights as assertable in the face of the incursions of the other. But *before* they can operate in that way, they presuppose a community in which such rights are recognized, and in which that recognition is itself subject to social processes (such as weighing conflicting rights). The claim that is expressed in the assertion of a right is conditioned by the social processes that ensure the *legitimacy of rights in general* by mediating conflicting claims. Those social processes are not themselves just legal processes, and while they have a vital formal openness to multiple determinability (many different factors can be brought to bear), they are, by the same token, open to manipulation. It is at this point that a certain kind of judgment must remain available to us: manipulation, false consciousness, systematically distorted communication, etc. This is no mere value judgment. It is a reminder that something we value ("freedom") will lose its legitimacy if the conditions of that legitimacy are interfered with.[33]

Nor is the pursuit of legitimacy here a return to a metaphysical grounding; it is a reflection of the grounds of any sociality at all. The claim that the value of individual freedom requires the satisfaction of various heteronymous conditions simply articulates the complex achievement that freedom consists in, one that rests on certain conditions of sociality the absence of which genuinely threatens freedom. The language of corruption, ideological distortion, etc., is appropriate, indeed required, to mark the operation of mechanisms that would promote the mere husk of a certain value (such as freedom) in the absence of its sustaining conditions.[34] The argument will be made, of course, that any particular story of legitimation will be just that, a particular story. And this is where a key source of "contradiction" arises: a freedom detached from its sustaining conditions is not true freedom.

Marcuse arrived at the idea of repressive desublimation as an attempt to explain how the project of freedom was derailed, how a certain logic did not work itself out as it might have (or *should* have!). Consumer capitalism bought off what would otherwise have been the revolutionary potential for structural transformation inherent in the demand for radical freedom. Should we still be haunted by this ghost? (A strange formulation!). We could resuscitate it as an unfinished project.[35] But there are many unfinished projects that are properly left unfinished (such as squaring the circle). What justifies resuscitating the project of freedom?

First, it remains a compelling story both to those already enjoying a version of it, and to those still suffering from overt oppression; second, freedom is a complex if fragile human value central to so many other hopes and values (democracy, social justice); and thirdly, and partly as a reflection of the above, it is a value that has been co-opted by the most powerful forces of capitalist globalization. This co-option both threatens the very value of freedom, and at the same time rearticulates the space in which these struggles will subsequently be worked through.

My claim here is that the co-opted versions of freedom (free trade, freedom of "speech" understood as a justification for the role of advertising, media manipulation, and propaganda in elections) lethally infect the logic of freedom, even as they mutate into becoming the mainstays of a world in which radical freedom has become an anachronism. A mere image of freedom displaces a more complex hope.

I might of course be accused of a purely nostalgic view of history, a logocentric projection of the future, one in which it is insisted that a certain logic (that of human freedom) be allowed to work itself through. Should we not welcome the breakdown of one logic and its creative transformation into another? Should we not welcome this historical creativity?

In the context of economic development, this is in effect the view expressed by a 1951 UN document:[36]

> Ancient philosophies have to be scrapped; old social institutions have to disintegrate; bonds of caste, creed and race have to burst; and large numbers of people who cannot keep up with progress have to have their expectations of a comfortable life frustrated.

If we imagine these words being used to justify the American Civil War, or the end of apartheid in South Africa, it is hard not to agree with them. And there is no doubt that this rhetoric is appealing. We imagine heroic journeys, great risks that paid off, big ideas that were scorned and later triumphed, the times when "they said it could not be done." But we have witnessed too many grand ideas that human history could have done without: The War to End All Wars, The Final Solution, Slavery in America, all that the names Korea, Algeria, Vietnam bring to mind, memories, traumas we do not need, events that haunt us even as we fail to learn their central lesson. Each of them has been dressed up in noble colors and the language of sacrifice. And in each case undoubtedly unexpected benefits flowed. But it would be a sorry consequence if we concluded that human history had to be like this, and that the rhetoric of sacrifice would just motor on, untroubled.

If we were to agree that our values get distorted when the conditions necessary for their realization are either denied or corrupted, we might well wonder whether it is not a parallel "reduction" of vision that occurs both in the march of economic globalization and in wartime. By the march of economic globalization I mean the coordinated operation of global instruments of economic development (such as the World Bank, the WTO, IMF). These institutions commonly act in concert to set conditions for economic development (credit) for entire states that effectively undermine the power of local democratic governance.[37] The "reduction" that takes place here happens by way of the imposition of economic and financial targets that discount the significance of other quasi-independent dimensions such as history, culture, environmental specificities, and many other local issues. Such a reduction can be justified by the claim that the economic is what is determinative "in the last analysis," that it is no different to insisting that engineers understand the laws of physics, whatever they are building.

Our time is out of joint, doubly so. In a contrived wartime, a time that has its own logic, and in a sense a different kind of time, we find many of the civilized values for which we have fought for so long set aside, we find the struggles for social justice suspended, the struggle against poverty and disease undermined, in order to assure ourselves of the more fundamental value of survival and security as a people, as a state, perhaps as a global community. It is said that until we have security, the institutions on which these other values rest could not be assured. Wartime is a time out of joint in that it turns everything into a joint, a juncture, a binary choice. Good against evil, friend against enemy, for us or against us—the most reductive logic. This time is doubly out of joint, because whether we think of the announced global war against terrorism or the surging war against Iraq, we are talking of a wartime that to many observers has been invented as a political strategy, serving a domestic agenda, what has been called a discretionary war. The polarizing logic of wartime does not press upon us as an inexorable fate to be borne with tragic stoicism, it is, rather, a voluntary exercise of strategic power, transparently reflecting specific long-term economic, military, and political interests, co-opting the language of freedom for its own ends.

There is a parallelism between these three reductions—the reduction of freedom to a value cut off from its heteronymous conditions of possibility, the subordination of political options in developing countries to the constraints of global economic models, and the calculated reduction of democratic life to the exigencies of wartime necessity. In fact, these three reductions are not merely parallel but complexly, and often paradoxically entangled.

I want to take up, finally, in this section, the logic of substitution operating in the promotion of free trade as an engine of freedom. From Milton Friedman to advocates of a Third Way such as Oxford Bengali economist Amartya Sen, there is a recurrent claim that freedom is inextricably tied to development, where development means global free market economic policies. I have already tried to analyze something of why this model is attractive, and at times even delivers a version of what it promises. But we cannot just bathe selectively in this rosy story. It is important also to place this aspect of globalization in the more paradoxical setting of the logics of contrariety I mentioned earlier. What excites us as a fantasy algorithm, the logic that raises all boats, should give us pause when too many of the boats sink, or founder with the number of people clinging to them, or when boatless people drown.

It cannot be dismissed as an attraction of the idea of market economics that individuals are understood not just as independent monadic substances, but rather in their very interdependence, and that their flourishing is recognized to be tied up with, and not threatened by, such interdependence. The division of labor make us all more than ever dependent on each other. But it is in just this recognition of the heteronymous condition of autonomy, combined with the inherent attractiveness of the analogy with a game with clear rules, that the danger lies. Market economics dangerously *idealizes* heteronomy, by reducing the complex dependencies on which survival and flourishing depend, to what is often a precarious engagement in markets that, far from being "free," are subject to all kinds of distortions and manipulations. To the extent that it is the recognition of the complexities of material heteronomy and interdependence that sustains real freedom, it is the idealizing mimicry of this recognition that makes market economics dangerous. Economic freedom does not simply need political freedom as an added bonus, a supplementary benefit; it cannot secure itself without it. And yet it can all too easily appear as a substitute for it.

The freedom that masquerades as free trade, as the freedom of the market, recognizes the need for relationality, and hence the way in which autonomy rests on a certain heteronomy. But heteronomy construed in this way not only does not supply any guarantees, it is subject to the structural instabilities of market forces that are themselves being manipulated, gamed, by powerful corporations. If radical freedom is a capacity to affect if not determine the conditions of one's own freedom, the freedom of the market meets that standard only for those in a position to control markets. At this point we find the transformed reemergence of one of Marx's central concerns—the ownership of the means of production, where "ownership" has been replaced by "capacity to determine," and "means of production" has turned into "opportunities for exchange." The result is very similar. Those who cannot much affect their opportunities to participate in market relations are deprived of freedom. When times are good, this disempowerment may be invisible. When times are tough, a new servitude becomes apparent.

We have described the gaming of markets as an aporetic contrariety, an internal development of the logic of the market. The failure of formal markets to capture in depth the complexity of human interdependency, even as, in some respects it contributes to it, opens economic globalization to all the problems associated with the application of schemes or models to the "real world." This application both transforms the real and sets up instabilities within it. If market economics is to become the basis of the new world order, development is not in itself freedom,[38] it requires assistance from political practices and institutions at every level. In many ways, Sen is aware of this, and yet, in a blistering critique of his claim that democracy prevents famine, Vandana Shiva writes (about rural India): "People are starving because the policy structures that defended rural livelihoods, and access to resources and markets, and hence entitlements and incomes, are being systematically dismantled by structural adjustment programs, driven by the World Bank, and by WTO rules imposing trade liberalization."[39] If what we have called participation in determining the conditions of one's well-being (access to resources, access to markets) could be called democracy, it is a democracy that can never be reduced to a formal schema. Such a "democracy to come"[40] needs to be as creatively rhizomal as the conditions we face are changing.[41] It will concern itself not just with relations of production, but also reproduction (empowering women through education). And it will draw strength from the work of local imaginative transformation of global cultural influences, as Appadurai suggests.[42] But in addition to these "horizontal" proliferations, a democracy to come cannot ignore the multiple layers and levels at which the conditions that make for war or famine are nourished or thwarted.[43] If we care about radical freedom, justice, or a democracy to come (and we must), we need to locate its possibility, its "impossibility," within the landscape that makes visible the structural obstacles to its pursuit, the contradictions and aporias that beset it, and why it may even be receding. The pursuit of such ends is one of the ways in which Marxism can productively haunt us, if productive haunting is not an oxymoron. The result would be a phronesis of contrariety.

THE ELEVENTH PLAGUE: ENVIRONMENTAL DESTRUCTION

In *Specters of Marx*, Derrida names ten plagues of the global order, but there is (at least) one more (and perhaps the real plague is that there is always one more): environmental destruction.

The traditional view of Marx's significance for environmental thinking and concerns is that it is negative, that Marx was an heir to the Enlightenment and its focus on human progress through subjugation and exploitation. More recently, work by Paul Burkett (*Marx and Nature*) and John Bellamy Foster (*Marx's Ecology*) has argued for a much more eco-friendly Marx. This Marx is a materialist, naturalist, and realist. Foster, for example, digs up Marx's neglected writings on capitalist agriculture and soil ecology, philosophical naturalism, and evolutionary theory, and shows how it is not just man who gets exploited by capitalist modes of production, but nature itself. The end of the peasant farmer, for example, meant the end of a direct cycle between animals, manure, and crops, and the need to add artificial fertilizers to a soil that would otherwise soon be exhausted.[44] We do not perhaps get an ecocentric perspective from Marx, but we do have an environmental materialism in which the fate of the natural world is clearly tied to the social relations of production, and one in which environmental degradation is clearly the outcome of the exploitation of nature simply as a raw material. This suggests that Marx has a pretty clear idea of the problem of sustainability, one of the central buzzwords in contemporary land use debates. The logic to which sustainability is a response is that of the otherwise inexorable depletion of resources, and the need to change practices that would have this consequence. This is an aspect of what we have called the recognition of the earth as a finite material totality. Practices that "work" under the condition of moving on, opening up new spaces, etc., no longer work under conditions of closure. Nature is the first source of the law of diminishing returns. Sustainability is the shape of a practice under the condition of finite closure.

There are many ways in which the degradation of nature[45] is clearly a consequence of the social relations of production, in the form of industrialization, the development of transport systems, property laws, the expropriation of the land of indigenous peoples, etc. Much of this story could be told within a classical materialist ontology. But it is equally true that the whole issue of environmentalism is inseparable from the logic of the specter. The value of nature today is inseparable from mourning, nostalgia for the way the world once was. Indeed, the "natural" is one of our words for the pure origin whose loss we mourn. It would be easy simply to dismiss these concerns as metaphysical artifacts, and certainly there are projects of environmental restoration that seem to rest on an arbitrary decision that some point in the past constitutes an ideal to which we should return.

But we would be crazy to allow our postmetaphysical caution to blind us to the fact that the natural world is indeed populated increasingly by ghosts. Not just by dead animals, but by extinct species. And the rate of extinction is only accelerating. Species are now becoming extinct before even being discovered. From an evolutionary point of view, we are witnessing a massive loss of *differentiation*. And with the loss of this differentiation we are losing the possibilities of further transformation. Every species that dies out is the loss of an adventure with the future. And with such loss of differentiation we also lose ecological complexity, and hence the diminution of constitutional relationality in nature. What this points to is not mourning for a lost purity, a privileged identity, but rather for a lost wealth of differential possibility. The time of industrialization is strangling evolutionary time. And the natural world is haunted by ghosts.

The spectral appears to us in the way our affection for nature is driven by the aesthetic of the sublime and the beautiful, justifying the preservation not so much of nature as of those vistas celebrated in eighteenth- and nineteenth-century European landscape painting (think of Constable or Cole), and of the wilderness in which a certain image of natural purity can be preserved. The privilege of these images has been contested within Western environmentalism by people such as Aldo Leopold[46] and Baird Callicott[47] who have tried to redirect us away from the visually flashy stereotypes of natural beauty, Bill McKibben's "eco-porn,"[48] toward the complex but modest swamps, and bogs, which are much less inviting, much less designed for human consumption. The lesson of Leopold's farm is that his nutrient-poor land sustains a much greater diversity of plant species than would rich land because no single species can command enough resources to take over.

The privilege of the sublime landscape, especially in American landscape painting, is a double-edged honor bestowed upon nature. It is a recognition of the value of a nature beyond human control. But at the same time it can and does function as a symbolic substitute and guarantee that our relation with nature is going well. The privilege of wilderness images has been contested too by third world environmentalists such as Ramachandra Guha,[49] for whom it reeks of an imperialist privilege blind to the true causes of environmental damage—overconsumption and militarism. The third world cannot afford this aestheticizing of a nature symbolically removed from human use.

But in addition to neo-Marxist critiques of the exploitation of nature as well as man, and the ambivalent logic of the specter, there is a third dimension to the deconstructive approach to the eleventh plague—that of environmental destruction. Deconstruction is filially tied not just to Marx, but equally to the legacy of structuralism, of Heidegger and of Levinas. And in each case, a common thread is the distance being marked from a certain "humanism." Key to this humanism is not just a certain anthropocentrism (of which residues remain in all these thinkers), but also a privileging of individual human intention, and the intellectual myopia to which this leads.[50] For environmentalism, this individualism generates a very specific logic of disaster, not a contradiction, not an aporia, but a catastrophe nonetheless. The shape of this logic is as follows: There is no significant environmental impact from any one person's action. As such there is nothing "wrong" with my doing this or that (say, driving an SUV). But the cumulative effects of each of us acting in this way spell disaster. So there is a disconnect between the whole space of individual desires and satisfactions, and the material consequences of their mass satisfaction. The ideological promotion of the individual consumer may have as its unintended consequence the destruction of the world. Environmental degradation is the consequence of the logic of individualism and the refusal to limit the scope of narcissistic humanism. What this shows, interestingly, is that what Marcuse called repressive desublimation does not merely short-circuit the interiority necessary for radical freedom, rather, the normalized pleasure that goes with commodity consumption provides an alibi for the destruction wreaked by cumulative effects.

CONCLUSION

My basic argument has been that deconstruction confirms and extends what is still alive in Marx and Marxism by fostering a phronesis of contrariety. This is a call to take seriously the problems and paradoxes that arise when, driven by often conflicting interests, we too enthusiastically apply models to the world in an effort to remake it. I have singled out Marcuse here both for his sense of the paradoxes of freedom, and for the antidote he provides to any manipulative deployment of the idea of radical freedom. I have tried to supplement Derrida's account of the ten plagues of the global order with a heavily abridged account of our destruction of nature.

The fundamental idea here is that we cannot deny to ourselves the philosophical tools for a critique of the new economic imperialism, tools that crucially draw on our Marxian legacy. Globalization intensifies contradictions of every sort, because we cannot just export our problems any more.

Although this intensification of contradiction—this recognition, through globalization, of the fragility of our finitude—can be expected to produce such documents as the U.S. National Defense Strategy, they are foolish and regressive responses to a genuinely critical moment in world history. Globalizing closure may yet provide the impetus for a revolution in the ways we act and think. It was in this spirit that Heidegger quotes Hölderlin's "where the danger is, grows the saving power also."[51] No more can we export our problems. They need to be dealt with here on earth—there is nowhere else to go.

Philosophy: The Antioxidant
of Higher Education

Imagine you have left your native country—with universal secondary education, selective higher education, and widespread healthy skepticism—and you find yourself in another country, highly advanced technologically, with mass higher education. You pick off the newsstand two widely circulated publications, one a paper, one a magazine. On the front page of the paper—a map of the solar system—with the location of Heaven clearly marked. Inside—a *photograph* of Heaven—(resembling Salt Lake City without cars). The magazine reports the results of a poll: that 81 percent of the population believe in heaven, and 88 percent of *those* believe they will meet their friends and family there. This is no thought experiment. The aliens have landed, and I am one of them.

I *assume* that what is of value in all education is *essential* in higher education—that it is not just a matter of communicating bodies of knowledge, vital though that is, but of imparting dispositions of critical inquiry. And it is the focus on ways of thinking, methods of investigation, powers of judgment, and complexity of response that makes higher education "higher." But how are we to reconcile the above data with the high percentage of the U.S. population that attends college? Either colleges do not, typically, have these Enlightenment goals, *or* they routinely fail to meet them. I claim that the Enlightenment ideals of higher education are subject to various kinds of corruption, and that philosophy would be the most powerful defense against these corruptions, were it not itself vulnerable to the same ailments. "Physician heal thyself" applies to the meta-physician too.

It used to be fashionable in England to contrast universities with training colleges. The former would educate minds, the latter would impart useful skills. But technological and social pressures are blurring that distinction.

Social life is increasingly being managed by information systems that require only the technical ability to participate in them. There is increasingly less need to understand how things work. My tax software asks me some bite-size questions and then constructs the finished return. Even the political process, traditionally an exercise of citizenship, is now run by electoral machines. It would not be surprising if "higher" education had adapted to accommodate our need to comfortably negotiate an increasingly complex humanly constructed real world. And then we might suppose that philosophy would have a diminishing role to play in education. If this story of an ever-more-programmed world is true, it is one that has crept up on us. If you put a frog in water and raise the temperature slowly, the frog will eventually be boiled alive. It adapts to every minute change in temperature; at no point is there a significant enough change to justify jumping out. Invisible increments add up, and the frog fries.

Education has to "adapt" to changing times. But, the frog adapted! To adapt successfully, the frog should have noticed something wrong, got a thermometer, kept records, and jumped. (The more direct analogy with global warming is unintended, but ominous.) I argue that it is philosophical attitudes, habits, and skills that can prevent our universities from being boiled alive.

Adaptation can be active and responsive or it can be reactive. Reactive adaptation responds to surface changes without grasping their shape and logic, allows the terms of the relationship to be dictated entirely by the other party. Active adaptation tries to grasp the law of change, not to be led by the nose, but to grasp and even create the opportunities that change brings. The shapes of change rarely stare us in the face. But critical reflection can draw them out and place even them in perspective. *Active* adaptation requires the critical capacities that are the natural but not exclusive property of philosophy. In the short term universities can do without philosophy, or make do with an emasculated rump of technical puzzle solvers. In the longer term, however, higher education will be brought to its knees if it turns its back on the critical reflection that is the hallmark of philosophy, and the effects on our broader cultural life will be disastrous. But this places the strongest demands and responsibilities on philosophy itself. What would philosophy have to be like to meet them?

Some worries: We live in an infantilizing culture, sadly one of our healthiest exports to the rest of the world. How? It promotes cartoon-level simplifications of complex problems, it confuses individualism with selfishness, imagines a freedom without responsibility, it cultivates an ever-reduced attention span, and it promotes ignorance and disdain of what is foreign— this applies to our own racial diversity, to relations between states, and to the rest of the world. And all this with complacency and good conscience. The United States of America is a bold experiment—a country forged out of revolution whose greatness depends on the way it sustains that legacy. This means consolidating and developing institutions that serve its founding values of freedom, justice, and equality of opportunity.

All institutions are subject to corruption. This applies to states, to the organs of state, to the universities and colleges that make up what we call higher education, and to philosophy itself. There is one specific sense and mechanism of corruption that I would like to isolate and discuss here— which, for want of a better phrase, I will call inaugural drift. I do not simply mean that the principles on which an institution was founded are lost sight of. It would be hopelessly prescriptive to call that corruption. After all, an institution might have been founded on narrow self-interest, and only subsequently discovered the values that made it great. Or it might constructively adapt its principles. Pressure groups that promoted a universal franchise that included women understandably broadened their scope after women were given the vote. No, I mean by corruption something more technical, perhaps more frighteningly predictable—that is, a change in the status of the rules that govern an institution's activity from being regulative to being constitutive. I once had a friend who invented a bidding system for the game of Bridge that was banned by the British Bridge Federation because it was too effective. The same could be said of modern electoral politics. There is a big difference between, on the one hand, presenting your views to the electorate and accepting consequent success or defeat, and, on the other, fine tuning one's expressed views to those which focus groups lead you to believe will maximize the chance of success. The same can be said of the tacit move from supposing that as a leader you are answerable to the nation—the whole electorate, including those who voted against you or did not even vote—to focusing your sense of subsequent obligation on those groups that elected you, or worse, financed your election. If institutions are set up to serve certain ends, and in the course of time, certain regulative rules or procedures are set in place the better to attain these ends, corruption occurs when these procedural rules take on a life of their own, and instead of having to justify their existence by reference to those original goals, they come to *constitute* a new game, a new reality. It is not just that the ends of the institution have changed, but rather that the structure in which *regulative rules serve independent ends* has been lost. If the letter of the law supplants the spirit of the law, what is lost is not just the original "spirit," but the dynamic relation between the two. This form of corruption—inaugural drift—hides under the banner of adaptation. In fact, as I have suggested, "active" adaptation would respond not to every impulse, but to the *law of change*. Institutions whose procedures maintain a living relationship to inaugural grounds are better suited to active adaptation than those "one-dimensional" institutions that most narrowly and shallowly seek to preserve themselves. Universities and colleges have enormous fundraising powers, for example, and it would not be impossible to gear admissions, teaching, and other policies wholly toward the business of raising money, as if the college were a corporation like any other. This would be an obvious example of corruption, though no law was ever broken.

An analogous one-dimensionalization occurs within the individual disciplines of universities and colleges. I was once confronted at an interdisciplinary seminar on the Sokal Hoax (the publication of a spoof postmodern essay by a scientist in an apparently reputable journal) with the insistent claim (by a natural scientist) that there were "truths out there" that no amount of post-Kantian, constructivist, or even deconstructivist exhortation on my part would budge. It was not that he was an epistemological realist, there was simply no intellectual space within which such issues were real to him. And he was not making a special limited claim about his slice of the world. There was just no sense that there might be disciplines that thrive on negotiating between different interpretations of the real—i.e., most of the arts and humanities. But even in natural science this epistemological naivete is a pedagogical disaster. To teach a student to understand a discipline as so much received knowledge rather than as an active interrogation of the world is to betray the charge of higher education, which is not to create consumers of knowledge, but its critics and creators. That should have been true at high school. How much more so at college! Of course we need to acquire knowledge before we can productively test and extend it. But what if this one-dimensional positivity about knowledge were normal in higher education? The fact that one can readily test students for their absorption of such knowledge and evaluate teachers for their capacity to convey it makes the business of delivering knowledge a ripe candidate for a source of corruption in higher education, one in which the less measurable virtues are subordinated to the more measurable. This is corruption in that it threatens the grounds for the existence of the institution itself.

If philosophy is the antioxidant of higher education, not just any mode of philosophizing will do. Humility is a great virtue, but being an underlaborer for the sciences will just deliver positivity again after a certain detour. The problem is that corruption endangers all institutions, including philosophy. There is a story about an Irishman outside a bar one night looking on the ground under a streetlight. A man asks him what he is looking for. He has dropped a coin. And where did you drop it? Actually, I dropped it round the corner, but this is where the light is, so I'm looking here. The most dangerous corruption of philosophy is the substitution of simple problems for complex ones. Yes, we can, as Descartes suggested, break down the complex into the simple the better eventually to solve the complex one. The danger is in the *substitution* of the simple for the complex without remainder. The history of empiricism, for example, looks awfully like the history of the substitution of emasculated models of experience for that extraordinary rich resource with which we begin. The temptation to substitute the simple for the complex is huge if we are promised for the first time solutions where we only had perplexity. But unless we can find a ladder back to the level of perplexity with which we began, and unless we can remember why we started philosophizing in the first place, we may be buying local success at the price of general failure. We may, for example, be able to *stipulate* a scheme of conceptual relatedness in some corner of the map, without having begun to address the difficulties as they arise on what Wittgenstein called the rough ground. I recall the anger of one of our graduate students when confronted with opposition to his declaration that "philosophy is just a game." Why was he so angry? The success of his whole life so far, including his graduate fellowship, had been predicated on this corrupt (and corrupting) assumption. Some philosophers advise: "Don't scratch where it doesn't itch." What kind of response would that have been to St. Augustine's avowal of puzzlement about time, whenever he tried to think about it? This slogan has a point in questioning the value of purely technical philosophical discussions, and there is, I believe, an important therapeutic dimension to philosophy. There is also a vital sense in which philosophical issues are not merely formal, but arise out of concrete human concerns. "Don't scratch where it doesn't itch" is a one-dimensional attitude. Sometimes we *should* itch, even if we don't. At other times we will start to itch madly once the scratching starts. And at yet other times, we may be in severe pain, but denying it so strongly that there seems to be nothing wrong. Philosophy is about making easy things difficult, not making difficult things easy. Just as institutions lose their way, and forget what brought them into being, so the same is true of each of us—that we necessarily lose ourselves in our habitual activity. The claim that the unreflected life is not worth living is not a recipe for a head in the clouds, but for finding effective ways of keeping ourselves open to the limits and conditions of our habits, and to other ways of seeing and thinking.

No one would dream of driving a car without binocular vision with which to judge depth and the speed of oncoming vehicles. Philosophy (and philosophical dispositions in whatever "department" they can be found) is the most powerful source of another kind of "double vision," one that allows us to combine knowledge with its constant critical interrogation; and this is the most powerful antidote to institutional corruption. But on this very point there is huge confusion. For the dogmatic mind, binocular vision appears as blurred vision, as a threat to faith, to certainty, to the prejudice that bears up entrenched habit. For the dogmatic mind, the demonstration of limits, of conditions of possibility, of difficulties, of tensions and ambiguities, is a destructive turn, to be resisted at all costs. It depicts the gods at war with each other, as Plato complained of Homer. Skepticism, critique, and deconstruction—as once were free inquiry, experimentation, and open public discussion—are seen as threats to the established order. In fact, however, they are threats to a dogmatic monocular way of inhabiting that order, and they are the handmaidens of *active* adaptation, of the true responsiveness to change that a tradition makes possible. That these "specters" are consistently misunderstood by non-philosophers is an indictment of philosophy's capacity to project its own best insights. What I am calling "double vision" is a knowing, a seeing and thinking *in a certain way,* an adverbial modification of an activity, not seeing two (or many) things and being unable to judge between them. All too many of the mock battles within contemporary philosophy rest on this error. Institutions that abandon their founding ideals without finding new ones are doomed to become the playthings of forces beyond their control. Institutions that no longer know the thrill of creation and innovation become the deaf sclerotic drones of a dead past. The management of change requires that we participate in the events that pass before us in the full awareness of what is at stake in this momentous play of forces. Double vision again. Critique is not the scourge of tradition, but the force that keeps its powers alive. Critique is not the enemy of faith but what prevents faith from falling into empty repetition. Critique is the enemy of complacency, of corruption, and of cultural decay. And philosophy is its home.

Finally, I would like to propose a way of shepherding together a number of the virtues that philosophy brings to education generally and to higher education in particular, under the umbrella of what Keats once called "negative capability." What he meant is quite profound: the capacity to endure uncertainty, to live with ambiguity, to keep alive questions to which one does not know the answers. Negative capability is not a synonym for intellectual laziness, a refusal or unwillingness to seek clarity where clarity is due, but rather a readiness to recognize the inherent limits, contextuality, and contingency of our knowledge, what Aristotle called the different kinds of precision appropriate to different disciplines. Negative capability is clearly not in itself negative, but a capacity, or disposition, to accommodate the negative. It is consonant with the recognition that there are times when the quest for certainty is pathological. If there are rarely rules for the application of rules, that does not rule out the need for judgment—*phronesis*—but makes it all the more important. Moreover, negative capability pervades numerous traditional philosophical values—freedom, toleration, patience, and openness. But philosophy cannot play the role of keeping institutions healthy and vibrant, keeping them free from the cancer of corruption, unless the healer heals herself. The choice is not between the caricatural options of analytic and continental philosophy—for each of these shelters both vital and moribund tribes—but between the humble, subtle, open, patient, adventurous, and judicious versions of each. I am far from recommending a kind of Rortyean ironic detachment. Instead of irony as detachment we should promote irony as a tolerance compatible with belief and commitment. To abandon the possibility of such a complex position, to say that this bicycle cannot be ridden, is to betray both philosophy and the culture it precariously serves.

Notes

INTRODUCTION

1. I have Pascal Massie to thank for bringing this to my attention (Summer 2002).

2. This may be the clue to the scene in which operational thinking flourishes. It allows us a hold over the future that it is essential for many of the systems we have established to be able to rely on. That hold is not based on (scientific) knowledge of nature, but on our ability to sustain a practical/informational complex to which this operational thinking does indeed adequately apply, for the most part. It would be instructive to compare the attack on the World Trade Center and the collapse of Enron in the lights of this formulation. The WTC was attacked as a symbol of the American domination of global capital markets. What is remarkable is that despite the demonstration of the vulnerability of such institutions, the large loss of life, and a temporary "loss of confidence," there seemed to be no real interruption of the operation of global trade or markets, implying that the information, and the systems in question, had no unique storage site. The response (on the part of the U.S. military) was to attempt to subject an underdeveloped country (Afghanistan) to its military/technological machine, which nonetheless kept running up against precapitalist tribal formations that limited its operational effectiveness (sheltering suspects, for example). And one can only speculate on the long-term damage to the interests of globalization effected by the political fallout from this military operation, not to mention the subsequent Iraq fiasco. In the case of Enron, its collapse made clear that those who advocated deregulation did so in order to be able to fix the markets in which they sold their energy. The phenomenon of "gaming"—engineering profits through artificially induced scarcity—exposes what we could call a black hole arising out of operational thinking. The fact that regulations do not regulate themselves suggests that such uncontrolled consequences will always be possible. My argument in the Postscript is somewhat parallel—that complex institutions (including universities and other educational institutions) are, in principle, subject to corruption (I define corruption technically as "treating regulative principles as constitutive"), and philosophical dispositions are well suited to counter this pathological tendency.

3. This formulation is taken from Heidegger's own introduction of the "step back" in "The Thing," in *Poetry, Language, Thought* (New York: Harper and Row, 1975), 181. Obviously, we are broadening the scope of this expression in this book.

4. It would be interesting in this context to bring together the various references philosophers have made to steps, paths, walking, etc. and the variations philosophers have played on this theme. To Heidegger's step back we would add Blanchot's *"pas au delà"* (the step [not] beyond), Kierkegaard's leap (of faith), Nietzsche's dance ("my style is a dance . . ."), and leap (". . . an overleaping mockery of symmetries"). To these we would have to add the many references to the path and the way *(Tao)*. Indeed, even the ubiquitous (for some iniquitous) word *method*, with its Greek root *hodos* (way), would have to be included. The question raised by this lexicon of paths and ways has to do with the status of its contribution to philosophical discourse, whether it is a wholly dispensable metaphorical legacy from a distant past or whether it reflects another way in which human embodiment is ineliminable from thought.

5. Our quotation from Keats on the first page of this *Introduction* comes from a letter he wrote to his brothers in 1817. Obviously, we are developing this notion in a somewhat different way; we are not, for example, foreswearing fact or reason, but (not surprisingly), the inappropriate grasp of their significance.

6. If negative capability has a tradition, Nietzsche is clearly one of its champions: "To be true to my nature, which is *affirmative* . . . I . . . set down the three tasks for the sake of which one requires educators. One has to learn to *see*, one has to learn to *think*, one has to learn to *speak* and *write*: the end in all three is a noble culture. Learning to see—habituating the eye to repose, to patience, to letting things come to it; learning to defer judgement, to investigate and comprehend the individual case in all its aspects . . . not to react immediately to a stimulus. . . . Learning to *see* . . . the essence of it is precisely *not* to "will," the *ability* to defer decision. . . . One will have become slow, mistrustful, resistant as a *learner*. . . . In an attitude of hostile calm one will allow the strange, the novel of every kind to approach one first—one will draw one's hand back from it" ("What the Germans Lack," Section 6, *Twilight of the Idols*). These remarks are perhaps a response to Heidegger's readings of him, *avant la lettre*.

7. At this point, of course, there is a clear parallel with at least the aims of Foucauldian genealogy.

8. Allow me to refer here to my *The Deconstruction of Time* (Evanston: Northwestern University Press, 2001) and *Time After Time* (Bloomington: Indiana University Press, forthcoming), where these issues become thematic.

CHAPTER ONE. IDENTITY AND VIOLENCE

1. This is no longer a view confined to the exotic jungle of deconstruction. It is central to more mainstream marginal discourse too. Its importance for thinking of sexual difference is made clear in José Medina's landmark paper, "Identity Trouble: Disidentification and the *Problem* of Difference," *Philosophy and Social Criticism* 29, no. 6 (2003): 655–80, and pursued more fully in his forthcoming *Speaking from Elsewhere*.

2. A remark by Bishop Butler which G. E. Moore made famous in his *Principia Ethica* (Cambridge: Cambridge University Press, 1922).

3. For a classic formulation of this claim, see Sartre's *The Transcendence of the Ego* (New York: Noonday, 1991).

4. I would not want to prematurely close off discussion about, say, the status of agency. In a political context, the response of someone such as Jean-Luc Nancy in *The Inoperative Community* (Minneapolis: University of Minnesota Press, 1991) has not been to show how unproblematic it is for such a self to be an agent, but rather to question the very idea of a productive agency (at least in the sense of attempting to enact a political program in constructing a community). Such a position suggests that there may be a way forward at least politically, even if the deconstruction of the self were to problematize the idea of agency.

5. I am reminded here of an example of Lacan's—the Moebius strip—a circular band, cut, twisted and rejoined, which then possesses only one surface, but at every point two sides. The two sides we could use to represent the empirical and transcendental—made of the same material but performing distinct functions, and at any chosen point operating at different levels. On such a model, although Kierkegaard's references to God's role in helping to constitute a self would be references to the necessity of a transcendental function, which could not, he claims, be provided entirely by the Self alone, we might come to wonder whether the construction of a wholly discontinuous power was necessary.

6. This claim is helpfully developed in Simone de Beauvoir's *The Ethics of Ambiguity* (New York: Philosophical Library, 1948), where she describes the various ways in which stunted development produces "sub-men."

7. I develop this idea in "Glimpsess of Being in Dasein's Development," *contretemps* 3 (2002) [online journal].

8. Heidegger's treatment of the importance of Hölderlin as such a resource in his *Contributions to Philosophy: (From Enowning)* (Bloomington: Indiana University Press, 2001) is a classic example of this thought.

9. See, for example, Nietzsche's account of eternal recurrence (e.g., in *The Gay Science*, section 341). See also my discussion of the eternal recurrence in *The Deconstruction of Time* (Evanston: Northwestern University Press, 2001).

10. For a fuller treatment of place, I would refer the reader to Ed Casey's *The Fate of Place* (Berkeley: University of California Press, 1999)

11. Here, one could try to think together the diaspora, the songlines of Australian aborigines discussed by Bruce Chatwin (in *Songlines*), Husserl on gypsies, and the American myth of the road, from Jack Kerouac to road movies and onward.

12. What we mean by modernity is clearly connected with secularization, with the displacement of religious belief and religious fellowship as the basis of our sense of self. If lived-identity rests on certain horizons of constancy, and if the maintenance of some of these horizons of constancy has been displaced from religion to the state and dependent institutions of civil society, then a great deal will hang on the maintenance of state functions. If these state functions disintegrate, then, in the absence of surviv-

ing buffering institutions, a cascade of consequences follow, and we can expect a return to the war of all against all from which the state had delivered us. It is not difficult to see the extreme and almost unbelievable violence that followed the breakup of Yugoslavia in this light, and the combination of genocidal "ethnic cleansing" with rape and torture camps suggests a desperate scramble for even the most primitive forms of selfhood. One is reminded of Sartre's dialectical accounts of the variety of concrete relations with others that follow the breakdown of love: sadism, masochism, hatred, etc.

13. See, e.g., Bataille, and also Derrida in "Eating Well," in *Who Comes After the Subject*, ed. Cadava (London: Routledge, 1991).

14. Here, the work of Bataille and Girard is obviously central. See for example George Bataille, *Inner Experience* (Albany: State University of New York Press, 1988), and René Girard, *Violence and the Sacred* (Baltimore: Johns Hopkins University Press, 1979). For an excellent discussion of their work, see Zeynep Direk, "Bataille on Sacrifice: Immanent and Transcendent Violence," *Bulletin de la Société Américaine de Philosophie de Langue Française* (2005). And for American poet Gary Snyder, sacrifice is intimately linked to the idea of the sacred, the point of resistance to "an endlessly expansive materialist economy" ("Good, Wild, Sacred," in *The Practice of the Wild* [San Francisco: North Point Press, 1990], 81).

15. And we must not discount here Jean-Luc Nancy's suggestion that it is precisely the sense of loss of community that founds our (residual?) sense of community today, however much of a myth that is.

16. This theme of a recognition-deficient culture is pursued at greater length in the next chapter, "The Philosophy of Violence :: The Violence of Philosophy."

17. At this point, one could begin to develop a philosophy of education, and indeed develop the consequences for a broader political philosophy, one that reminded us that whatever values we espouse, we are committed to valuing the conditions they presuppose. And if a free market does not supply the conditions for real freedom, they must be met in other ways.

18. Compare Heidegger's view that for Dasein Being is always a question.

19. The "Führer principle" promised identity through identification.

20. As Richard Kearney points out in his *Poetics of Imagining* (New York: HarperCollins, 1991), 225, referring to the Shoah and to Primo Levi. The issue of witnessing is also addressed in his *On Stories* (London: Routledge, 2002).

21. I discuss this in "The Economy of Time," in *Time After Time* (forthcoming).

22. In *The Kristeva Reader*, ed. Toril Moi (Oxford: Blackwell, 1986).

23. I owe this suggestion to Joe McCahery, of the Law School, then of the University of Warwick, now University of Tilberg, Leuven.

24. See Ricoeur's *Oneself as Another*, trans. Kathleen Blamey (Chicago: University of Chicago Press, 1992), especially the Fifth Study.

25. See Jacques Derrida, *On the Name* (Stanford: Stanford University Press, 1995)

26. The structure of this "problem" is captured and perhaps clarified, if not resolved, by that of the Moebius strip. A narrative about narrative is both of a different order (on the opposite side of the strip), and also of the same order (sharing a continuous surface).

27. I have in mind here Rorty's *Contingency, Irony, Solidarity* (Cambridge: Cambridge University Press, 1989).

CHAPTER TWO. THE PHILOSOPHY OF VIOLENCE :: THE VIOLENCE OF PHILOSOPHY

1. See my *Thinking After Heidegger* (Cambridge: Polity, 2002), much of which is occupied with this question. There are various antidotes to the violence of conceptuality: Openness to experience (what Merleau-Ponty meant by hyper-reflection, and the primacy of perception), listening to the speaking of language (to use Heidegger's formulation), or a certain stylistic/performative exuberance (Nietzsche) are just some of the ways philosophers have taken.

2. Suppose a man is reported missing in action. His distraught wife eventually remarries, moves away, and lives happily ever after. The soldier, who is very much alive, cannot trace his wife. Her new marriage continues in its undisturbed happiness only because her ex-husband cannot find her. A potentially devastating counterfactual is never realized. The ignorance of the new couple is bliss. I claim it really was bliss, even though it was based on ignorance. For there always are, or can be, destructive possible counterfactuals in the wings of any supposedly stable state.

3. This raises the question of how to distinguish relative strengths of claim. There are some cases in which this seems to be able to be done convincingly, such as Solomon's solution to the two women claiming to be the mother of the same baby.

4. The question of the negotiability of loss is central to many issues—political conflict, psychological trauma, even the experience of the passage of time. See Nietzsche on *ressentiment*, Heidegger on being-towards-death.

5. Cf. the idea that the analysis ends when the patient realizes it could go on forever.

6. An early version of the chapter "Identity and Violence" appeared in *On the Work of Edward Said: Cultural Differences and the Gravity of History*, ed. Keith Ansell-Pearson, Benita Parry, Judith Squires (London and New York: Lawrence, 1997). His death on September 25, 2003, was a blow to the search for peace in the Middle East, and to American public life.

7. Bentham's utilitarian motto was "Calculemus!" ("Let us calculate!").

8. This refers to events in the spring of 1998.

9. This implication of this is best captured in the problematic phrase "conditional unconditionality."

10. For an extended discussion, see my "Vigilance and Interruption: Derrida, Gadamer, and the Limits of Dialogue," chapter 7 of *Philosophy at the Limit* (London: Unwin Hyman, 1990).

11. A popular but excellent introduction to negotiation theory (and practice) is Roger Fisher et al., *Getting to Yes* (Harmondsworth: Penguin, 1991).

12. See Theodor Adorno, *Dialectic of Enlightenment* (with Max Horkheimer) (London: Continuum, 1976); Jean-François Lyotard, *The Postmodern Condition* (Minneapolis: University of Minnesota Press, 1985).

13. See Nietzsche's *Thus Spoke Zarathustra* (Harmondsworth: Penguin, 1961), 161.

14. As I was writing an early draft of this chapter there came news of a black man dragged to death on the streets of a small town in Texas (Spring 1998).

15. The manipulation of this structure of displacement was most evident in the targeting of Iraq in response to 9/11, and the repeated attempts to associate Bin Laden and Saddam Hussein in the mind of the American public.

16. Kant, "Idea for a Universal History with a Cosmopolitan Purpose," in *Kant's Political Writings*, ed. Hans Reiss (Cambridge: Cambridge University Press, 1970); Hegel, *Phenomenology of Spirit*, trans. A. V. Miller (Oxford: Oxford University Press, 1977); Sartre, *Being and Nothingness*, trans. Hazel Barnes (New York: Philosophical Library, 1956).

17. Although there are analogous examples in nature. Suppose you work very hard to clear land, plant crops, and eventually something grows—you might treat this as "reward for (recognition of) all my hard work." It would be wise not to immediately discount this formulation. It may be that what is being captured is, at the very least, the peculiarly human capacities for delayed gratification, for planning ahead, for investment for the future, which alone make sense of all that labor. Nature is recognizing this in the sense that at this complex level, you have established some sort of relation with nature.

18. See "Concrete Relations with Others," in *Being and Nothingness*, op.cit. supra.

19. Cf. Bertrand Russell, *Mysticism and Logic* (London: Unwin, 1963) on the importance of being able to live with uncertainty, and the ethical meaning of ancient skepticism.

20. Heidegger's essay *Gelassenheit* (1959) has been translated as *Discourse on Thinking*, trans. John Anderson and Hans Freund (New York: Harper, 1966).

21. Theodor W. Adorno et al., *The Authoritarian Personality* (New York: Harper, 1950).

22. Those who advocate the legalization of drugs argue plausibly that what is called the war on drugs is a mask for a massive state dependency on the continuation of the drug trade, a true dance with the devil.

23. At the opposite extreme, think of (1) the role of honor in traditional European war, (2) arguments against assassination of enemy leaders—that there needs to be trust finally to make peace.

24. In *Heidegger: Basic Writings*, ed. David Farrell Krell (London: Routledge and Kegan Paul, 1978)

25. *Being and Time*, trans. Joan Stambaugh (Albany: State University of New York Press, 1996) (*Sein und Zeit* [Tübingen: Max Niemeyer Verlag, 1953]).

26. "The Anaximander Fragment," trans. David Krell and Frank Capuzzi, in *Early Greek Thinking* (New York: Harper and Row, 1976) ("Der Spruch des Anaximander," in *Holzwege* [Frankfurt: Vittorio Klostermann, 5th ed, 1972]).

27. *An Introduction to Metaphysics*, trans. Ralph Mannheim (New York: Anchor, 1961), 125–49 (hereafter IM) (*Einführung der Metaphysik* [Tübingen: Max Niemeyer Verlag, 1953]).

28. Ibid., 125.

29. Ibid., 126.

30. Ibid., 131.

31. Ibid., 130.

32. Ibid., 130.

33. "Violence and Metaphysics," in *Writing and Difference*, trans. Alan Bass (Chicago: University of Chicago Press, 1978) (originally in *L'écriture et la différence* [Paris: Editions du Seuil, 1967]). On this question, I would particularly draw attention to Hent de Vries's *Religion and Violence* (Baltimore: Johns Hopkins University Press, 2002), especially chapter 2, "Violence and Testimony." There are few better treatments of the religious and philosophical problem of violence.

34. See Jacques Derrida, "The Future Can Only Be Anticipated in the Form of an Absolute Danger," in *Of Grammatology*, trans. Gayatri Chakravorty Spivak (Baltimore: Johns Hopkins University Press, 1976) 5.

35. "Force of Law—'The Mystical Foundation of Authority,'" trans. Mary Quaintance, in *Deconstruction and the Possibility of Justice*, ed. Drucilla Cornell et al. (New York: Routledge, 1992).

36. *Being and Time* 352/*Sein und Zeit* 384.

37. See chapter 3, "The Voyage of Reason," in my *Thinking After Heidegger* (Cambridge: Polity, 2002).

38. Kristeva makes this distinction in "The Semiotic and the Symbolic," Part 1 of *Revolution in Poetic Language* (New York: Columbia, 1984). By the symbolic she means that level of language at which meaning, rules, and grammar operate. The semiotic refers to a nonsignifying dimension within the symbolic, reflecting "the basic drives recognized by psychoanalysis as they discharge themselves into language prior to any actual linguistic signification" (*Revolution*, 24).

39. In *Philosophy and Truth*, trans. D. Breazeale (Atlantic Highlands: Humanities, 1979) ("Uber Wahrheit und Luge im aussermoralischen Sinne").

40. This "control over phenomena" will later be named the will-to-power.

41. See his *The Visible and the Invisible*, trans. Alphonso Lingis (Evanston: Northwestern University Press, 1968) (*Le Visible et l'invisible* [Paris: Gallimard, 1964]).

42. I have to report that violence noticeably erupted at one point in the questions that followed an early version of this chapter presented as a lecture at Bochum

in 1998. I was passionately condemned by one speaker for trying to explain Heidegger's remarks about factory farming. This is hardly surprising—a seventy-minute monologue is hardly a model of the free exchange of ideas. And what I said is not without consequence, practical as well as symbolic. Rather than being disappointed, I was, on reflection, grateful that there are still institutions in which passionate disagreement does not end in bloodshed.

43. For a considerable expansion of these remarks, see my "Comment ne pas manger: Deconstruction and Humanism," in *The Animal as Other*, ed. Peter Steeves (Albany: State University of New York Press, 1999). Also, "Thinking with Cats," in *Animal Philosophy*, ed. Atterton and Calarco (London: Continuum, 2004), which discusses Derrida's "The animal that therefore I am (more to follow)."

44. "Eating Well," trans. Peter Connor and Avital Ronell, in *Who Comes After the Subject*, ed. E. Cadava et al. (New York: Routledge, 1991).

45. "Symbolic" dimension is not quite right. What Derrida and Heidegger have in common here is the claim that our ways of treating of animals embody broader patterns of significance.

46. The subversion of the independence of the United Nations by the United States, the refusal by the United States to ratify the World Court (as of 2002), would be examples of this difficulty.

47. Vicki Hearne, *Adam's Task* (New York: Vintage, 1987).

48. These comments are my response to strongly voiced objections to such an expression made to me by Karin de Boer (*Collegium Phaenomenologicum*, 2000). While I doubt that what I say here will allay her doubts, I hope at least that my reasons for persisting in speaking of the "animal holocaust" are at least clearer. Any timidity one might have had in broaching the parallels between the Jewish and animal holocausts is rendered merely quaint after the bravura performance of Elizabeth Costello in J. M.Coetzee's *The Lives of Animals* (Princeton: Princeton University Press, 1999).

49. The very cry "Never again!" to the Jewish holocaust, argues against a rigid insistence on its singularity. Who could seriously restrict this proscriptive demand to a chosen people, to a certain magnitude, to a particular mechanism without cheapening and diluting the depth of the outrage. For Jews, it is understandable that they might have in the forefront of their minds: "We must do everything we can to ensure that this never again happens to us." But the deeper ethical and political message precisely demands our vigilance to all the translations and transformations of holocaust. The Jewish holocaust was not the first and has not been the last. Singularity—ethically, historically, and (if you will) spiritually—marks every event in which through incomprehensible violence, pain, and suffering it jumps out of every concept, name, or representation with which we attempt to capture it. If "Never again!" is to be allowed its full reach, what it teaches us is not merely how easily educated humans can conjure up and carry out genocidal projects, but how a veneer of legitimacy can blind ordinary people to the most outrageous and horrific acts being carried out in their midst. We might hope that we have now been sufficiently alerted to the shape of this particular horror that it may not easily return. But we have no reason whatsoever to

suppose that the desire not to know the terrible things being committed in one's name, the willingness to accept what is endorsed by authority—that any of these fundamental human failings have changed one bit. It is in the light of this that those who champion the rights of animals have been tempted to draw analogies with the Jewish holocaust. Yiddish Nobel Prize–winning author Isaac Bashevis Singer did not find the comparison difficult. As one of his characters, Herman, put it, "In their behavior toward creatures, all men were Nazis. The smugness with which man could do with other species as he pleased exemplified the most extreme racist theories, the principle that might is right" (from *Enemies, A Love Story*, 1989).

50. There are real and important differences between what we persist in calling the animal holocaust, and genocide. If genocide is the deliberate attempt to exterminate a species, then clearly our agricultural practices (which kill 10 billion chickens a year, 500 million turkeys, 3.5 million cows, etc. just in the United States) are not genocidal at all, despite the large numbers. There is no attempt to wipe out a species, just to control the breeding, genetic characteristics, conditions of life, and time of death technologically. As for the rapid rate of destruction of animal species on earth, this is occasionally genocidal (attacks on West Nile virus, smallpox, malarial mosquitoes, and, at times, wolves), but intentional destruction is dwarfed by the foreseen and unforeseen consequences of actions (draining marshes, building cities, logging forests) that do not have any genocidal intentions. But if we think hard about the intelligence and capacities for exercising reason that we believe distinguish our own species, these unintended consequences begin to take on the character of culpable negligence.

51. Let me add, to prevent any misunderstanding, that what I have called "silent, invisible violence" takes many other contemporary (and sadly quite traditional) forms: mass incarceration and the failure of social incorporation to which this testifies (at epidemic proportions in China and the United States), the violence of globalization (a rising tide raises all boats, but those without boats may drown), and the violence we are perpetrating on our descendants, the inheritors of this planet. There is a genuine conceptual question here—whether we can describe as "violent" every case of predictable, even well-known, but unintended damage, and whether there is not a certain attempt to persuade in such a definition of violence. Not all negligence is culpable. But where that culpability is diminished by systematic disinformation and the spreading of ideological rationalizations for violence, we would surely only need a more stratified grasp of the structure of violence.

52. See my *Thinking After Heidegger*, op. cit.

CHAPTER THREE. WHERE LEVINAS WENT WRONG

This chapter was first presented as a paper at the Levinas Conference, Emory University, Atlanta, October 15, 1999. I am grateful to the organizers, Antje Kapust, Eric Nelson, and Ken Still for inviting me before they realized what I would say.

1. This should not be interpreted as an attempt to *reduce* Levinasian ethics to the conditions that may have prompted its formulation. It may be that *all* significant ethical beginnings are particular, and that what is distinctive about a philosophical

elaboration or articulation is the way in which this generalizes from that particular beginning. Our question could be formulated as: What shape has the elaborative generalization taken in this case? What does it close down as it opens up?

2. Heidegger, *What is Called Thinking?* [1954], trans. Fred Wieck and J. Glenn Gray (New York: Harper and Row, 1968), 77. Heidegger's words are "einmal das Entgegengehen und dann das Dagegenangehen."

3. Levinas, *Time and the Other* [1947], trans. Richard Cohen (Pittsburgh: Duquesne University Press, 1987), 63 (hereafter TO).

4. The Discovery Channel is an American TV channel devoted to nature and wildlife.

5. This interview can be found in Derrida, *Points . . . : Interviews, 1974–1994* (Stanford: Stanford University Press, 1995).

6. See my "Comment ne pas manger: Heidegger and Humanism," in *Animal Others: On Ethics, Ontology, and Animal Life*, ed. H. Peter Steeves (Albany: State University of New York Press, 1999).

7. The classic contemporary paper on this matter is Christopher D. Stone's "Do Trees Have Standing: Towards Legal Rights for natural Objects"[1972], in Joseph DesJardins, *Environmental Ethics* (Mountain View: Mayfield, 1999). See also John Llewelyn, *The Middle Voice of Ecological Conscience* (London: Macmillan, 1991), 148–50 and passim.

8. Edmund Husserl, *Cartesian Meditations* (The Hague: Nijhoff, 1960).

9. See Derrida's *Aporias*, trans. Thomas Dutoit (Stanford: Stanford University Press, 1993) for the argument that if being able to die in the full sense ("as such") is definitive for the distinction between humans and animals, and if that involves our grasp of the meaning of what it is to die, the distinction may be in trouble.

10. See Heidegger, *Being and Time*, trans Joan Stambaugh (Albany: State University of New York Press, 1996), section 26, H122.

11. Levinas, *Existence and Existents*, trans. Alphonso Lingis (The Hague: Nijhoff, 1978).

12. "The Old and the New," TO, 136.

13. Richard Kearney's "Dialogue with Emmanuel Levinas" (hereafter DEL) can be found in *Face to Face with Levinas*, ed. Richard A. Cohen (Albany: State University of New York Press, 1986).

14. Ibid., 24.

15. See Robert Bernasconi's paper in *Addressing Levinas*, ed. E. Nelson et al. (Evanston: Northwestern University Press, 2004).

16. DEL, 21.

17. TO, 75.

18. J. P. Sartre, *Being and Nothingness* [1943] (London: Methuen, 1958), 564.

19. TO, 74.

20. Ibid.

21. TO, 75.

22. Ibid.

23. TO, 82.

24. Ibid.

25. DEL, 21.

CHAPTER FOUR. THE FIRST KISS

I would like to thank Jonathan Rée and Jane Chamberlain for their helpful input on a fledgling version of this chapter.

Abbreviations are employed in this chapter as follows: EO = *Either/Or*, trans. Alastair Hannay (Harmondsworth: Penguin, 1992); FT = *Fear and Trembling*, trans. Alastair Hannay (Harmondsworth: Penguin, 1985). I have capitalized First Kiss where it refers specifically to Kierkegaard's account of it.

1. *Concluding Unscientific Postscript*, trans. Hong and Hong (Princeton: Princeton University Press, 1992), 117.

2. The first two issues emerge early on in the practical sphere of accountancy. (Imagine owing someone more cows than you possess.) And it is not difficult to see how these concepts could have aroused passions, as numbers take on a life of their own. Uncanny feelings must have accompanied the development of credit—sentiments that still linger. These associations suggest that to the extent that arithmetic is tied to the practice of counting, it will inherit the developing social significance attached to counting and accounting. And it would not be a wholly original claim to suggest that the strangeness associated with these concepts might be tied to the mercantile social transformations they heralded. But what about the third question we posed, that of the *first* number? Aristotle is said to have declared that "2" is the first number. And we can imagine various arguments against "1": because it is exhausted by its ontological significance as unity or singularity, because until there is a second number, the first cannot be the first, because first means first of a series. On this argument, the first number is "2," which then retrospectively confers that status on "1." The special status of small numbers only grows when we realize that the counting abilities of some animals, and some indigenous peoples, and our own capacity for counting-at-a-glance are all confined to small numbers—usually seven and under. It suggests that numbers operate qualitatively before taken up into quantity.

3. I recommend for further reading "The Lore of Number," by Julian Barit, in *From Five Fingers to Infinity*, ed. Frank Swetz (Peru, IL: Open Court, 1994)

4. Here I quote the irresistible interpollation of an anonymous reviewer on reading this manuscript. For this and numerous other insightful comments, I am most grateful.

5. *John Donne*, ed. John Hayward (Harmondsworth: Penguin, 1964), 23.

6. This forces philosophers to a critical reexamination of Herman Hupfeld's lyrics in the theme song "As Time Goes By" in *Casablanca* (1942). In a world in which so much is changing, his argument goes, some "fundamental things" can be relied on: "A kiss is still a kiss." Notwithstanding his creative deployment of what Erasmus Schöfer (discussing Heidegger) called "tautology as *figura etymologica*," Hupfeld's brilliant inversion of the more common sense of the fleetingness of love is nonetheless defective in failing to grasp the inherent fragile projective temporality of the kiss.

7. It is illuminating to note that the same sort of remark can also be made in response to Freud's claim that the processes of the unconscious have no reference to time. The apparent insulation of primary processes from the passage of time, time as it "goes by," only conceals the most powerful drive to master our mortal immersion in time.

8. The capacity for rejuvenation is close to what Kierkegaard means by "repetition" in his book of that name, which is at the heart of his phenomenology of time. There is, indeed, something of a paradox in the idea of committing oneself to spontaneity. But we can commit ourselves to trying to cultivate those conditions that nourish spontaneity—and this is far from being a merely formulaic resolution of the paradox. Compare Derrida's treatment of the "impossibility" of the marriage vows in his essay on "Perjury" in *Without Alibi* (Stanford: Stanford University Press, 2002). We have tried to capture the same idea in terms of conditional unconditionality.

9. See "Of Old and Young Women," in *Thus Spoke Zarathustra* (Harmondsworth: Penguin, 1961), 91.

10. *Stages on Life's Way*, ed. Hong and Hong (Princeton: Princeton University Press, 1988), 134.

11. In *Martin Heidegger: Basic Writings*, ed. D. F. Krell (New York: Routledge, 1978).

12. Without in any way wanting to reduce Kierkegaard's complex view of women to his own relation to his mother, a relation complicated by his father's later confessions of impropriety toward his mother (and probably worse), and by Kierkegaard's struggle to deal with the psychic inheritance of his father, the complexity and intensity of life chez Kierkegaard does give us a powerful example of the extreme circumstances under which some thinkers have had to construct their fundamental images of self, identity, gender, the other, women, etc. Such circumstances may, however, be closer to being the normal state "writ large" than we might think. It is for this last reason that a biographical reductionism is almost always naive.

CHAPTER FIVE. THINKING GOD IN THE WAKE OF KIERKEGAARD

1. Those of us who deserted Sartre on reading *Being and Time, Letter on Humanism*, and then Sartre's own confession of the petty-bourgeois concerns of the author of *Being and Nothingness* may have come to need such proof.

2. See "The Singular Universal"[1964], in *Kierkegaard: A Collection of Critical Essays*, ed. Josiah Thompson (Garden City: Anchor, 1972), 231–65 (hereafter SU).

3. *The Gift of Death*, trans. David Wills (Chicago: University of Chicago Press, 1995), 108 (hereafter GD). John Caputo, in his *The Prayers and Tears of Jacques Derrida* (1997) argues that this is a view of God that Derrida ultimately rejects. This argument came to my attention too late to be dealt with in detail here.

4. Ludwig Wittgenstein, "On Heidegger on Being and Dread," in *Heidegger and Modern Philosophy*, ed. Michael Murray (New Haven: Yale University Press, 1978) (hereafter OHBD).

5. See F. P. Ramsey, "Last Papers of Philosophy," from his *Foundations of Mathematics and Other Logical Essays* (1931), quoted in Cyril Barrett's excellent *Wittgenstein on Ethics and Religious Belief* (Oxford: Blackwell,1991), 22.

6. OHBD, 81.

7. *Tractatus Logico-Philosophicus*, trans. D. F. Pears and B. McGuinness (London: Routledge, 1961) (hereafter TLP).

8. Quoted from his *Notebooks*, 72–75. See Barrett, 97.

9. Barrett, 100.

10. TLP 6.432 (quoted in Barrett, 94).

11. TLP 6.45 (quoted in Barrett, 73).

12. *Being and Time*, section 29.

13. Compare Heidegger's reference to the ontico-ontological difference, the difference between (particular) beings, and Being.

14. This is close to what Heidegger tried to generalize as the relation between Being-toward-death and authenticity. We might suppose that Sartre's disagreement over the significance of death has to do with him thinking that mortality can be subordinated to our (broader) finitude, in which every choice is a "petit mort." We might also think that the true significance of the Abraham/Isaac story lies in seeing it as a particularly graphic dramatization of self-sacrifice.

15. SU, 241ff.

16. SU, 243.

17. SU, 244. See below, where we take up the question of Kierkegaard's own discussion of immortality (in *Concluding Unscientific Postscript*).

18. Another version of this claim may be found elaborated in Heidegger's distinction (which he insists is not a [mere] difference of category) between Being and beings, in *Being and Time*. It is well known that Heidegger subsequently came to rue this attempt at constructing a fundamental ontology, as if one could improve on traditional systematic metaphysics while keeping the constructive mode of exposition. His later more allusive, "poetic" style is an attempt to form a new way of writing in keeping with the recognition that it is precisely in the character of the *way* (the how) that "truth" lies. Lacan claimed that Freud's hydraulic language (of libidinal flows and blockages) reflected a certain contingent restriction on available models, and that had Saussure's work been available to him, he might have found a linguistic model preferable. I am making an analogous argument about Kierkegaard's religious language, that

it captures vital distinctions in a way that seems to preserve them, but actually sets up a different kind of struggle against their loss, one in which the struggle is more likely to be won, but the victory Pyrrhic. On this argument the institutionalization of religious thought against which Kierkegaard railed is already to be found in the very concepts constitutive of religious discourse.

19. See G. W. F. Hegel, *Phenomenology of Spirit*, trans. A. V. Miller (Oxford: Clarendon, 1977), 111ff (section on Lordship and Bondsman).

20. This suggests to me a cascade of translations of any "divine" absolute, with Christianity bringing God to earth in Christ, and then an interpretation of Christ as a way of being human, which would be radicalized in Zarathustra, or (see later) in a certain way of reading Kierkegaard's knight of faith.

21. In *Being and Nothingness*, 533–34, he explicitly repudiates Heidegger's sense that we can make something of our death. Instead, Sartre says we should recognize it as something absurd. In fact, I suspect that Sartre misunderstands Heidegger's position here. It is only in a rather technical sense that Heidegger makes something of our Being-toward-death. It is not so much a grounding as an abyssal moment—an ungrounding.

22. "He is continually making the movement of infinity, but . . . with such precision and assurance that he continually gets finitude out of it . . ." (*Fear and Trembling*, trans. Howard V. Hong and Edna H. Hong [Princeton: Princeton University Press, 1983], 40–41).

23. This theme can be found in various places: *Fear and Trembling* (why Abraham had to remain silent), in *The Concept of Irony* (with special reference to Socrates), and *Concluding Unscientific Postscript* (esp. the section "A Contemporary Effort" where the communication of inwardness is at stake).

24. SU, 257–58.

25. SU, 264.

26. "Economimesis," "From Restricted to General Economy," "Comment ne pas parler," "Sauf le nom," "Passions," *Of Spirit, Aporias,* and *The Gift of Death.*

27. See Jacques Derrida, *Speech and Phenomena*, trans. David Allison (Evanston: Northwestern University Press, 1973).

28. This kind of position has been developed by such thinkers as Mark C. Taylor, John Caputo, and Sylvane Agacinski. More recently, as we shall see, by Jacques Derrida himself.

29. *The Gift of Death*, trans. David Wills (Chicago: University of Chicago Press, 1995), 6.

30. Ibid., 8.

31. There are remarkable parallels between Patočka and Nietzsche's discussion in *The Genealogy of Morals* of the production of a subject with interiority, through Christian asceticism. For Derrida's purposes, what is central is the way this allows us to demonstrate the interweaving of history and economy. It allows us to begin to think that something like a self-present responsible subject might not be a simple given, but

a complex historical product lodged in, and explicable only within a certain economy (of gift, of sacrifice).

32. Note that Derrida had himself used this very expression *(fair trembler)* in *Of Grammatology* (1967) to describe his central aim in that book: "to *faire trembler* the value of presence." If it is now clearer that to be caused to tremble need not just be thought of in terms of questioning a previously unquestioned value, but may instead serve to constitute a (dialectically?) more complex version of that value, this would support the idea that Derrida was never engaged in a destructive critique of phenomenology, but rather in a genealogical and economic enrichment of its axiomatics.

33. Remarkably, Derrida here is reworking the structure of the Look (Gaze) that Sartre described in *Being and Nothingness*, the experience there of how other people pose a constant threat to my status as a free subject by incipient engulfment. Derrida is arguing that this structure of exposure is not merely disruptive but productive of a certain subjectivity. A more recent parallel would be Foucault's discussion of the exemplary structure of Bentham's proposal for a panopticon, in which the prisoners exposed in cells ringing an inner courtyard are all visible.

34. One obvious way in which this gap begins to be bridged is realizing that the relation of dependency sustained by both a child's relation to a father and to God (God the Father) is, if not actually imaginary, at least to an *image or ideal* of the father (or of God). These kind of considerations make us less tempted to go in for any simple *reduction* of one dimension to another.

35. GD, 57.

36. Ibid.

37. Here, Derrida himself is being very cryptic. Is he talking about God or about Kierkegaard's father? Is I deliberately vague?

38. GD, 58.

39. See Jacques Derrida, *On the Name* (Stanford: Stanford University Press, 1995), especially "Sauf le nom," a wide-ranging essay that broadens the discussion of the name of God with further reference to Angelus Silesius and negative theology.

40. GD, 61.

41. GD, 66.

42. GD, 67.

43. See Derrida, *On the Name.*

44. The economic dimension is classically captured by Hobbes when he wrote that "words are wise men's counters—they do but reckon by them; but they are the money of fools" (*Leviathan* [1651] [London: Collins, 1962], 78). What is distinctive about the economic consideration of religious discourse—maintaining a space of otherness, while risking constructive nonsense—is that the optimism of Hobbes's reference to reckoning is equally misplaced. Religious discourse requires constant vigilance; we cannot calculate some kind of discount rate.

45. GD, 68.

46. Ibid.

47. Ibid.

48. GD, 69.

49. GD, 68.

50. GD, 71. See my essay "Much Obliged," in *Philosophy Today* (Spring 1997), where I pursue similar worries.

51. GD, 77.

52. Ibid.

53. GD, 78.

54. The analogy, obviously, is with Wittgenstein's "Don't ask for the meaning, ask for the use." Interestingly, we might suppose that this formulation would deliberately avoid saying, "Meaning *is* use," but Wittgenstein was willing to say that too, and arguably was concerned not just with practical recipes for avoiding confusion but getting clear about why they worked. See Hans-Johann Glock, *A Wittgenstein Dictionary* (Oxford: Blackwell, 1996), 377.

55. GD, 108.

56. GD, 108–109.

57. See Nietzsche, *The Genealogy of Morals* (New York: Vintage, 1969), 141.

58. *The Sickness unto Death*, trans. Howard V. Hong and Edna H. Hong (Princeton: Princeton University Press, 1980), 14.

59. *Concluding Unscientific Postscript to Philosophical Fragments*, 2 vols., trans. Howard V. Hong and Edna H. Hong (Princeton: Princeton University Press, 1992), I, 202 (hereafter CUP).

60. CUP, 203.

61. CUP, 199–200.

62. *Philosophical Fragments or A Fragment of Philosophy*, trans. David Swenson (Princeton: Princeton University Press, 1946), 31.

63. CUP, 201.

64. Ibid.

65. I am reminded of Nietzsche's letter to his friend Rohde, in which he says, "If eternal return is true, or if it is believed to be true [then everything in one's life is changed]," which suggests a similar thought about the power of organizing beliefs.

66. See his *Aporias*, trans. Thomas Dutoit (Stanford: Stanford University Press, 1993), 16.

67. I will deal elsewhere with the fascinating implications of Derrida's discussion of faith in "Faith and Knowledge: the Two Sources of 'Religion' at the Limits of Reason Alone," trans. Samuel Weber, in *Religion*, ed. Jacques Derrida and Gianni Vattimo (Stanford: Stanford University Press, 1998). Part of what Derrida is arguing here is that faith is "already" present in the structure of the "we" that we take for granted.

68. CUP, 555ff.

69. CUP, 557.

70. CUP, 561.

71. Ibid.

CHAPTER SIX. DIONYSUS IN AMERICA

1. Charles Scott's books include *Boundaries in Mind* (Crossroad/Herder and Herder, 1982), *The Question of Ethics* (Bloomington: Indiana University Press, 1990), *The Language of Difference* (New York: Prometheus, 1987), *On the Advantages and Disadvantages of Ethics and Politics* (Bloomington: Indiana University Press, 1996), *The Time of Memory* (Albany: State University of New York Press, 1999), *The Lives of Things* (Bloomington: Indiana University Press, 2002). I also refer to "Wonder and Worship," *Soundings* (Fall 1970).

2. "Time and Being," in *On Time and Being* (New York: Harper and Row, 1972), 24.

3. See chapter 5 above, "Thinking God in the Wake of Kierkegaard."

4. See "The Singular Universal" [1964], in *Kierkegaard: A Collection of Critical Essays*, ed. Josiah Thompson (Garden City: Anchor, 1972), p.264

5. Twilight of the Idols (Harmondsworth: Penguin, 1968), 53.

6. There is often, in philosophy, a strategic choice between working within a tradition, trying to exploit its own possibilities of transformation, its own desire to avoid paradox and stultification, and making a break with that tradition. I have been unable to let go of Derrida's early diagnosis of the situation in which he said that there is no possibility of choosing between the strategies of immanent transformation and the *pas au-delà*. The rupture, the step beyond, continues to make appeals to versions of values it leaps beyond. I do think it may be necessary to give the appearance of rupture to bring about an internal transformation. As for my own investment in readings that return, it is my sense that there is something—perhaps the embodied economy of our desire—that is in play both in humanism and in its overcomings. And it may be that what we call humanism is nothing but these same desires at the end of the day, at their point of weakness, a condition that will befall every thought, including this, including Scott's.

7. I allude here to the title of Nietzsche's essay—"On the Uses and Disadvantages of History for Life" (1874)—on which Scott's title plays.

8. The Moebius strip, a looped band with a single twist in it, has everywhere two sides and but one surface. It nicely illustrates the possibility that the empirical and transcendental *could be opposed at every point,* and yet work on the same surface.

9. Scott (1970).

10. Ibid.

11. Foucault, "Theatrum Philosophicum," in *Language, Counter-Memory, Practice*, ed. Donald Bouchard (Ithaca: Cornell University Press, 1977), 165.

12. Scott (1990), 1.

13. Scott (1996), 1.

14. Chalmers Johnson's book *Blowback: The Costs and Consequences of American Empire* (New York: Owl, 2004) focuses sharply on these unintended consequences of what we may charitably suppose to be benign action. The term *blowback* was invented by the CIA.

15. I have the suspicion that every powerful thought rests on logical distinctions that presuppose a commitment to the philosophy of representation. This is perhaps particularly true of the thought that would break with representation.

16. Scott (1970), 322.

17. Scott (1999), 2.

18. Ibid., 3.

19. In Foucault's *Language, Counter-Memory, Practice*, op.cit.

20. Aldo Leopold, *A Sand County Almanac* (New York: Ballantine, 1946), vii.

21. This section is an expanded version of a response to Charles Scott's "Starlight in the Face of the Other," presented to the APA December 1998.

22. "Starlight in the Face of the Other" appeared in Scott (2002).

23. I show here that there are a plurality of constituent parts to which we could be said to "return," which undercuts the privilege of the stars. But in fact this whole sense of our "returning"—ashes to ashes, dust to dust—is deeply problematic. I am tempted to agree that constituent dependency, as we might call it, is always *potentially* at least the basis for constructive dialogue between an achieved form and the matter that makes it up. But there is no guarantee at all that we will learn anything from such a dialogue in any particular instance. The picture is complicated in an intriguing way when we realize, as I have been told, that the star-stuff of which we are made is not that of stars that gently fade away as they burn out, but that of supernova stars, and their cataclysmic explosions. But if we can inscribe trauma in our stellar past, it is surely the violence locked away in that past that is more interesting than the mineral elements involved.

24. Foucault, *The Archaeology of Knowledge* (London: Tavistock, 1972), 210–11.

25. Op. cit., 210.

26. Scott (2002), 105.

27. In Nietzsche, *Philosophy and Truth*, ed. and trans. Daniel Breazeale (Atlantic Highlands: Humanities, 1979).

28. Ibid., 87–88.

29. Scott (2002), 102.

30. One could argue that if, without us, the universe or its parts would have no meaning, then it is here "for us" in a phenomenological if not theological sense. I am arguing that good phenomenology here needs to remember precisely that the universe has no intrinsic meaning, even if it may have shape, pattern, etc. Whatever is "for us" at the level of meaning is "from us."

31. Vicky Hearne, *Adam's Task* (New York: Harper, 1994).

32. In "L'animal que donc je suis," in *L'animal autobiographique*, ed. Marie-Louise Mallet (Paris: Galilée, 1999), 251–301. A shortened version of this essay appears in *Animal Philosophy* (see below).

33. For a sustained discussion of the gaze of the cat, see my "Thinking with Cats," in *Animal Philosophy*, ed. Peter Atterton and Matthew Calarco (New York/London: Continuum, 2004)

34. Scott (2002), 101.

35. Ibid., 100.

36. *Existence and Existents*, trans. Alphonso Lingis (The Hague-Boston: Nijhoff, 1978), 56.

37. Scott (2002), 104.

38. Levinas (1978), 56–57.

39. I refer here to Sartre's short essay "Intentionality: A Fundamental Idea of Husserl's Phenomenology" [1939], trans. Joseph P. Fell, *Journal of the British Society for Phenomenology* 1, no. 2 (May 1970): 4–5.

40. Rudolf Bernet, "The Traumatized Subject," Research in Phenomenology XXX (2000): 160–79. Both Levinas and Bernet here bring home the difficulty, if not impossibility (as we saw in chapter 2), of positively managing the value of violence, for here, trauma does violence to a narcissism that may itself be said to nourish violence.

41. Scott (2002), 111.

42. I allude to her famous remark on hearing that French peasants had no bread: "Let them eat cake."

43. Bernet (2000), 20.

44. In fact, it may be that the question of trauma is the most productive bridge between identity and violence (see chapter 1)—in particular explaining both the source of rigidity in identity, and the intractability of violence. It is reported that a large percentage of Palestinian suicide bombers are boys (some girls) who have witnessed their father's humiliation at the hands of Israeli troops. In this crystal we can find refracted not just trauma, violence, and identity but death and sacrifice, perpetuating generational cycles of repetitive violence. "What the young man did not say was that he was burning with a desire for revenge. He was a tearful witness to a scene when his father was beaten by Israeli soldiers twelve years ago. He was six years old. He would never forget his father, being taken away, bleeding from the nose" (Dr. Eyad El Sarraj, director, Gaza Community Mental Health Program, Gaza City, Palestine. Quoted in *Peacework* May 2002, *http://www.afsc.org/pwork/aboutpw.htm*).

45. "The 'Uncanny,'" in Sigmund Freud, *On Creativity and the Unconscious* (New York: Harper, 1958), 133.

46. "The Mouth: A New Opening for Philosophy," to appear in *Things at the Edge of the World* (in preparation).

47. Breazeale (1979), 79.

48. I do not know how appropriate it is here to express one's indebtedness, to thank the person one could have read more thoroughly, more perceptively, even more critically. But I do thank Charles for the quality of his philosophical friendship. He has been a friend in Nietzsche's sense, sternly rebuking me when the occasion called for it. I will not lightly forget him telling me as we looked out from the terrazzo toward Assisi that what I had just said was the worst thing he had ever heard from me. I had suggested that if Martians landed on our planet and we asked them where they came from they would say, "Earth." It took a few glasses of bourbon and a cigar to sort that out, but my philosophical sensibility has been changed by the powers and the spirits raised by our many conversations over the years.

49. Breazeale (1979), 79.

CHAPTER SEVEN. NOTES TOWARD A
DECONSTRUCTIVE PHENOMENOLOGY

1. Such as the *British Society for Phenomenology* (UK), the *Society for Phenomenology and Existential Philosophy* (U.S.).

2. This chapter first saw the light at the annual meeting of the British Society for Phenomenology in Oxford in 1997. *Renewing Phenomenology* was the theme of the conference.

3. See for example, Husserl's essays "Philosophy as a Rigorous Science" [1911] and "The Crisis of European Man" [1935], in *Phenomenology and the Crisis of Philosophy*, trans. Quentin Lauer (New York: Harper and Row, 1965).

4. Husserl's understanding of phenomenology is radically tied to that of beginning (again). See for example his *Cartesian Meditations*, section 2, "The necessity of a radical new beginning of philosophy," or the "real 'beginnings'" he talks about in *Ideas*, section 18. It is noteworthy that Heidegger took over Husserl's language in this respect almost verbatim: "[T]he philosopher . . . is precisely the genuine and constant 'beginner,'" and "beginning has its 'time.' To begin for another time is senseless" (1921–1922) (Gesamtausgabe 61 13, 186). Quoted in Van Buren, *The Young Heidegger* (Bloomington: Indiana University Press, 1994).

5. See for example Sartre's *Being and Nothingness* [1943], subtitled "An essay in phenomenological ontology" (London: Methuen, 1958).

6. Ricoeur's essay "Phenomenology and hermeneutics" [1975] (in his *Hermeneutics and the Human Sciences* [Cambridge: Cambridge University Press, 1981]) makes it clear that Ricoeur sees his hermeneutics as an antidote to phenomenology's idealistic *interpretation* at Husserl's hands in his middle period. And yet "hermeneutics is erected on the basis of phenomenology" (p.101).

7. See for example Husserl's *Cartesian Meditations* [1929], trans. Dorion Cairns (The Hague: Nijhoff, 1960).

8. See Heidegger's *Identity and Difference* [1957], trans. Joan Stambaugh (New York: Harper and Row, 1969) where he distinguishes the dead abstract unmediated A = A of strict identity from the more revealing "belonging together" of sameness.

9. See Derrida, "Afterword: Towards an Ethics of Discussion," in *Limited Inc* (Evanston: Northwestern University Press, 1988), 147, and Heidegger, *Being and Time* [1927], trans. Macquarrie and Robinson (Oxford: Blackwell, 1967), H23/4, E44.

10. See Sartre's *Existentialism and Humanism,* trans. Philip Mairet, in *The Existentialist Tradition,* ed. Nino Languilli (Garden City: Anchor Doubleday, 1971), 406: "Existentialism . . . [cannot be regarded] as a pessimistic description of man . . . no doctrine is more optimistic."

11. Here, Heidegger famously says that "[e]ven today, this term 'intentionality' is no all-explanatory word but one which designates a central *problem." Phenomenology of Internal Time-Consciousness* (Bloomington: Indiana University Press, 1966), 15.

12. In *Philosophy in France Today,* ed. Alan Montefiore (Cambridge: Cambridge University Press, 1983). As the title suggests, Levinas here "starts from certain standpoints found in Husserlian phenomenology" (p.100).

13. I am tempted to talk here of a playground, to emphasize that this "ground" while not a foundation is also not an abyss (Ab-grund)—more an arena of fundamentally orienting concern.

14. See Merleau-Ponty's account of the primacy of perception in the book of that name, Derrida's reference to pressure and imminence (note 39 below), Kierkegaard on dread, Heidegger on mood, etc. See also chapter 2, "The Return of Experience," in my *Thinking After Heidegger.*

15. See esp. Heidegger, *Being and Time* [1927], section 7, "The Phenomenological Method of Investigation." Moreover, Levinas writes in his preface that "the presentation and the development of the notions employed owe everything to the phenomenological method," and "Husserlian phenomenology has made possible this passage from ethics to metaphysical exteriority," in *Totality and Infinity* [1961], trans. Alfonso Lingis (Pittsburgh: Duquesne University Press, 1969), 28–29.

16. In his conversations with Philippe Nemo (*Ethics and Infinity,* trans. Richard A. Cohen [Pittsburgh: Duquesne University Press, 1985]), he endorses "phenomenology in the largest sense of the term . . . a radical reflection . . . the recall of forgotten thoughts." In Richard Kearney's *Dialogues with Contemporary Continental Thinkers* (Manchester: Manchester University Press, 1984), Levinas writes, "[F]rom the point of view of philosophical method and discipline, I remain to this day a phenomenologist" (p. 50).

17. In *Totality and Infinity,* 256–66.

18. See Derrida, *Edmund Husserl's* Origin of Geometry: An Introduction [1962], trans. John P. Leavey (New York: Nicolas Hays, 1978); *Speech and Phenomena* [1967], trans. David Allison (Evanston: Northwestern University Press, 1973).

19. See Derrida, *Positions* [1972], trans. Alan Bass (Chicago: University of Chicago Press, 1982).

20. Marion's best known work is *God Without Being,* trans. Thomas A. Carlson (Chicago: University of Chicago Press, 1991). This remark was reported to me in conversation with Philippe van Haute (Amsterdam, 1997).

21. See for example Husserl's *Cartesian Meditations* [1929], trans. Dorion Cairns (The Hague: Nijhoff, 1960).

22. A recent letter to the TLS (May 9, 1997) talks of Derrida "refuting" Husserl. The idiocy continues.

23. See Heidegger, *On the Way to Language* (New York: Harper and Row, 1971): "The three lectures that follow . . . are intended to bring us face to face with a possibility of undergoing an experience with language" (p. 57).

24. Taken from *Of Grammatology*, 158. This claim, and its persistent misunderstanding, is taken up again in a slightly different way in the "Afterword" to *Limited Inc*, 136 (see above).

25. Husserl, *Ideas* [1913] trans. Boyce Gibson (London: George, Allen and Unwin, 1931), section 55.

26. Rodolphe Gasché, *The Tain of the Mirror* (Cambridge: Harvard University Press, 1986).

27. See Ricoeur's *Time and Narrative*, trans. Kathleen McLaughlin and David Pellauer (Chicago: University of Chicago Press, 3 vols, 1984–86).

28. The scare quotes around "acts" are vital. Husserl is insistent that we are not talking about "real" activities in time, but acts in an ideal or formal sense.

29. See Blanchot's *The Writing of the Disaster*, trans. Ann Smock (Lincoln: University of Nebraska Press, 1986).

30. See Levinas, *Totality and Infinity* (see note 14 above).

31. See Husserl's *Ideas* [1913], section 49. This is the subject of an extraordinary short paper by Levinas: "Simulacrum: The End of the World," in *Writing the Future*, ed. D. C.Wood (London: Routledge, 1990).

32. See Derrida, *Aporias*, trans. Thomas Dutoit (Stanford: Stanford University Press, 1993), *Given Time: 1. Counterfeit Money*, trans. Peggy Kamuf (Chicago: University of Chicago Press, 1993); *The Gift of Death*; "Force of Law: The 'Mystical Foundation of Authority,'" in *Deconstruction and the Possibility of Justice*, ed. D. Cornell et al. (New York: Routledge, 1992).

33. *Of Grammatology*, trans. Gayatri Spivak (Baltimore: Johns Hopkins University Press, 1976), 60–61.

34. These quotes come from *Aporias*, and from *The Gift of Death*, op.cit.

35. Husserl's shifts on "experience" are fascinating. Even within *Ideas* [1913], we find him attacking the value of "experience," associated first with empiricism, and its restriction of experience to facts of nature (section 19), and then later allowing a much broader sense: "Under *experience* in the *widest sense* we understand whatever is to be found in the stream of experience, not only therefore intentional experiences . . . but all the real phases to be found in this stream . . ." (section 36).

36. Blanchot, *The Writing of Disaster* (see above): "[S]ince the disaster always takes place after having taken place, there cannot possibly be any experience of it"

(p.28); Giorgio Agamben, *Infancy and History: Essays on the Destruction of Experience* [1978], trans. Liz Heron (London/New York: Verso, 1993).

37. See Derrida, *Aporias* (see note 30 above), 15. See also "The Return of Experience," chapter 3 of my *Thinking After Heidegger* (Cambridge: Polity Press, 2002).

38. See note 2 above for the sources of these and similar remarks.

39. Derrida, *The Other Heading*, trans. Pascale-Anne Brault and Michael Naas (Bloomington: Indiana University Press, 1992), 28.

40. See Derrida's most explicit embracing of a concern with the nonhuman animal in "'Eating Well': or the Calculation of the Subject," in *Who Comes After the Subject?* ed. Eduardo Cadava et al. (London: Routledge, 1991). See my reply "Comment ne pas manger: Deconstruction and Humanism," in *The Animal as Other*, ed. Peter Steeves (Albany: State University of New York Press, 2000).

41. For a fuller treatment of this theme, see the next chapter, "Responsibility Reinscribed (and How)."

42. *The Other Heading*, 4–5.

43. See my paper, "Much Obliged," in *Philosophy Today* (1997).

CHAPTER EIGHT. RESPONSIBILITY REINSCRIBED (AND HOW)

1. See for example: *The Other Heading*, trans. Pascale-Anne Brault and Michael Naas, (Bloomington: Indiana University Press, 1992); "Force of Law: The 'Mystical Foundation of Authority,'" *Cardoza Law Review* 11 (1990); *Limited Inc* (Evanston: Northwestern University Press, 1988); (with Jean-Luc Nancy), "'Eating Well,' or the Calculation of the Subject: An Interview with Jacques Derrida," in *Who Comes After the Subject*, ed. Eduardo Cadava et al. (New York and London: Routledge, 1991); *The Gift of Death*, trans. David Wills (Chicago: University of Chicago Press, 1995); *Aporias*, trans. Thomas Dutoit (Stanford: Stanford University Press, 1993).

2. See "*Comment ne pas manger:* Deconstruction and Humanism," in *The Animal as Other*, ed. Peter Steeves (Albany: State University of New York Press, 2000), and in my *Thinking After Heidegger* (Cambridge: Polity, 2002).

3. "Eating Well."

4. He continues by saying, "A limited, measured, calculable, rationally distributed responsibility is already the becoming-right of morality" ("Eating Well," 118).

5. *The Gift of Death*, 69f.

6. Derrida has himself made much of similar strategies—I am thinking especially of his use of "indécidables" in his early writing.

7. In *Martin Heidegger: Basic Writings*, ed. David Farrell Krell (London: Routledge and Kegan Paul, 1978).

8. In *Heidegger and Modern Philosophy*, ed. Michael Murray (New Haven: Yale University Press, 1978).

9. Gilbert Ryle, *The Concept of Mind* (Harmondsworth: Penguin, 1963).

10. "To talk of a person's mind is not to talk of a repository which is permitted to house objects that something called 'the physical world' is forbidden to house; it is to talk of the person's abilities, liabilities and inclinations to do and undergo certain sorts of things . . . in the ordinary world" (ibid., 190).

11. In *Heidegger and Modern Philosophy*.

12. See Martin Heidegger, *Being and Time*, trans. Joan Stambaugh (Albany: State University of New York Press, 1995).

13. See his *Ideas: General Introduction to Pure Phenomenology* [1913] (London: George Allen and Unwin, 1931), ch. 1.

14. I mean by "categorial distinctions" distinctions between orders or types of knowledge, of relationship between or to things. This includes both distinctions between different categories, and between "categories" and other "things." Grammatical categories are included here when they are deemed to be philosophically significant.

15. I'm trying to avoid saying "systematic philosophy" so as to include nonconstructive even antisystematic philosophers such as Nietzsche and Derrida.

16. The anticipations of Derrida in Sartre, and other parallels between them are of great interest. See especially various writings by Christina Howells, including her "Conclusion: Sartre and the Deconstruction of the Subject," in *The Cambridge Companion to Sartre*, ed. Christina Howells (Cambridge: Cambridge University Press, 1992) and "Sartre and Derrida: Qui perd gagne," *JBSP* 13, no. 1 (1982). An interested reader might start with such a remark as, "Man is free because he is not himself but presence to himself." (*Being and Nothingness*, "Being and Doing: Freedom," 440). This shows Sartre thinking self-presence precisely *not* as self-coincidence, but as something like the difference-from-self that Derrida called "differance" and used to probe the value Husserl had given to self-presence.

17. J-P. Sartre, *Being and Nothingness* [1943] (London: Methuen, 1958), 441.

18. Jacques Derrida, *Speech and Phenomena* [1967], trans. David Allison (Evanston: Northwestern, 1973), 103.

19. *Limited Inc.*

20. The expression *proto-ethics* is used for example by John Llewelyn in his brilliant *The Middle Voice of Ecological Conscience* (London: Macmillan, 1991). I do not begin to do justice here to his grasp of the multidimensionality of our responsibilities, not least to nonhuman animals.

21. See Robert Bernasconi and David Wood, eds. *The Provocation of Levinas: Rethinking the Other* (London: Routledge, 1988).

22. Ibid., 173.

23. And, *pace* Llewelyn, it is hard to sustain the exclusion of other living beings from any account of the space of our concern.

24. *The Gift of Death*, 69.

25. For a more developed discussion of the way philosophical concepts structure the texts in which they occur, couched in terms of textual reflexivity (exemplification, reflective modification, and totalization) and different kinds of operators (boundary regulators, structural and transformational operators) see my "Philosophy as Writing: The Case of Hegel," in *Philosophy at the Limit* (London: Unwin Hyman, 1990), ch. 4.

26. Sartre's claim *(Being and Nothingness)* that good faith is a form of bad faith seems very close here.

27. Compare here Derrida's treatment of Kant's distinction between acting *in conformity* with duty, and acting *out of respect for* law. See "Force of Law: The Mystical Foundation of Authority," *Cardoza Law Review* 11 (1990): 949.

28. Ibid.

29. See his *The Visible and the Invisible* [1964] (Evanston: Northwestern University Press, 1968), 38,46.

CHAPTER NINE. WHAT IS ECOPHENOMENOLOGY?

Versions of this chapter were presented at the IAEP conference at Penn State, October 2000, and at the Philosophy and Religious Studies department of the University of North Texas, December 2000. I am grateful to those whose comments improved it. A shorter version of this chapter was published in *Research in Phenomenology* XXXI (2001) and yet another version in *Eco-Phenomenology: Back to the Earth Itself*, ed. Ted Toadvine and Charles Brown (Albany: State University of New York Press, 2003).

1. See Donna Haraway's discussion in *How Like a Leaf: Interview with Donna Haraway* (with Thyrza Goodeve) (New York: Routledge, 1999).

2. A translation of what Husserl called *die sache selbst.*

3. Here, we would attempt to think through Heidegger's various formulations of the animal's relation to the world as *weltarm*, or *weltlos.*

4. I have not yet found this word in any dictionary, though it appears in various ways on the Internet, sometimes in essays in linguistics, and sometimes in the names of websites. It is an attempt to get at the root sense of such words as complexity, implexity, and perplexity. And something of its intended sense can be divined from the SOED entry for *plexus:* "A structure [in the animal body] consisting of a network of fibres of vessels closely interwoven and intercommunicating."

5. Imagination is the central connection between space-boundary questions, and boundary/level transformation.

6. My tacit reference here is to Merleau-Ponty's *The Visible and the Invisible* (Evanston: Northwestern University Press, 1969). We also note the importance here of Merleau-Ponty's *La Nature: Notes, Cours Du College De France.* trans. Robert Vallier (Evanston: Northwestern University Press, 2003).

7. Are we in effect endorsing here Heidegger's view of the animal as poor-in-world *(Weltarm)?* I have argued against just this view in "Comment ne pas manger:

Deconstruction and Humanism," in my *Thinking After Heidegger* (2002). Doesn't an ant really fail to see the tree? Shouldn't we rather say that she succeeds in relating to the tree in an ant-ish way? It may seem that I have invited this trouble unnecessarily. The ant/tree example illustrates spatially a part/whole relation that I am trying to think temporally. In relation to the temporality of the tree, we are as myopic as ants are in relation to its spatiality. A more careful account of its spatiality would linger on the ways ants have better access to a trees spatiality—tunneling underground, even under the bark—while we typically are restricted to external, above ground perception. But I have to admit that when it comes to time, I have a more robust sense of the privilege bestowed by something such as the human power of temporal synthesis, which, I believe, allows us to grasp the living nature of the tree, a nature that is "invisible" precisely because it is temporally extended and articulated,

8. Cf. births, marriages, and deaths, the common thread that joins newspapers to religions.

9. Rainer Maria Rilke, *Duino Elegies*, trans. J. B. Leishman and Stephen Spender (London: The Hogarth Press, 1963), 103.

10. Ibid., 104.

11. There are paradoxes in the idea of "ordinary experience" that I cannot entirely resolve here. Someone might object, for example, that (surely) ordinary experience is precisely what is most rich. It is just our philosophical representation of it that is impoverishing. There is something right about this. The value of phenomenology, however, rests precisely on its claim to be able to bring out this wealth of subtlety without reductive schematization. The need for phenomenology lies not just in the dangers of such schematization, whether from science or from philosophy. It also responds to the dullness with which we often *live* our ordinary experience, however rich and subtle it may potentially be.

12. I do concede that within the extremes of absolute speeding up and slowing down, varying the "rate" of our perception often yields remarkable insight. Historical reflection is an example of this, as is slow-motion photography. I would contend, however, that the interest in these temporal prostheses comes in having things shift from one category to another (e.g., thing-event-process) not to any radical breakdown of the categories themselves. In my example of the tree, I claimed that through temporal synthesis we see it as the kind of thing (vegetative organism) that it really is.

13. I use this phrase in the face of my own misgivings. In my view it marks an indispensable site, even if that is a site of interrogation and dispute.

14. See my paper "Time-shelters: An Essay in the Poetics of Time," in *Time and the Instant,* ed. Robin Durie and David Webb (Manchester: Clinamen Press, 2001).

15. I am thinking here of Aristotle's idea that metaphysics, unlike the particular sciences, deals with being qua being.

16. When we speak of "something more than causality" we are trying to address changes in the clay that impact its own capacity to sustain complexity or relational-

ity. Compression of soil can drive out air and water and so transform it from being something that sustains life to something dead. Or something malleable that can sustain an impression that something hard cannot. We are not so much escaping from causality here as introducing dimensions of significance which, though tied up with causality, begin to allow us to speak of "for the clay," whether or not it is information that is at stake.

17. A classic treatment of this question can be found in J. Baird Callicott's "Holistic Environmental Ethics and the Problem of Ecofascism," in *Environmental Philosophy: From Animal Rights to Radical Ecology*, 3rd ed., ed. J. Baird Callicott, Michael E. Zimmerman, George Sessions, Karen J. Warren, and John Clark (Upper Saddle River, NJ: Prentice-Hall, 2001), 111–25.

18. See Arne Naess, "The Deep Ecological Movement: Some Philosophical Perspectives," in *Environmental Ethics*, 2nd edition, ed. Botzler and Armstrong (New York: McGraw-Hill, 1998), 438–39.

19. This claim needs serious qualification. When a map is drawn showing which parts of the Amazon rainforest are to be clear-cut, and what profit will accrue, representation is playing a key role. And capitalism in general, not to mention the information revolution, is driven precisely by representation. Nature seems to be that realm in which representation is not yet fully developed.

20. Hence the significance of the legal, and often scientific expression *ceteris paribus*—"other things being equal."

21. What is at stake here could hardly be overemphasized. Descartes' opposition to that part of Harvey's theory of the circulation of the blood that posited ventricles in the heart pumping by muscular contraction (rather than, as Descartes claimed, by rarefaction by a "dark fire" in the heart), was so great that he insisted in a letter to Mersenne in 1639 that "if what he had written about the movement of the heart should turn out to be false, then the whole of his philosophy was worthless." As I understand it, Descartes sees that part of Harvey's *De Motu Cordis* as departing from his own strictly mechanistic understanding of nature. I quote here from Anthony Kenny, *Descartes: A Study of His Philosophy* (New York: Random House, 1968), 201–202.

22. "What is Phenomenology?" Preface to *Phenomenology of Perception*, trans. Colin Smith, (London: Routledge and Kegan Paul, 1962).

23. Given that emergency conditions seem to license the abandonment of democratic safeguards in political life, it is not wholly implausible to suppose that the heart of politics might become the manipulation of situations so as bring about such emergency conditions. Although this is not straightforwardly treated as a crime, it ought to be understood as a treasonous betrayal of the responsibilities of leadership. The classic elevation of reptilian thinking into a fundamental political principle can be found in Carl Schmitt, *The Concept of the Political*, trans. George Schwab (Chicago: University of Chicago Press, 1996).

24. This is a reference to Ed Casey's work on the phenomenology of the naive glance, *The World at a Glance* (forthcoming, 2005).

25. For the classic statement of the tension between individual motivation and collective interest, see Garrett Hardin, "The Tragedy of the Commons," *Science* 162:1243–48.

26. These worries are increasingly the concern of mainstream science. John Schellnhuber recently reported (August 2004) the identification of twelve vulnerable "hotspots," areas which act like massive regulators of the Earth's environment, and which are being impacted by human activity.

27. The obvious response to the suggestion that we might have to suspend democratic institutions is that this is a hollow fear, because democratic institutions now operate only as a sham even in Western societies. But it would be a mistake to generalize too much from the American experience where indeed it is hardly possible to find democratic institutions unsullied by the extrademocratic influence of big money. It is clearly for this reason that so many activists are looking to novel ways of influencing public opinion.

CHAPTER TEN. GLOBALIZATION AND FREEDOM

I thank Jacques Derrida, Wilson Dickinson, John Stuhr, and William Partridge for their comments on an earlier version of this chapter.

1. See Heidegger, *Contributions to Philosophy (From Enowning)*, trans. Parvis Emad and Kenneth Maly (Bloomington: Indiana University Press, 2001), 3.

2. The process of rehabilitating suspect language has been proceeding apace in recent years, both with Derrida's willingness to speak of justice and responsibility, albeit in new ways, and, for our purposes more directly, with Jean-Luc Nancy's deployment of the word *freedom*, in, for example, *The Experience of Freedom* [1988], trans. Bridget McDonald (Stanford: Stanford University Press, 1993), which proposes the ungrounded fact of existence as freedom.

3. Jacques Derrida, *Specters of Marx: The State of the Debt, the Work of Mourning, and the New International*, trans. Peggy Kamuf (London: Routledge, 1994), 75 (hereafter SM).

4. Herbert Marcuse, *One Dimensional Man: Studies in the Ideology of Advanced Industrial Society* (London: Sphere, 1964) (hereafter ODM).

5. ODM, 3.

6. See http://www.whitehouse.gov/nsc/nss.html.

7. All these phrases are from SM, 50–52.

8. ODM, 13.

9. A barbarous phrase, perhaps, but to the point, and close cousin to the idea of negative capability (Keats) that informs this book. By a "phronesis of contrariety" I mean a sophisticated capacity for negotiating the practical contradictions (of freedom in the modern world). It bears comparison with Derrida's "going through the undecidable."

10. The possibility (indeed, inevitability) that systems of rules, from democracy to "free market capitalism," will be "gamed," that is, exploited for ends that subvert the legitimizing basis of the system, is one of the key "contrarieties" we are faced with.

11. Cf. Derrida, "There is nothing outside the text" (*Of Grammatology*, trans. Gayatri Spivak [Baltimore: Johns Hopkins University Press, 1976], 158). He will subsequently insist that there is no "inside" either.

12. "Terra nullius" ("no man's land") was the legal fiction Cook used in 1770 for the expropriation of the land of aboriginal Australians. This was reversed in *Mabo v. Queensland* No. 2 (1992).

13. For a classic account, see Gerard O'Neill, *High Frontier: Human Colonies in Space* (Garden City: Anchor, 1982). Also, as an example of popular folly, see Hal Lindsey, *The Late Great Planet Earth* (Grand Rapids, MI: Zondervan, 1970).

14. To call this a "need" raises the question of just what kind of need this might be. On my view, all such "needs"—the need for an *other* space to escape to, the need for a scapegoat (an other to exclude [see Foucault, Girard])—reflect the operation of economies or logics that are not themselves necessary, but which we find ourselves caught up in, and which somewhat problematically often determine the shape of our struggles against them.

15. It is ironic that in the place where preemptive action would really be useful—global warming—it is said that the evidence is not there! Compare decades of claims about the link between smoking and cancer.

16. See Chalmers Johnson, *Blowback: The Costs and Consequences of American Empire* (New York: Owl Books, 2003). "The term 'blowback,' invented by the CIA, refers to the unintended consequences of American policies. Chalmers Johnson lays out in vivid detail the dangers faced by our overextended empire, which insists on projecting its military power to every corner of the earth and using American capital and markets to force global economic integration on its own terms" (Publisher).

17. See Derrida, *Of Grammatology*, 158.

18. For an active intervention on just such lines, see Donna Haraway, "A Cyborg Manifesto: Science, Technology, and Socialist-Feminism in the Late Twentieth Century," in her *Simians, Cyborgs, and Women: The Reinvention of Nature* (New York: Routledge, 1991).

19. "Trade expansion will help us all. . . . As they say on my own Cape Cod, 'A rising tide lifts all boats.' And a partnership, by definition, serves both partners, without domination or unfair advantage. Together we have been partners in adversity—let us also be partners in prosperity" (President John F. Kennedy, June 24, 1963; The Paulskirche, Frankfurt, Germany).

20. Preemptive war is an example of a mode of action that (a) reduces contrariety to domination and conquest, (b) engages in moral expulsion (cf. you are for us or against us, good v. evil), (c) assertively abandons universalizability, (d) projects a global and world-historical framework, (e) triumphally proclaims the end of history and the beginning of enforcement. Those who lament the lack of intelligence of their leaders are not asking for the moon. The need for intelligence is predicated on the

need to be able to navigate the waters of complexity without being tempted by regressively oppositional thinking.

21. The status of the frame and framing requires a fuller treatment at another time. For Heidegger, of course, the frame (*Gestell*) is the hallmark of the technological epoch. For Iyengar—see his *Is Anyone Responsible?* (Chicago: University of Chicago Press, 1994)—it is a key conceptual tool in political science. And in Lakoff's *Moral Politics* (Chicago: University of Chicago Press, 1999) it has both a political and a broader metaphysical import.

22. Both of these examples refer to Kierkegaard's discussions in *Fear and Trembling*, trans. Alastair Hannay (Harmondsworth: Penguin, 1985).

23. This is how I understand Heidegger's (and Hölderlin's) invocations of the gods—possibilities that exceed the frames of our anticipation—the "impossible." See for example, Heidegger's *Contributions to Philosophy*.

24. For a contemporary restatement of this position, see Michael Albert and Robin Hahnel: "What is true is that capitalism either will not, or cannot satisfy essential human needs for the majority of people on the planet. Capitalism will not satisfy the need for basic economic security for most of the third world and a growing underclass in the advanced economies. Capitalism cannot satisfy the need for self-managed, meaningful work that an increasingly educated populace demands. Capitalism cannot satisfy needs for community, dignity, and economic justice. And capitalism cannot keep itself from devouring the environment, or generating an international climate that fosters conflict and war instead of peace and cooperation," from their "In Defense of Participatory Economics," *Science and Society* 66, no. 1 (Spring 2002). Cf. "Milton Friedman, in *Capitalism and Freedom*, told us that the way to preserve freedom is to centralize information and disperse power. This is the essence of participatory economics" (Albert and Hahnel). For a brilliant account of how global poverty undermines the legitimacy of the new world order, see Robert Bernasconi, "The Philosophy of Poverty and the Poverty of Philosophy," presented to the World Congress of Philosophy, Istanbul, 2003.

25. In his April 1924 pamphlet, *Foundations of Leninism*, Stalin wrote: "For the final victory of socialism, for the organization of socialist production, the efforts of one country, particularly of a peasant country like Russia, are insufficient; for that, the efforts of the proletarians of several advanced countries are required." This publication was later withdrawn from circulation after Stalin had proclaimed Socialism in One Country. And Lenin wrote, "Complete victory of the socialist revolution in one country is inconceivable and demands the most active cooperation of at least several countries" (V. I. Lenin *Collected Writings*, Vol. 28 [Moscow 1977], 151).

26. No doubt for some I am being too evenhanded here in taking seriously the idea that free trade could enhance freedom. As ex-World Bank colleague William Partridge writes, "[W]hen that global elite speak of 'free trade' they do not mean 'freedom' in the sense in which you use it, if you examine their actions. Trade is not actually designed to be free—they mean that the global is free to invade the local, but the local is not permitted to penetrate the global. It is more than just lack of level playing field: such participation is legally prohibited by the globalization process and cod-

ified in legislation, treaties, subsidies and tax policies. Free trade in the Orwellian language of globalization should actually be translated as protectionist policies of the global elite" (personal communication).

27. Francis Fukuyama's *The End of History and the Last Man* (New York: The Free Press, 1992) was pointedly the object of Derrida's critique in *Specters of Marx*.

28. His classical defense of liberalism was *Capitalism and Freedom* (Chicago: University of Chicago Press, 1962).

29. The case of Enron and the California energy market, is a classic case. Enron collapsed in 2002.

30. Noreena Hertz writes: "[O]f the world's 100 largest economies, 51 are now corporations, only 49 are nation states. . . . The sales of General Motors and Ford are greater than the GDP of the whole of Sub-Saharan Africa, and Wal-Mart, the US supermarket retailer, now has a turnover higher than the revenues of most of the states of Eastern Europe" (*The Silent Takeover: Global Capitalism and the Death of Democracy* [New York: Harper, 2003]).

31. See Amartya Sen's *Development as Freedom* (Garden City: Anchor, 1999).

32. This formulation is taken from Heidegger's critique of Descartes in section 19 of *Being and Time* (Oxford: Blackwell, 2000).

33. It may be said that this whole language of conditions and grounding is symptomatic of the problem, that we are proposing a new (or a resurrected) architectonic foundationalism, which will merely reproduce all the problems of schematization and representation. If the idea of legitimacy points to some sort of underpinning, some sort of capacity for justification by reference to circumstances and conditions, is it not the idea of legitimacy that we should be setting aside? Here, we arrive at a line in the sand, which, if we cross, will change everything. We may admit that any value wrapped up with legality, with law, with legislation, is inseparable from such constituted authorities as the state, or from bodies (such as the UN) that ultimately derive their authority from states. We may conclude then, that there is nothing natural or pure or free from "representation" about such notion as legitimacy, or right, or justice. But instead of concluding that as a consequence these notions are fatally corrupted, we might just as easily conclude that the appropriation of this language by the powers that be is at least in part an acknowledgment of its power to move us. The idea that any power to move us is just an internalization of social norms does not need to be challenged by positing some primitive natural sense of justice. Any social order whatsoever will generate some sense of fairness, justice, the equitable, or it would not qualify as a social order. These ideas are genuine human achievements, not the gifts of particular regimes. They move us, even to the point of allowing us to question their local instantiations, because the order we endure is but a version of a condition of order we could not endure without. We demand justice even against the state because the state's legitimacy fundamentally rests on its success in honoring the promise of justice that any social order must fulfill. This is to say that the claim of legitimacy is one that marks the border between the moral and the political, between individual or collective experience and social structures.

34. For this reason, we share Habermas's concern with "systematically distorted communication."

35. Marcuse was perhaps adapting to America what Heidegger said about German idealism's never having been refuted, it was just that the German people were not up to it. The same sentiments, of course, have been expressed about communism—that the failure of the Eastern Europe experiment does not refute the idea, though it probably should discourage attempts at analogous implementation.

36. Cited by anthropologist Arturo Escobar. See Amartya Sen, "Why Half the World is Hungry," *The Observer*, June 23, 2002.

37. See the analysis of the devastating treatment of Argentina by the World Bank, by Greg Palast in *Harper's Magazine*, March 2003.

38. Amartya Sen's classic work in this context is *Development as Freedom*.

39. She continues, "After the Great Bengal Famine of 1942, which killed more than 2 million people, India's policies put livelihoods and food security first. . . . The economic 'reforms' under globalization reverse these reforms by corporatizing agriculture, displacing small peasants and removing limits on land ownership" (*The Observer*, June 23, 2002).

40. "Democracy to come" is an expression of Derrida's. See, e.g., *The Politics of Friendship*, trans. G. Collins (London: Verso, 1997).

41. Consider here the rise of Internet activism as an antidote to growing authoritarianism even in democratic societies.

42. See Arjun Appadurai, *Modernity at Large: Cultural Dimensions of Globalization* (Minneapolis: University of Minnesota Press, 1996).

43. The question of war and its economic equivalence (such as sanctions) is all the more important when considering these questions. Wendell Berry argues unfashionably for self-sufficiency as an antidote to globalization, with trade only after local needs have been met. Sen thinks this is a misunderstanding. Famine is not lack of food, but lack of money. But he then goes on to say, "There are situations in which self-sufficiency is important, such as during wars [he refers to the UK in WWII]. . . . But that is a very peculiar situation. . . ." Would that this were so.

44. For an articulate championing of the virtues of a return to just such an economy, see Wendell Berry, *The Gift of Good Land* (San Francisco: North Point Press, 1982).

45. To speak responsibly of the "degradation" of nature would require another paper, or book. Obviously, at one extreme, the implicit normativity of this expression could be contested. At one level, poisoning a lake just redistributes molecules. (Compare Hume: "'Tis not contrary to reason to prefer the destruction of the whole world to the scratching of my finger" [*A Treatise on Human Nature*]). In some sense "nature" merely adjusts. I identify nature with the potential for creative adaptation and transformation, which is reflected in biodiversity. On this basis, degradation of nature = loss of the ecological complexity associated with biodiversity.

46. See Aldo Leopold, *A Sand County Almanac* [1949] (New York: Ballantine, 1986); Baird Callicott, *Beyond the Land Ethic: More Essays in Environmental Philosophy* (Albany: State University of New York Press, 1999).

47. See Callicott, *Beyond the Land Ethic.*

48. See Bill McKibben, *The End of Nature* (New York: Doubleday, 1989).

49. Ramachandra Guha, *Environmentalism: A Global History* (New York: Addison-Wesley, 1999).

50. See my "*Comment ne pas manger:* Deconstruction and Humanism," in *Thinking After Heidegger* (Cambridge: Polity, 2002), ch. 9.

51. Martin Heidegger, *The Question Concerning Technology* (New York: Harper, 1977), 28.

Index

absence, 2
achievement, 7
    conceptual, 7
    existential, 7
activity, (action), 32, 41, 75, 134, 156, 167
Adorno, Theodor, 27, 33
Agamben, Giorgio, 136
agency, 2, 13, 23, 73, 174, 197n4
alienation, 17, 60
alterity, 54, 64–65, 68–69, 100, 118, 122, 127. *See also* Levinas; other; otherness
ambiguity, 4
ambiviolence, 27
Anaximander, 40
animal(s), 47–51, 53, 56, 60, 62, 125, 146, 158, 164–65, 185, 202n45, 217n40, 219n7
    animal holocaust, 49–50, 202n48, 203n50. *See also* Holocaust
    cat, 121–22
anxiety, 20, 22, 77, 124, 141
apologetics, 43. *See also* theology
aporia, (aporetic), 20, 33, 74, 83, 100, 106, 109, 136, 140, 148, 171, 178–79, 186
    breakdown, 175
    contrariety, 183. *See also* contrariety
    See also experience; time; responsibility

Aristotle, 7, 17, 164–65, 194, 205n2
arrival
    too late, 1
    "always already," 1. *See also* origin
art, 4, 39, 55, 81, 122–23
asymmetry. *See* Levinas
atheism, 104. *See* Sartre
Aufhebung, 96
Augustine, St., 86, 193
authenticity, 92, 110, 207n14
autonomy, 3, 17, 93, 179, 183

Bataille, George, 198n14
being, 38, 54–56, 86, 104, 122, 141
    meaning of, 56, 76
Benjamin, Walter, 41
Bergson, Henri, 4, 63, 65–66
Berkeley, George, 160
Berlin, Isaiah, 17
Bernasconi, Robert, 60, 64
Bernet, Rudolf, 124–25
Blanchot, Maurice, 19, 24, 131, 136, 196n4
boundary, (boundaries), 8, 21, 23, 69, 75, 77–78, 104, 158, 161, 166, 174
    bodily, 161
    of the thinkable, 177
    of thinghood, 151, 155
    See also real, the
Burke, Edmund, 17
Burkett, Paul, 184

Callicott, Baird, 185
capitalism, 6, 224n24
Caputo, John, 207n3
Carnap, Rudolf, 141
Christianity. *See* religion
communitarian, 17, 23. *See also*
  liberal
community, 6, 17–18, 63, 97, 101,
    135–36, 162, 197n4, 198n15
  and identity, 12
  global, 182
  See also religion
Concept(s), (conceptual, conceptualiza-
    tion), 2–4, 27, 44, 142, 156, 165,
    219n25
  construction, 4
  operational, 2
  relatedness, 193
  scheme, 2, 22
  violence of, 44–46, 69
condition(s), 12, 15–16, 62, 94
  background, 31–33, 51
  formal, 18
  human, 17, 33, 67
  material, 18
  of legitimacy, 180
  of possibility, 2, 8, 14, 78, 182, 193
  of sociality, 180
  for projection, 15
  See also negotiation
consensus, 28–30
  breakdown of, 32
contingency, 4, 90, 92
contrariety, 175–76, 223n10. *See also*
  aporia; logic; *phronesis*
critique, 8
culture, 23–25, 35. *See also* politics

Darwin, Charles, 60
  social Darwinism, 60
death, 16–17, 55, 59, 64–65, 79–80,
    90–91, 95. *See also* Heidegger
deconstruction, (deconstructive) 2–3, 8,
    18, 28, 40, 132, 135, 140, 170,
    186, 192–93, 196n1
  of phenomenology, 95
deep ecology, 161–63, 166–68

Deleuze, Gilles, 22, 74, 109, 112–13,
    120, 150
democracy, (democratic), 17, 176, 180,
    223n10
  democracy to come, 183–84
  institutions, 167, 222n27
  society, 168
dependence, (dependent, dependency),
    59, 87–89, 121, 126, 179, 212n23
  See also independence
Derrida, Jacques, 1–2, 5, 8, 19, 22, 24,
    27, 39–41, 47, 51, 55, 74, 85–86,
    89, 95, 97–98, 112–13, 121,
    131–37, 139–48, 164, 169,
    170–71, 174, 209n32
  a-venir, 135
  carnophallogocentrism, 47, 55
  différance, 3
  God, 95–104, 107, 209n39. *See also*
    God
  responsibility, 139–48, 222n2. *See*
    also responsibility
  messianism, 171, 176–77
  spectral, the, 175, 185–86
  ten plagues, 184–86
  undecidable, the, 110, 176, 222n9
Descartes, René, 13, 54–56, 59–60, 101,
    192, 221n21
description, (descriptive), 2
desire, 76
despair, 14, 20, 91, 104
difference, 6, 12–13, 99, 134, 175
  philosophies of, 74
  sexual, 196n1
differentiation, 185
Dionysus, 116
dogmatism, 46
Donne, John, 76
double inscription, 142–44, 146–47
double vision, 194
dualism, 141

economy, (economic), 5, 17, 21–22, 40,
    73, 83, 85–86, 91, 93, 95, 97, 99,
    108, 135, 164, 208n31
  and identity, 12
  and closure, 166, 168

and oppression, 6
of mutual recognition, 12. *See also*
    recognition
of responsibility, 98. *See also* respon-
    sibility
of subjectivity, 106
of violence, 39–40. *See also* violence
eco-phenomenology. *See* phenomenology
education, 189–94
    higher education, 189–94
    institutions of, 191–94, 195n2
    philosophy of, 198n17
embodiment, 149, 159, 196n4
empiricism, 192
engagement, 5, 7, 151
    with the world, 3, 15, 109, 141, 151,
        172, 176. *See also* world
Enlightenment, the, 6, 19, 24, 33, 40,
    69, 179, 184, 189
environmental destruction, 184–86
epistemology, 87, 156, 192
epoché, 137
essence, (essentialism, essentialist), 13,
    24, 29, 42, 132, 174
    and identity, 18. *See also* identity
ethical, the, 4–6, 8, 53–54, 99–100. *See
    also* ethics; Levinas
ethics, 1, 5, 28, 53–54, 57–59, 62–63,
    66, 69, 75, 113, 117
    proto-ethics, 145, 218n20
    See also ethical, the; Levinas
ethnicity, 11–12
    and difference, 12
    and violence, 177
    ethnic cleansing, 11, 61, 198n12
    See also identity
ethos, 5
event, the, 66–68, 77
    eruptive, 153, 155
    founding, 82
    inaugural, 36–37, 81
evil, 55–56
exclusion, 19
existentialism, 91, 94, 132
experience, 5, 73, 132–33, 135–36, 142,
    151, 216n35
    aporetics of, 134. *See also* aporia

impossibility of, 136
    See also innocence; Scott
exposure, 137, 145, 147–48

face-to-face relation, 57, 63, 66, 76, 145
    See also Levinas
faith, 16, 75, 89, 116, 177. *See also*
    Kierkegaard
family, 22–23
feminine, the, (femininity), 53, 64, 66
Feuerbach, Ludwig, 60
finitude
    celebration of, 151, 153–55, 168
    fragility of, 187
force, 6
Foster, John Bellamy, 184
Foucault, Michel, 47, 109, 111–14, 117,
    119, 126, 153, 196n7
foundationalism, (foundation) 4,
    225n33. *See also* ground
frame, 176–77, 224n21
    dependency, 176
freedom, 6, 17, 42, 58, 69, 93–94, 142–44,
        170, 177, 180–81, 183, 194, 222n2
    economic, 169, 177, 183
    political, 169, 177, 183
    radical, 170, 179, 184, 186
    value of, 170
Frege, Gottlob, 134
Freud, Sigmund, 33, 60, 62, 82, 126,
    170–71, 206n7
    Unheimlich, 115–16, 125
Friedman, Milton, 177, 182
Fukuyama, Francis, 177

Gadamer, Hans-Georg, 31
Gasché, Rodolphe, 135
genealogy, 114, 136, 196n7
generosity, 54, 68, 114
genocide, 36, 42, 53, 56, 68–69,
    198n12, 203n50
gift, the, 54–55, 74, 79, 95–96, 102–3,
    135, 175
Girard, René, 198n14
globalization, 6, 23, 169–70, 172,
    174–76, 180, 186–87, 195n2
    and closure, 173

goal, 7
God, 1, 43, 59–60, 85–89, 96–105, 110, 124, 170, 177, 197n5, 209n34
  God-talk, 86, 89, 94. *See also* Wittgenstein
  See also Derrida
good will. *See* will; Kant
ground, (grounding, grounded), 4, 45, 58, 69, 88, 101, 133, 142, 174, 179–80, 215n13. *See also* origin; transcendental; plurality; phenomenology
Guha, Ramachandra, 185
guilt, 5, 42, 121–22, 124, 126
  morality of, 5
  philosophy of, 118. *See also* Levinas

habit(s), 2, 16, 79, 151, 193
Hearne, Vicki, 48, 121
Hegel, G.W.F., 3–4, 16–17, 20, 22, 27, 34–35, 54–55, 74–75, 89–91, 94, 147, 151, 167, 172, 177
  master and slave, 3, 81
Heidegger, Martin, 1–2, 5, 8, 22, 33, 37–43, 46–49, 51, 54–56, 58–59, 63–64, 77, 81, 87, 89, 93, 104, 109–10, 112, 122, 132–33, 139–40, 142, 147, 153, 161, 186–87, 196n4
  being-toward-death, 56, 65, 94, 199n4, 207n14, 208n21. *See also* death
  Destruktion, 40, 132
  Gelassenheit, 34, 64, 133
  language, 2, 64, 134–35, 170, 199n1
  and the Holocaust, 42, 44, 47–48
  Nothing, (*das Nichts*), 141
  nourishment, 54–55, 58
  reading, 54
  thinking, 1, 3, 136. *See also* thinking
  See also world
Heraclitus, 32, 38
hermeneutics, 21, 214n6
  circularity of, 21
  of suspicion, 114
heterogeneity, 24
heteronomy, 182–83

history, 3, 8, 18–21, 39–40, 46, 49, 85, 91–93, 95, 110, 119, 132, 173, 180–81, 208n31
  and teleology, 170
  historiography, 38
  inaugural, 36–37
  primordial, 38
Hitler, Adolf, 39, 62
Hobbes, Thomas, 60, 209n44
Hoffmann, E.T.A., 126
Hölderlin, Friedrich, 187
Holmes, Oliver Wendell, 69
Holocaust, the, 28, 43–44, 50, 62, 202n49. *See also* animal; Heidegger
home, 15
  homelessness, 15
Homer, 193
homogeneity, 12
hope, 56, 106, 171
horizon, (horizonality), 15, 20, 23, 79, 95, 110, 124, 133, 161
  of constancy, 197n12
  of continuity, 15
  of predictability, 16
  See also temporality
hospitality, 68, 116
humanism, 5, 8, 60, 111, 123, 170, 179, 186, 211n6
  violence of, 44, 47–50
Husserl, Edmund, 5, 57, 67, 95, 131, 133–36, 139, 142, 158
  intentionality, 3. *See also* intentionality
hyper-reflection. *See* Merleau-Ponty, Maurice

idealism, 120, 122–23, 126, 133–34, 177
identity, 6, 11–13, 15–17, 21, 24, 37, 41, 63, 132, 161, 170.
  constitution of, 13, 18, 116, 133, 174
  crisis, 16
  formation, 21–22, 28, 41.
  human, 39
  national and ethnic, 6, 16, 45
  numerical, 12
  personal, 12–14, 97, 135

political, 12
qualitative, 12
self-identity, 15, 25
See also community; economy
imperialism, 19
inauguration, 38–41
inaugural drift, 191
See also event; history; power; tradition; violence
independence, (independent), 59, 88
See also dependence
innocence, 73, 80. *See also* experience
inside/outside relation, 171–72
intentionality, 32, 34, 132, 135, 150, 159–60, 168
limits of, 133
See also Husserl
interpretation, 37–39, 99, 107, 124, 147
public, 55. *See also* public
schemes, 176
self, 20
See also hermeneutics
Irigaray, Luce, 77

Jentsch, Ernst, 125
justice, 1, 40–41, 50, 54, 74–75, 83, 94, 100, 139–40, 180, 191, 222n2, 225n33

Kafka, Franz, 17
Kant, Immanuel, 31, 34, 43, 48, 50, 67, 87, 106, 112, 134, 146–47, 152, 192
causality, 142–43
good will, 174
unsocial sociability, 34, 36, 47
Kearney, Richard, 60, 198n20
Keats, John, 1, 196n5
negative capability, 1, 4, 34, 148, 194, 222n9. *See also* negative capability
Kierkegaard, Søren, 1, 5, 19–20, 22, 54, 65, 73–108, 116–17, 206n8, 206n12
aesthetic, the, 5, 73–74, 76–80, 82–84

ethical, the, 73–74, 77–80, 83–84
See also ethical, the
faith, 3, 78, 83, 85, 196n4. *See also* faith
indirect communication, 80, 94, 96, 102
religious, the, (religion) 5, 80,82, 86, 89, 97, 104–7, 197n5, 207n18
See also religion
religiousness A and B, 107, 110
selfhood/subjectivity, 14, 85, 92, 102–3, 106–7, 117. *See also* self; subject
See also repetition; paradox
kiss, 73–77, 79–83, 154
Kristeva, Julia, 22
semiotic, the, 3, 44
symbolic, the, 210n38

Lacan, Jacques, 112, 197n5, 207n18
La Mettrie, Julien Offroy de, 56
language, 3, 16, 30–31, 38, 45–46, 66, 95, 98, 119, 133–34, 139, 144, 147
limits of, 76, 86
metaphysical, 170
See also God; Wittgenstein
law(s), 4, 16, 41, 44, 69
of context, 164
See also rule
Leibniz, Gottfried Wilhelm, 31, 86
Leishman, J.B., 153–54
Leopold, Aldo, 117, 185
Lessing, Gotthold Ephraim, 1, 116
Levinas, Emmanuel, 5, 8, 22, 39–41, 47, 53–68, 73, 102, 116, 118, 121–26, 131–32, 135–36, 140, 144, 179, 186, 203n1
asymmetry, 53, 63, 65, 67–68
il y a, 59, 122–23
infinite responsibility, 5, 53, 59, 63, 67–68, 116. *See also* responsibility; obligation
See also ethics; ethical, the; other, the; face-to-face relation
Lévi-Strauss, Claude, 16, 21
liberal, (liberalism), 17, 23, 171. *See also* communitarian

life, 56, 90, 93, 115
  forms of, 3, 17, 111
  meaning of, 87, 94
limit, (limitation), 2, 146, 152, 193
  liminology, 158, 161
  of human understanding, 177
logic, 7, 12–13, 16–17, 69, 85, 93, 114,
    141–42, 144, 158, 171, 176
  binary, 166, 168, 182
  of aporia, 171
  of contradiction, 171
  of contrariety, 182. See also contrari-
    ety)
  of destruction, 171
  of deterritorialization, 172, 174
  of history, 172, 177
  of individualism, 186
  of the market, 183
  of the spectral. See also Derrida
  of substitution, 182
  of wartime, 182
loss, 133, 135
love, 55, 65, 73, 77–79, 154, 177
Lyotard, Jean-François, 6, 24, 27, 33

MacIntyre, Alasdair, 17
Marcuse, Herbert, 143, 169–71, 174,
    176, 179–80, 186, 226n35
Marion, Jean-Luc, 133
marriage, 76, 78, 80–83
Marx, Karl, (Marxism) 17, 60, 74, 94,
    170–72, 176–77, 184, 186
mathematics, 7, 74, 120, 127, 162
McCarthyism, 170
McKibben, Bill, 185
meaning, 31
  construction of, 5
  See also being
Medina, José, 196n1
memory, 15, 19, 21, 28, 32, 49, 115–17
Merleau-Ponty, Maurice, 111, 131,
    160–61, 165
  perception, 3, 199n1. See also per-
    ception
  hyper-reflection, 3, 27, 45, 148,
    199n1
metaphor, 117

metaphysics, (metaphysical), 2, 6, 12,
    56, 95, 110–11, 158, 164, 168,
    179
method, (methodology), 7–8
  philosophical, 28
Mill, John Stuart, 56
Moebius strip, 147, 172, 197n5, 199n26,
    211n8
morality, 23, 63, 66–67

Naess, Arne, 161
Nancy, Jean-Luc, 47, 55, 197n4,
    198n14, 222n2
narrative, 18, 20, 24–25, 41, 153,
    199n26
  deconstruction of, 19, 24
  incompleteness of, 5
naturalism, 149–51, 159, 168, 184
nature, 3, 5–6, 19, 34, 36, 60, 127,
    149–50, 158, 165, 173, 176, 184,
    195n2, 200n17
  degradation of, 226n45
negative capability, 6–7, 69, 196n6. See
    also Keats, John
negativity, 4, 132
negotiation, 29–31
  background conditions of, 30
Nemo, Philippe, 124
Newton, Isaac, 175
Nietzsche, Friedrich, 3, 5, 8, 16, 19, 21,
    24–25, 38, 43, 45, 61, 81, 95, 99,
    109–11, 118–20, 127, 142–43,
    196n4, 199n1, 208n31
  "active forgetting," 17
  affirmation, 82
  eternal recurrence, 33, 154, 197n9
  ressentiment, 32–33, 199n4
  revaluation of all values, 109, 111
nihilism, 21
normativity, (normative), 21, 75
nourishment. See Heidegger
number, 74–75

obligation, 57–59, 65, 68, 99–100, 121,
    125, 140, 146–47, 153. See also
    responsibility; Levinas
Ockham, William of, 88

ontology, (ontological), 5, 28, 32–33, 38, 53, 56–60, 66–67, 69, 92, 156, 185
    difference, 141–42, 147. *See also* Heidegger
    primacy of, 127
onto-theology. *See* theology
openness, (opening), 5, 15, 57, 77, 83, 89, 93, 101, 103–5, 121, 139, 147, 166–67, 194
organized integrity, 157
origin, 19, 27, 38–39, 41, 45, 89, 116, 185. *See also* arrival; ground
other, the, (Other, the) 22, 34, 35, 53, 56–59, 63–69, 76, 97, 104, 110, 116, 118, 122, 124, 126, 133, 140, 146
    See also alterity; Levinas; otherness
otherness, 5, 57, 59, 64, 69, 118, 127
    See also alterity, Levinas; other, the
overcoming, 109, 114
Owen, Wilfred, 44

pacifism, 32. *See also* peace
paradox, 80, 86, 93, 96, 100–1, 107, 110, 176, 179. *See also* Kierkegaard
Parmenides, 38
Pascal, Blaise, 60, 118, 126
passivity, 2, 64, 75, 135
Patočka, Jan, 96, 208n31
peace, 6–7, 11, 20, 28, 38, 40, 46, 51, 69, 169–70, 200n23
    fragility of, 28, 36
    See also pacifism
Peirce, Charles Sanders, 11, 25, 74
perception, 149–50. *See also* Merleau-Ponty
performance, 8, 90, 109
    emancipatory, 117
phenomenology, 2, 5, 59, 64, 82, 123, 131–37, 139, 142, 149–51, 153, 159, 163, 165, 167–68, 177, 220n11
    deconstructive phenomenology, 8, 131–37. *See also* deconstruction
    eco-phenomenology, 5, 150–51, 154–55, 158, 161, 166, 168
    of eros, 133

grounding, 89
    psychoanalytical phenomenology. *See* psychoanalysis
    renewal of, 131–32
    transcendental phenomenology, 133
philosophy, 4, 6, 11, 21, 27, 30, 39, 43–44, 57, 95, 112, 131, 139, 190–94
    and definition, 8
    and engagement, 85
    of mind, 12
    of violence, 69
    See also method
phronesis, 3, 32, 110, 172, 176, 194
    of contrariety, 172, 175–76, 184, 186, 222n9. *See also* contrariety
physis, 28
pity, 113
Plato, (Platonism), 13, 28, 82, 93, 109, 134, 153, 165
    recollection, 82
plurality, 24, 83
    of grounds, 24. *See also* ground
poetry, 37, 55, 135
politics, (political), 6, 17, 68, 165, 169, 191, 225
    activity, 19. *See also* activity
    critical political culture, 24
    institutions, 63
positivism, 141
positivity, 4–5, 91, 132
possibility, (possibilities), 5, 8, 14, 75, 90, 124. *See also* condition
postmodernism, 8
power, 16, 19–20, 30, 36, 38, 63, 68, 104–5, 111
    inaugural, 39
    overpowering, the, 38
practice, (practices), 5, 8, 28, 56
    linguistic or discursive, 86, 117
    human, 31, 142
    and philosophy, 4, 5, 28
    social, 86, 119
    transformatory, 109. *See also* performance
prescription, (prescriptive), 2, 5
pre-Socratics, 74

private, 20–21. See also public
progress, 175
promise, 41, 78
proscription, (proscriptive), 5
psychoanalysis, 57–58, 136
    psychoanalytical phenomenology, 34
psychology, 17, 97
    transcendental psychology, 135
public, 20–21, 134
    meaning, 13
    See also private; interpretation

Ramsey, Frank Plumpton, 86
Rawls, John, 23
reading. See Heidegger, Martin
real, the, 4, 8, 66, 192
    boundaries of, 6. See also boundary
    repression of, 169
reason, 6
receptivity, 2
recognition, 28, 32, 34–36, 44, 54, 58,
    63, 69, 117, 179, 187
recollection. See Plato
reflection
    conceptual, 2
    critical, 4
relativism, 3
religion, (religious), 15–16, 74, 86,
    96–97, 171, 176
    belief, 16, 197n12
    community, 20
    Eastern forms, 51, 57
    fundamentalism, 177
    Judeo-Christian, 59, 85, 89–90, 92,
        94–96, 103, 107, 111, 143,
        208n18, 208n20
repetition, 4, 13, 28, 33–34, 41, 73–74,
    75, 78, 80, 82, 90–91, 96, 112, 154,
    206n8
representation, 2–3, 7, 19, 30, 77, 85,
    103, 114–15, 155, 165
responsibility, (responsibilities), 1, 4–5,
    28, 55, 59, 63, 96, 98–100,
    103–5, 110, 133, 136, 139–48,
    179
    aporia of, 98. See also aporia
    ethical and political dimensions, 139

limits of, 144
    See also aporia; Derrida; economy;
        Levinas; obligation
ressentiment. See Nietzsche
revolution, 4, 6, 28, 32, 41, 177
rhythm
    coordination of, 151, 154–55, 168
Ricoeur, Paul, 8, 19–20, 22, 131, 135,
    160, 214n6
Rilke, Rainer Maria, 153
Rorty, Richard, 21, 194
rule(s), 4–5, 119. See also law
Ryle, Gilbert, 141–42
    category mistake, 141, 146

sacrifice, 16–17, 93, 96–99, 103, 108,
    135, 207n14
    language of, 181
    rhetoric of, 181
Said, Edward, 18–19, 24
Sandel, Michael, 17
Sartre, Jean-Paul, 34–35, 64, 74, 85–86,
    89, 91–95, 102, 104, 110, 123,
    131, 142–44, 170, 175, 207n14,
    208n21
    becoming-an-atheist, 85–86, 95, 110,
        116
Scott, Charles, 5, 109–27
    experience, 114–15. See also experi-
        ence
    materiality, 118, 121–23
secret, (secrecy), 85, 96–99, 102–3
self, 13, 15, 17, 67, 145, 170
    absorption, 58
    boundaries of, 116. See also boundary
    deconstruction of, 197n4
    disruption of, 116
    metaphysical, 18
    presence, 95
    reflexivity of, 20
    selfhood, 13–14, 17–18, 113, 115
        See also Kierkegaard
    See also interpretation; identity
Sen, Amartya, 23, 182–83, 226n43
sensation, 45
Sessions, George, 161
Shakespeare, William, 118

Shiva, Vandana, 183
silence, 88, 98–99, 102
singularity, 19–20, 45, 79, 94, 96, 98, 100–1, 103, 106, 110, 154
skepticism, 19, 189, 193
Smith, Adam, 178
Snyder, Gary, 198n14
society, 18, 47, 169
  structures of, 225n33
Socrates, 18, 106, 132
Sophocles, 38, 40–41
soul, the, 13, 92
Spinoza, Benedict, 60
state, the, 17, 177, 191, 197n12
step back, the, 1–5, 7–8
structuralism, 186
struggle, 7, 18, 175, 180
  and freedom, 169
  class, 177
  for existence, 169–70
  life and death, 90, 93
  political, 136
subject, the, (subjectivity), 6, 13, 22, 59, 64–65, 91, 95, 98, 115, 117–19, 122, 124–25, 146, 148–49, 170
  structures of, 104–5
  See also Kierkegaard
substance, 59, 141

Taylor, Charles, 17
technology, 55, 62, 111
temporality, 7, 56, 116–17, 151, 153, 173
  temporal horizon, 151, 153, 155, 168. See also horizon
thematization, 2, 20
theology, 43, 59–60, 86, 89, 95
  negative, 94–95
  onto-theology, 59
thinking, 38, 66
  operational, 3, 195n2
  oppositional, 54, 224n20
  See also Heidegger
time, 4, 6–8, 13, 20, 32–34, 36, 46, 63–66, 69, 73–75, 77–78, 116, 131, 151, 154, 167, 173, 181–82, 193
  as event, 155
  as physis, 155

aporias of, 135. See also aporia
  horizon of, 56. See also horizon
  invisibility of, 151–53, 155, 168
  pathologies of, 28, 32, 36, 51
  plexity of, 151
  See also Heidegger
totality, 127
tradition, 23, 38–39, 59, 85, 114, 139–40
  of inauguration, 40
tragedy, 20
transcendence, (transcendental) 14, 22, 58, 67, 76, 88, 90, 92, 103, 110, 112, 121, 132, 134
  grounds, 21, 94
  principles, 112
  quasi-transcendental, 135. See also Gasché
  questions, 22
trauma, 32–34, 63, 96, 124–26, 150–51, 199n4, 212n23, 213n44
truth, 3, 22, 40, 121, 127
Tse-tung, Mao, 58

value, (values), 17, 21, 30, 56, 62, 73, 79, 91, 111, 113, 115, 144, 146, 161–62, 170, 180–81, 194. See also Nietzsche
violence, 6–7, 11, 18, 22, 24, 27–28, 31–51, 55–56, 61, 67–69, 124–25, 198n12, 203n51, 213n44
  inaugural, 37, 39–40, 51
  instituting, 38–39
  nonviolence, 27–28
  See also concept; economy; humanism
virtue(s), 5, 27, 79, 194
visibility, 152–53

war, 32, 44, 56, 169, 171, 175, 182, 184, 223n20, 226n43
Walzer, Michael, 17
Whitman, Walt, 117
will, 31. See also Kant
Wittgenstein, Ludwig, 1, 5, 19, 28, 86–89, 94, 104, 210n54
  "dependency," 97, 105

Wittgenstein, Ludwig *(continued)*
   language-games, 3, 86–87, 92. *See
     also* language; God
   rough ground, 1, 3, 193
  world, 3, 54–55, 67, 75, 83, 87–90, 107,
     121, 132–33, 137, 142, 149–50,
     155

being-in-the-world, 15, 89, 90, 94,
   104, 107, 133, 135, 137, 141,
   165. *See also* Heidegger
  meaning of, 87, 94
  See also engagement
writing
  under erasure, 140